WHAT YOUR COLLEAGUES ARE SAYING ABOUT GOTTLIEB'S *ASSESSMENT* SERIES . . .

Assessment in Multiple Languages: A Handbook for School and District Leaders

"Margo Gottlieb provides resolutions and resources to tackle the most important dilemma in educating multilingual learners equitably—their assessment. By presenting cases that highlight the different issues that school and district leaders face when gauging the learning of multilingual learners, Gottlieb shows her encyclopedic understandings of the condition of their education today and the role that monolingual assessments have played in unfairly judging them. But in addition, Gottlieb demonstrates her commonsense and imaginative approach to ensure that multilingual learners are assessed fairly. Every assessment dilemma is given resolutions, as Gottlieb gently guides school and district leaders to perceive assessment from the students' multilingual perspective, and then provides them with the resources they would need to act differently."

—Ofelia García
Professor Emerita
The Graduate Center, City University of New York

"Assessment in Multiple Languages: A Handbook for School and District Leaders *is a must for any school leader who wants to turn students' and teachers' multilingualism into an educational advantage. The discussion is packed with practicable ideas and resources for language assessment that are informed by research and professional experience.*"

—Constant Leung
Professor of Educational Linguistics
King's College London, School of Education, Communication and Society

"Assessment in Multiple Languages: A Handbook for School and District Leaders *is a must-read for all students in education administration programs in higher education, for policy makers, and for current school administrators. A foremost expert in multilingual education and assessment, Margo Gottlieb uses a combination of research-based assessment principles combined with useful 'can do' examples that will be of great use for administrators and other educators serving multilingual learners. In dismantling inequity and evoking educational change, Gottlieb invites us to balance assessment approaches with strategies that are inclusive of 'assessment as, for, and of learning . . . from the classroom to the boardroom.' I recommend her book highly.*"

—Joel Gómez
President and CEO
Center for Applied Linguistics

"Assessment in Multiple Languages: A Handbook for School and District Leaders *approaches the issue of assessment from the multilingual learners' perspective. Excellent approach! Reframing language education models and understanding the basics of assessment of learning are topics all school and district leaders will find most helpful for supporting multilingual learners in difficult times. The book contains key resources for planning, gathering, and conducting assessments: planning curriculum, interpreting information, providing feedback in multiple languages, and taking action based on assessment results."*

—Margarita Espino Calderón
Professor Emerita
Johns Hopkins University

"Assessment in Multiple Languages: A Handbook for School and District Leaders *is a must-read for anyone who cares about equitable and meaningful assessment for multilingual learners. Margo Gottlieb makes a compelling case for assessing these students in multiple languages. Through insightful case studies presented as dilemmas, and a rich, comprehensive collection of tools and resources, the book offers everything the reader needs to get started with or to transform existing assessment practices."*

—Andrea Honigsfeld
Associate Dean, Educational Leadership for Diverse Learning Communities
EdD Program, Molloy College

"Who says assessment happens only in English? Margo Gottlieb demonstrates again why she is the go-to source for the equitable assessment of multilingual students. Assessment in Multiple Languages: A Handbook for School and District Leaders *provides school leaders with an invaluable 'how-to manual' for organizing and implementing a common, ongoing assessment program in any language that not only is more complete and informative for instructional feedback but also moves the needle toward excellence and innovation in our schools."*

—Tim Boals
WIDA Founder and Director
Wisconsin Center for Education Research

"Assessment in Multiple Languages: A Handbook for School and District Leaders *is a true deep dive into the importance of assessment in multiple languages—a moral imperative to ensure appropriate assessments are created for and serve culturally and linguistically diverse students. Our educational leadership and policy makers must utilize this important work for ensuring accountability and commitment to supporting effective instructional practice.*

"Assessment in Multiple Languages: A Handbook for School and District Leaders *is an answer to prayer. It is a moral imperative for tackling social justice issues that currently exist with assessments developed and produced for native monolingual English speakers and forced upon our culturally and linguistically diverse student populations.*

"If we are truly interested in knowing our students' academic, linguistic, and sociocultural competence, then we must capture and understand their proficiencies through all of their languages.

"Who knew that there could be a common assessment for multiple languages? This new resource is timely, as there is a growing voice to strengthen and expand K–12 dual language immersion education. Developing a large-scale

testing system on the tenets and guidance of this resource that works for DLI is now within reach!"

—David Rogers
Executive Director
Dual Language Education of New Mexico

Classroom Assessment in Multiple Languages: A Handbook for Teachers

"There are strong cultural, academic, and linguistic arguments for a pluralistic approach to working with bi/multilingual learners. While such an approach has been conceptualized by many for curriculum and pedagogy, the domain of assessment has proven to be more difficult. In Classroom Assessment in Multiple Languages: A Handbook for Teachers, *Margo Gottlieb addresses this gap in the field from a theoretical and practical perspective. She challenges all educators, including those who consider themselves monolingual or may speak languages other than those of their students, to approach assessment through a multilingual lens. The book uncovers common myths about multilingual assessment and provides practical strategies for educators to ensure fair and valid assessments for multilingual learners. A great resource for teachers and teacher educators."*

—Ester de Jong
Professor, ESOL/Bilingual Education
University of Florida, College of Education

"At its core, Classroom Assessment in Multiple Languages: A Handbook for Teachers *puts forth a vision of assessment for multilingual learners that is collaborative, inclusive, and, most importantly, equitable. Margo Gottlieb not only presents a comprehensive guide to align assessment, curriculum, and instruction, but her vision of this process honors the voices, as well as the linguistic and cultural assets, that students bring to learning. The ESPEJO Curriculum Model, with its 'mirrored' cultural and linguistic curricular components, is a powerful example of this inclusive and respectful approach that creates a fully reflective portrait of the 'student as curriculum.'"*

—John F. Hilliard
President and Founder
Paridad Education Consulting

"Margo Gottlieb's Classroom Assessment in Multiple Languages: A Handbook for Teachers *is a relevant and responsive book that challenges the monolingual bias of assessment in the United States. Full of scenarios and dispelling of myths, Gottlieb provides both theoretical underpinnings and practical strategies for multilingual assessment, which allows educators to be agents of assessment change in their own contexts. The book's focus on social justice and equity for multilingual learners comes at a time when bilingual programs are growing in the United States, while there is a similar growing need for assets-based multilingual assessments that honor what students do know and are able to do in their mother tongues."*

—Ivannia Soto
Whittier College/California Association for Bilingual Education (CABE)

"Classroom Assessment in Multiple Languages: A Handbook for Teachers *is a powerful and very needed resource in today's multilingual learning spaces. Margo Gottlieb demonstrates the importance of maintaining an assets-based lens while empowering educators to continue to fight for equity. This resource is unlike other professional books about assessment as it offers multidimensionality as we've never seen it—by leveraging our students' linguistic assets and using assessment for, of, and as learning. This book features deeply reflective questions to help you as an educator, as well as instructional teams and administrative leadership, to grow and develop culturally and linguistically responsive and assets-based pedagogy. This is a must-read for today's empowered educator and change agent!"*

—Carly Spina
District EL/Bilingual Instructional Coach
Glenview School District 34

"At long last, a book on K–12 assessment that takes an honest and comprehensive look at how the assessment needs of multilingual learners differ from those of monolingual learners. Margo Gottlieb, building on a lifetime of wisdom regarding assessment for language learners, provides insightful, practical, and accessible advice for teachers and school leaders. She shares an abundance of tools and resources for putting responsibility for learning and reflection into the hands of teachers and school leaders and, most importantly, into the hands of the multilingual students themselves. Classroom Assessment in Multiple Languages: A Handbook for Teachers *is no ordinary book of K–12 assessment practices; Gottlieb's book exudes affirmation, respect, and value for our multilingual learners. This is social justice in practice."*

—Lisa Tabaku
Director, Global Languages and Cultures
Center for Applied Linguistics

"When I started working with the complete beginners for the first time, I taught in English, interacted with them in English, assessed them in English, and provided feedback in English. No wonder they struggled so much in my class. I wish I had this guide to help me rethink how I assess language learners who are literate in their home language. Margo Gottlieb has been leading our field for decades now, and with this work, she continues to help us shift our thinking about how we assess with an assets-based approach. Like her extensive body of work, Classroom Assessment in Multiple Languages: A Handbook for Teachers *adds the equity piece when assessing language learners."*

—Tan Huynh
Secondary Social Studies and EAL Teacher

"Colleague Margo Gottlieb shows us what can be done when we truly challenge our monolingual biases in favor of creating schools where the multilingual identities of our richly diverse student and family communities are truly honored and valued. She adeptly moves us away from measuring students' successes and failures based on their performance on high-stakes tests to assessing the uniqueness

of their strengths and capacities as they engage in classroom-based projects, performances, and products. Whether we teach in person, remotely, or both, Classroom Assessment in Multiple Languages: A Handbook for Teachers *should be the go-to source of responsive assessment practices for a multilingual world."*

—Debbie Zacarian
Founder
Zacarian & Associates

Assessment in Multiple Languages

Assessment in Multiple Languages

A Handbook for School and District Leaders

Margo Gottlieb

Foreword by Patricia Morita-Mullaney

FOR INFORMATION:

Corwin

A SAGE Company

2455 Teller Road

Thousand Oaks, California 91320

(800) 233-9936

www.corwin.com

SAGE Publications Ltd.

1 Oliver's Yard

55 City Road

London EC1Y 1SP

United Kingdom

SAGE Publications India Pvt. Ltd.

B 1/I 1 Mohan Cooperative Industrial Area

Mathura Road, New Delhi 110 044

India

SAGE Publications Asia-Pacific Pte. Ltd.

18 Cross Street #10-10/11/12

China Square Central

Singapore 048423

Printed in the United States of America

ISBN 978-1-0718-2766-6

Library of Congress Control Number: 2021907641

President: Mike Soules

Associate Vice President and Editorial
    Director: Monica Eckman

Program Director and Publisher: Dan Alpert

Senior Content Development
    Editor: Lucas Schleicher

Associate Content Development
    Editor: Mia Rodriguez

Project Editor: Amy Schroller

Copy Editor: Melinda Masson

Typesetter: Hurix Digital

Proofreader: Dennis Webb

Indexer: Integra

Cover Designer: Candice Harman

Marketing Manager: Sharon Pendergast

This book is printed on acid-free paper.

21 22 23 24 25 10 9 8 7 6 5 4 3 2 1

Contents

Foreword   xviii
Patricia Morita-Mullaney

Preface   xxi

Acknowledgments   xxxii

About the Author   xxxiii

Chapter 1: Looking at Assessment Through the Lens of
Multilingual Learners   1

The Dilemma: But English learners isn't an appropriate
term (or label), and initial screening only in English isn't
an accurate depiction of who our multilingual learners
are and what they can do!   2

Federal Influence on Terminology and Assessment   4

Federal Legislative Directives   4

The Name Game: Implications for Assessment   7

The Power of Labels   10

Reframing Language Education Models   13

Linguistically and Culturally Sustainable Schools   16

The Resurgence of Bilingual and Dual Language Education   17

Multilingual Education   17

Research That Supports Bilingualism/Multilingualism   17

Competing Theories and Views of Assessment   18

Creating Language and Assessment Policies   21

School Policy   21

District Policy   22

Multilingual Learners and Social-Emotional Learning   23

Tips for Assessment in Multiple Languages   23

Facing the Issue: Rethink Terminology and Language
Education Models   24

For School Leaders   25

For District Leaders   25

Resolving the Dilemma: Accentuate Equitable Assessment
Practices for Multilingual Learners!   25

Resources for School and District Leaders

Resource 1.1 The Link Between Subgroups of Bi/Multilingual Learners and Assessment   27

Resource 1.2 Categorizing Terminology: References to Students, Languages, Teachers, and Programs   28

Chapter 2: Getting Started With Assessment in Multiple Languages   30

The Dilemma: But I only speak English! How can I be expected to communicate in other languages?   30

How Language Policy Informs Assessment in Multiple Languages   32

Effective Leadership in Programs Cultivating Multiple Languages   33

Supporting Multilingual Learners During Difficult Times   34

The Assessment Cycle in Multiple Languages   35

Purposes for Assessment Involving Multilingual Learners   37

    The Role of Standards   37

    Initial Assessment for Multilingual Learners   38

Data Associated With Assessment *as*, *for*, and *of* Learning   43

    Assessment *as* Learning   43

    Assessment *for* Learning   44

    Assessment *of* Learning   45

Understanding the Basics of Assessment *of* Learning   46

    Validity for Large-Scale Testing   46

    Reliability   48

Evoking Systemic Change Through Social Justice   48

Facing the Issue: Advocate on Behalf of Your Multilingual Learners and Their Families   49

    For School Leaders   49

    For District Leaders   49

Resolving the Dilemma: Enlist Families and the Community in the Assessment Process!   50

Resources for School and District Leaders

Resource 2.1 Conducting an Assessment Audit for Multilingual Learners   51

Resource 2.2 Collecting Language Samples in Multiple Languages as Part of the Enrollment Process   52

Resource 2.3 Planning the Flow of Assessment Data for Multilingual Learners Throughout the School Year   53

Resource 2.4 Gathering Information on Multilingual Learners for Planning Assessment in Multiple Languages   54

Resource 2.5 Thinking About Assessment as, for, *and of Learning*   56

Chapter 3: Planning Curriculum and Assessment in Multiple Languages   57

The Dilemma: The students are returning to school speaking a mix of languages!   58

Stimulating Assessment in Multiple Languages
Through Distributive Leadership   60

Assessment as an Expression of Curriculum Design   61

    Features of Effective Curricula for Multilingual Learners   62

    Purposes for Assessment in Multiple Languages for
    Units of Learning   63

    Universal Design for Learning: Maximizing Accessibility
    for Multilingual Learners   65

Resources for Curriculum and Assessment in
Multiple Languages   66

    Multiliteracies and Multimodal Resources   66

    Translanguaging   67

A Multilingual Curriculum Framework With
Embedded Assessment   68

    Integrated Learning Goals/Targets   70

Common Assessment for Schools and Districts   72

    Co-planning Common Assessment in
    Multiple Languages   75

    Planning Interim Assessment   78

Student Assessment Portfolios in Multiple Languages   78

Facing the Issue: Utilize Multilingual Learners' Resources
to Maximize Their Language Learning   81

    For School Leaders   81

    For District Leaders   82

Resolving the Dilemma: Put Trust in Your Multilingual
Learners' Language Use!   82

Resources for School and District Leaders

*Resource 3.1 A Rating Scale: Integrating Assessment
in Curriculum Design for Multilingual Learners*   84

*Resource 3.2 Planning Assessment in Multiple
Languages for a Unit of Learning*   86

*Resource 3.3 A Rating Scale for Planning Common
Assessment in Multiple Languages*   87

*Resource 3.4 A Checklist for Planning Common
Assessment in Multiple Languages*   88

*Resource 3.5 Planning Multilingual Portfolios to
Represent Assessment* as, for, or of *Learning*   89

Chapter 4: Collecting and Organizing Assessment Information in
Multiple Languages   91

The Dilemma: Discrimination abounds against
multilingualism and multiculturalism . . . What can we do?   92

The Role of Leadership in Collecting Data in
Multiple Languages   95

    Creating and Applying a Theory of Action Tool
    for Assessment in Multiple Languages   95

Advice for Collecting Data in a Post-Pandemic World   96

Improving Accessibility in Data Collection   98

    Revisiting Universal Design for Learning   98

Revisiting Resources for Assessment in Multiple Languages   100

    Using Multiliteracies in Data Collection   100

    Using Multimodalities in Data Collection   101

    Using Translanguaging in Data Collection   103

Co-planning Data Collection in Multiple Languages   106

Collecting and Organizing Common Assessment in
Multiple Languages   107

Organizing and Assembling Assessment Portfolios in
Multiple Languages   111

Facing the Issue: Collect Data in Multiple Languages Using
Multiple Resources to Form a Convincing Body of Evidence   113

    For School Leaders   113

    For District Leaders   113

Resolving the Dilemma: Take Responsibility for Diminishing
Discrimination for Multilingual Learners and Their Families!   114

Resources for School and District Leaders

*Resource 4.1 Creating a Theory of Action Tool for
Assessment in Multiple Languages*   115

*Resource 4.2 Using Images in Collecting Common
Assessment Data*   116

*Resource 4.3 Using Multiliteracies and Multimodal
Resources in Assessment* as, for, *and* of *Learning*   117

*Resource 4.4 A Checklist for Co-planning Data Collection
in Multiple Languages*   118

*Resource 4.5 Adding Multimodal Communication Channels
to Common Assessment*   119

*Resource 4.6 Collecting Initial Common Assessment Data
(for Students in Grade 3 and Beyond)*   120

Resource 4.7 Assessment Portfolio Considerations   121

Chapter 5: Interpreting Information and Providing Feedback in
Multiple Languages   122

The Dilemma: There simply aren't enough qualified
language teachers, so let's place multilingual learners in
"special education" classes for support.   123

Examining Data in Multiple Languages   125

    Interpreting Different Types of Data Involving
Multilingual Learners   126

Common Assessment in Multiple Languages   131

    Interpreting Student Work With Uniform Criteria
for Success   131

    Interpreting Translanguaging in Common Assessment   134

    Interpreting Common Assessment in Multiple
Languages With Qualitative Rubrics   135

Collaboration in Providing Consistent Feedback   136

    Providing Feedback During Times of Stress and Duress   138

    Creating a Schoolwide Culture of Critique:
Language for Feedback   138

Interim/Annual Assessment in Multiple Languages   140

    Interpreting Language Proficiency Data Through a
"Can Do" Lens   141

Standardized Testing: Reassessing Validity Claims   144

Interpreting Data in Multiple Languages for
Local Accountability   145

    Capstone Projects   145

    Student Assessment Portfolios in Multiple Languages   145

Facing the Issue: Never Consider Special Education as an
Option for Multilingual Learners (Unless Duly Warranted)   148

    For School Leaders   148

    For District Leaders   148

Resolving the Dilemma: Use Multiple Data Approaches,
Sources, and Languages When Assessing Multilingual Learners!   149

Resources for School and District Leaders

Resource 5.1 Interpreting Classroom, Interim/Common,
and Annual Data by Assessment Approach   150

Resource 5.2 Collecting, Recording, and Interpreting
Information on Multilingual Learners' Languages and
Literacies in Content-Based Assessment   151

Resource 5.3 A Checklist of Descriptors for
Common Assessment   152

Resource 5.4 Ideas for Multilingual Projects for Common
Assessment, Standards, and Criteria for Success   153

Resource 5.5 Annotating Multilingual Learners' Use of
Multiple Languages Across Three Dimensions   154

Chapter 6: Evaluating and Reporting Assessment Information   155

The Dilemma: But how can we evaluate the effectiveness of
instruction or programs for multilingual learners in multiple
languages if we only depend on results from assessment in
one language?   156

An Equity Framework for Assessing Multilingual Learners   158

Another Single Story, A Different Scenario: State
Reclassification Criteria   161

Creating Assessment-Capable Students and Schools   163

Evaluating Linguistically and Culturally Responsive
Assessment Practices   164

The Role of Rubrics in Evaluating and Reporting
Assessment Results   166

    Designing Student-Centered Rubrics   167

Reporting Assessment Results   169

    Classroom Assessment   171

Common Assessment Across Classrooms 172

Interim School or District Assessment 173

Annual State Assessment 175

Reconsidering Grading Practices 177

Multilingual Learners' Role in Evaluation and Reporting 179

Facing the Issue: Consider the Many Stories of
Multilingual Learners and Their Families 180

For School Leaders 180

For District Leaders 180

Resolving the Dilemma: Never Evaluate Evidence or Programs
for Multilingual Learners Based on a Single Story! 180

Resources for School and District Leaders

*Resource 6.1 Designing an Equitable Assessment
Framework for Multilingual Learners* 182

*Resource 6.2 Evaluating Assessment-Capable
Classrooms, Schools, and Districts* 184

*Resource 6.3 Linguistically and Culturally Responsive
Assessment and Reporting of Data: A Rating Scale* 185

Resource 6.4 Student-Centered Rubrics 186

*Resource 6.5 Reporting Results From Measures of
Assessment of Learning* 187

Resource 6.6 Principles for Grading Multilingual Learners 188

Chapter 7: Taking Action Based on Assessment Results 189

The Dilemma: The "'COVID slide' may be especially
troublesome for English-language learners, the 5 million
students still learning English in the nation's K–12 schools"
(Mitchell, 2020). How will schools and districts measure
multilingual learners' "COVID slide"? 189

Action 1: Engage in Reflective Practice and Inquiry 192

Reflect on and Inquire About Students'
Social-Emotional Learning 194

Action 2: Determine Priorities in Assessing in
Multiple Languages 195

Engage in District- and Schoolwide Professional
Learning on Assessment Literacy 196

Action 3: Challenge the Status Quo in Assessment: Take the
Multilingual Turn 198

Transform Assessment Practices 198

Action 4: Assess Multilingual Learners From a
Strengths-Based Lens 199

Apply an Assets-Based Philosophy to All
Multilingual Learners 199

Action 5: Enact Effective Assessment Practices in
Multiple Languages 201

Exert Locus of Control Through Assessment *as*,
for, and *of* Learning 202

Let Multilingual Learners Take the Lead 202

Give Teachers Autonomy in Communities of Practice 203

Determine Program Effectiveness Based on Assessment in Multiple Languages 204

Consider Principles for Assessment in Dual Language Contexts 205

Action 6: Use Assessment Data in Multiple Languages to Leverage Systemic Change 206

Evoke Systemic Change Through Assessment 206

Envision Systemic Change for Multilingual Learners 207

Instill Systemic Equity and Excellence for All Students 209

Apply Assessment *as*, *for*, and *of* Learning in Your Setting 210

Taking Action: Lessons Learned From Crises 211

Facing the Issue: Consider Crises as Eye-Opening Opportunities for Multilingual Learners 212

For School Leaders 212

For District Leaders 212

Resolving the Dilemma: Provide Equitable Educational Opportunities to All Minoritized Students, Including Assessment in Multiple Languages for Multilingual Learners! 212

Resources for School and District Leaders

Resource 7.1 Taking Action Based on Assessment Results in Multiple Languages 215

Resource 7.2 Determining Priorities in Assessing in Multiple Languages 216

Resource 7.3 Planning a Student-Led Conference Supported by a Teacher and Family Member 218

Resource 7.4 A Learning System Centering on Multilingual Learners 219

Glossary 220

References 230

Index 248

 online resources All end-of-chapter resources are available for download at resources.corwin.com/assessingMLLs-LeadersEdition

Foreword

At first glance, the title *Assessment in Multiple Languages* may conjure a technical image of furnishing standardized tests in the many languages of the multilingual students in our school communities. The term *assessment* is so tied to high-stakes testing that we move toward this narrative quickly, neglecting that assessment is something that we do with great dexterity with our multilingual students at the classroom level and often in collaboration with the school and district level. We make content and language decisions, integrate related scaffolds, and heterogeneously group our students. Our nimbleness as educators and leaders of multilingual learners is adaptive, responsive, and ongoing. Together, we work at the heart of assessment. Margo Gottlieb's comprehensive handbook of assessment *as*, *of*, and *for* multilingual learners is the practical resource for school and district leaders.

The Greek construct of *assidere* is a helpful heuristic in consideration of our multilingual students. *Assidere* in Greek means "to sit beside," so assessment is literally sitting alongside our students (Stefanakis, 2002). Unlike standardized tests that tell us a few things once a year, assessment focuses on how our multilingual learners understand and perform content and language, which includes their home language(s) and ways of thinking that differ from our own. With that understanding, we are in a constant state of change at the classroom, building, and district level.

At the heart of such nimble decision making for multilingual learners are English and multilingual teachers, instructional coaches, building principals, and multilingual directors who may or may not share the same languages with their multilingual learners. These educators have different roles and responsibilities, but also different positionalities within their settings—or, more simply, how they are ascribed within their institutions. An enduring challenge is often the dissonance or even clashes between multilingual teachers and general education colleagues and principals. Multilingual teachers often speak with a particular discourse, drawing from their training and expertise in working alongside multilingual learners. In contrast, most general education teachers and administrators have limited training in how to conceptualize teaching and learning of multilingual students. This is compounded by the lack of pre- or in-service training in how to best serve and engage with multilingual students, families, and dedicated specialized staff. Such dissonance or tension between the specialist and the generalist comes from individuals amplifying particular parts of their professional identities. The multilingual educators amplify their specialty: multilingual instruction and assessment. The administrators amplify theirs: leadership around assessment. Yet the aim of the specialist and the leader is really about arriving at *congruence*, pointing to how specialty and leadership can intersect and how each unique set of individuals can engage more fully in conversations about assessment of multilingual learners. The enduring question: How can we intersect leadership with that specialized orientation toward multilingual learners as we assess alongside our multilingual students?

Working toward this intersection involves a commitment to "set aside" so we can "sit beside" a newer way of thinking and leading assessment for our multilingual students. In Gottlieb's new book, *Assessment in Multiple Languages: A Handbook for School and District Leaders*, she reframes how assessment can be shaped more responsively and to center the needs, rights, and identities of multilingual students. As we have experienced and are experiencing the impact of the COVID-19 pandemic, our attention to the rights of our multilingual students and families is even more critical than ever.

Gottlieb starts the book by discussing the language ecology of schools and how it is foundational in creating a linguistically inclusive environment. Oftentimes the orientation and instructional practice is monoglossic, where only English is used for teaching and assessing. This de facto or standardized policy then takes on a life of its own, and decisions about teaching, learning, and assessment are framed by such ideologies. Some are so nuanced and subtle that they escape notice of educational leaders. Others are more overt or "linguicist" in orientation, where languages other than English are disrespected and diminished. Gottlieb states, "There might be some movement from a deficit to an assets- or strengths-based position for marginalized minoritized students in terms of educational discourse, but, in large part, it has yet to manifest itself in mainstream pedagogy and even less so in assessment" (p. X). To this end, Gottlieb challenges educational leaders to make this incremental change not only with specialized multilingual teachers, but within the entire school infrastructure, informing a new and responsive way to think about the assessment of multilingual students.

In Chapter 1, Gottlieb has an explicit discussion of language planning and policy. Most educational leaders are attuned to educational policies at the national level and how those are interpreted and practiced at the local level. Yet, without explicit discussion about language planning, educational policies morph into being the language plan for the school, obscuring and dismissing the rights and linguistic resources of multilingual students.

Gottlieb points out that the Every Student Succeeds Act allows for native language testing. The Migrant Policy Institute (2020) reports that 31 states and the District of Columbia use such native language tests, yet challenges persist as these tests may not align with the language of instruction in their schools. For example, taking a state exam in Spanish may be furnished and allowed, but if students have limited to no access to such instruction in Spanish, then there is a mismatch in the instruction and assessment cycle, or what Abedi (2004) calls an issue with construct validity. We are not really testing what we think we are testing if the original instruction was not set up to be inclusive of languages other than English, where multilingual students would have more access to the content. Gottlieb addresses this mismatch of instruction in one language and assessment in another by discussing alignment at the classroom, school, district, and state level, providing leaders with discussion prompts for inquiry.

Instructional provisions in languages other than English seem like a far stretch if teachers do not speak the languages of their students, but Gottlieb shows in Chapter 2 that this challenge can be tackled. By creating a robust enrollment process for all students, the language practices can be gathered by multiple personnel to create a linguistic portrait of multilingual learners. She examines the role that standards play along with intake information about the linguistic resources of students and families. Importantly, she ends this chapter detailing how to engage families reciprocally in the assessment process as they are critical partners in the *assidere* of assessment.

Chapter 3 involves the careful planning of curriculum and assessments in multiple languages. Gottlieb emphasizes that by having resources in the languages of the students, we have a more comprehensive portrait of their language repertoires. In so doing, teachers and leaders can more easily ascertain content understanding along with their growing proficiencies in multiple languages.

Chapter 4 details how leaders can organize the collection of assessment information. Gottlieb emphasizes that organizing and collecting such information must be grounded in linguistically, racially, and ethnically inclusive principles. Recognizing that schools are often sites for reproducing the social inequalities of the greater society (Anyon, 2005; Berlak & Berlak, 1981), this is central to properly informing what to organize and collect. Centrally, Gottlieb stretches what we think to be worthy of measurement, stretching us to think about the inclusion of multilingual and multimodal representations of learning. Students can perform and represent their content and language knowledge in creative and sophisticated ways. Such suggestions tie directly back to Gottlieb's opening chapters about language policies, where representations of content and language can include all the language resources of our multilingual students.

In Chapter 5, Gottlieb discusses how we interpret assessments and offer feedback to students and families across their many languages. Gottlieb emphasizes that this should include multiple sources of information that are coherently brought together to create an assessment portrait of each multilingual student. Merely focusing on the large-scale state exam provides an inadequate picture of what students are understanding and performing within content and their languages.

In Chapter 6, Gottlieb furnishes leaders with specific ideas on how to share information with educators and families. Notably, she always comes back to how the multilingual students can be the central leaders as they share a portfolio of their assessments that include summative, formative, and performance-based representations of their learning across their languages.

In the final chapter, Gottlieb summarizes her work stating that the core of leading assessment for multilingual learners includes the following actions: (1) engage in reflective practice and inquiry; (2) decide priorities in multiple languages; (3) challenge the status quo in assessment; (4) assess multilingual learners for a strengths-based perspective; (5) enact effective assessments in multiple languages; and (6) use assessment data to leverage systemic change. Gottlieb helps us—as educational leaders of assessment of, for, and with our multilingual students—pivot toward a more linguistically inclusive paradigm. *Assessment in Multiple Languages: A Handbook for School and District Leaders* is the practical planning resource for school and district leaders as it walks methodically through all the ways we need to think differently about assessment and how to implement such changes. Packed full of technical steps, it is also guided by the latest research in the teaching and learning of multilingual learners.

—**Patricia Morita-Mullaney**
Associate Professor
Purdue University

Preface

En tiempos de crisis, los inteligentes buscan soluciones, y los inútiles culpables.

In times of crisis, intelligent people seek solutions, and useless people [look for] those to blame.

—Anonymous

▶ Stop the violence against women and girls—now! A message in an outdoor space in Oaxaca, México

The Dilemma

What do we do as educational leaders to counteract inequity and social injustice of marginalized students?

Every new school year brings a sense of renewal and hope in the minds of educators. Due to prevailing uncertainty, frustration, and stress, the most recent academic years may be considered exceptions. It has been especially

(Continued)

(Continued)

troubling given the global reach of COVID-19 affecting the health, economics, and educational systems of societies and nations. The pandemic has disrupted and penetrated so many aspects of our personal and professional lives . . . and it has been compounded by a visceral backlash of racial injustice and inequity.

The lockdown to avoid getting infected and spreading the virus has forced us into a new virtual reality. Changing our modus operandi to successful online or hybrid teaching has been a long-term process and, given our will to be the best educators we can be, has forced us to revisit our values. Confronting a reset button at a distance and a whole new set of virtual resources to rely on has been perplexing to all stakeholders across educational systems, from states to classrooms and from superintendents to students and family members.

Let's view this unique time in our history as an opportunity to do something different rather than reclaim the normalcy of a pre-COVID world. We can actually take advantage of school closures and the challenges of online learning by turning our attention to the inequities and social injustices in education. In particular, let's focus on those disturbing issues of underrepresented and underprivileged students, such as their inaccessibility to technology and unreliability of high-speed internet. Let's look at today with a do-good spirit in an era of potentially unbridled equity. What we need is out-of-the-box thinking, not a return to practices that stymie multilingual learners because they are not able to use their full linguistic repertoires to learn in school.

Ana Patel is a district leader in a county serving elementary, middle, and high schools who has spent time with educators reflecting on the troublesome conditions and events of the recent past and their impact on students, families, and educational systems. Together the group has not only discussed oppression and racial injustice but has also asked what they might do to disrupt these hateful crimes on humanity in their own communities. They have investigated how to change policies that have perpetuated the marginalization of students and their families to promote stakeholder collaboration and voice.

The leadership team now plans to extend their courageous conversations to tackle linguicism and discuss how to shift the mindset of educators to be more affirming of the district's multiple languages and cultures. Their goal is to elevate the status of multilingualism and dual language/multilingual education starting with their mission, vision, and values and then extending this philosophy to a variety of evidence-based instructional and assessment models. Ultimately, as part of their equity agenda, the district team plans to initiate a comprehensive revamping of their assessment system to be inclusive of the multiple languages of their student population.

- In what ways does this scenario resonate with you?
- What is your stance for educating, in particular assessing, multilingual learners?
- What are you doing as an educational leader to move the equity needle for multilingual learners?
- How might assessment in multiple languages help fulfill the goal of advancing equity across the school system?

Let the truth be known. Science has verified that children are born with the capacity for developing multiple languages and their exposure to multiple languages has positive effects on their brain development, executive functioning, and social interaction. Yet, in large part, the United States clings to a monoglossic (monolingual) belief where we equate language and literacy with English. The empirical bases for the bilingual advantage, evident in child development and beyond, must be brought to the forefront of educating multilingual learners—from recent arrivals to the United States to those who have sustained language loss through generational assimilation.

There might be some movement from a deficit- to an assets- or strengths-based position for marginalized minoritized students in terms of educational discourse, but, in large part, it has yet to manifest itself in mainstream pedagogy and even less so in assessment. Now is the time to convert those negative impressions that have been perpetuated through baseless claims into positive action. These pervasive social justice and equity issues must be righted for our bi/multilingual learners and their families. One small contribution to this cause is assessment in multiple languages, as instruction, in order for multilingual learners to have enhanced access and opportunities for educational advancement. That is the goal we have set for *Assessment in Multiple Languages: A Handbook for School and District Leaders.*

Assessment in Multiple Languages is a companion to *Classroom Assessment in Multiple Languages: A Handbook for Teachers* (Corwin, 2021). This book, designed especially for educational leaders, is organized around the assessment cycle using a parallel format and organization; however, it has totally new content. Its intent is to foster collaboration among educators to jumpstart and sustain assessment in multiple languages across schools and districts. Together the two-volume compendium offers distinct perspectives and a full complement of assessment resources for educators of multilingual learners in elementary and secondary settings.

PURPOSES OF THE BOOK

Assessment in Multiple Languages portrays a multiphase equitable assessment cycle for multilingual learners at school and district levels. The purpose of the book is to spark school and district leaders to take action in planning and enacting assessment in multiple languages that is vital for the educational success of multilingual learners. By examining an assessment cycle focused on equity, local accountability systems inclusive of multilingual learners become built around unique language and assessment policies that underscore linguistic and culturally sustainable practices.

According to federal legislation, educational accountability rests with states and districts for determining school performance by setting annual goals to increase student achievement, high school graduation rates, individual student growth targets, and English language proficiency milestones. Goals must also be applied to student subgroups—racial/ethnic groups, gender, students with disabilities, English learners, and low-income students. These guidelines may frame educational accountability; however, we question their equity for multilingual learners due to their exclusion of multiple languages and multiple measures as part of the equation.

Like *Classroom Assessment in Multiple Languages*, this book challenges the monolingual or monoglossic bias that pervades our society and educational psyche, especially when it comes to assessment. It is a cry for equity and social justice that sets out to change language hierarchies in schools and districts by assuming bilingualism is the norm for multilingual learners. Thus, *Assessment in Multiple Languages* sets out to frame linguistic and cultural resources of multilingual learners as strengths and for school and district leadership to engage in transformative practices that lead to assessment in multiple languages.

ANOTHER ASSESSMENT BOOK: WHY?

I admit it—I seem to be addicted to writing about assessment for multilingual learners. It started with my dissertation when I developed a trilingual assessment in Spanish, Lao, and English to contribute to the language education field and prove that indeed a reliable and valid multilingual assessment is possible. It has been followed by many books and umpteen chapters and articles, yet I am still not convinced how educators can best be informed about the linguistic and cultural assets of multilingual learners and how to convert that information into action. The following pages are one more attempt to lasso educational leaders into believing, advocating, initiating, reforming, or transforming their assessment practices in multiple languages.

Most assessment books for K–12 educators deal with assessment *of* learning, addressing high-stakes tests, the scores that are generated, and the consequences from the inferences that are drawn from the results. Equity, or as the case may be inequity, is a prominent issue that comes to mind when examining large-scale testing involving multilingual learners. In this book, we highlight how common assessment across classrooms that is designed by school or district teams can also be assessment *of* learning. Coupling that with assessment *for* and *as* learning, we present a complete and balanced compendium of assessment approaches to be nurtured and supported by school and district leadership. Figure 1 shows one way to depict this triad of assessment approaches with multilingual learners assuming a central position.

Assessment in Multiple Languages is a much-needed resource for educator leaders who work in schools or districts with multilingual learners at a distance or face-to-face. It envisions the assessment cycle within an educational system and

FIGURE 1 Assessment *as, for,* and *of* Learning for Multilingual Learners

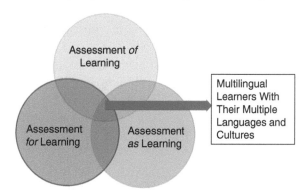

addresses assessment-related issues that schools and districts typically tackle, such as student classification and reclassification criteria. All in all, these two related assessment books allow for the dissection, discussion, and resolution of dilemmas that impact the world of multilingual/dual language/bilingual/language education.

AUDIENCES AND THEIR EXPECTATIONS

Educators of multilingual learners, in particular school and district leaders, who are confronted with assessment challenges are the primary audience for this book, although there is wide applicability across stakeholder groups. Figure 2 describes the potential uses of this book for different audiences.

FIGURE 2 Audiences for *Assessment in Multiple Languages*

DESIGNED FOR:	TO:
Multilingual families and communities	Become aware of their civil and educational rights; engage in assessment-related activities
Teachers and coaches	Advocate and collaborate on designing, enacting, and evaluating assessment in multiple languages
Assessment, data, or instructional coaches	Contribute to and give feedback on planning, enacting, and evaluating assessment practices for multilingual learners in one or multiple languages; facilitate interpretation of data
Coordinators/directors of language programs and curriculum	Use impact data to improve school or district language programs; help craft and share language policy; formulate principles and policies for assessment in multiple languages; embed assessment into curriculum
School leaders, principals, and assistant principals	Co-plan common assessment with multilingual learners in mind coupled with professional learning opportunities for teachers to reliably evaluate student work
District leaders	Mentor schoolwide/districtwide educational programs; update the mission, vision, and values of the school/district to be inclusive of dual language/multilingual education
Teacher educators	Prime pre-service and in-service teachers for working with multilingual learners, including assessment in multiple languages

Overall, like its classroom companion, this book crosses the fields of general education, language education, and assessment. As a result, educators who delve into *Assessment in Multiple Languages*, whether independently or in collaboration with other school leaders, will:

- Understand the legal precedence, rationale, and evidence for assessment in multiple languages for their multilingual learners

- Add to their assessment practices and policies at school and district levels

- Embed assessment *as*, *for*, and *of* learning into their school and district plans

- Realize how social-emotional, conceptual, and language development are tied to assessment for multilingual learners

- Empower teachers to engage in the assessment cycle in multiple languages and make evidence-related decisions

- Be inclusive of multilingual learners and their families throughout the assessment process

ORGANIZATION OF THE BOOK

Each opening scenario, as in this preface, opens with a multimodal representation of a current dilemma that has implications for assessment. Its purpose is to spark lively discussion between school and district leaders on how to initiate, enhance, or reimagine assessment practices in multiple languages for multilingual learners. It is followed by First Impressions, probing questions to encourage educators' response to the dilemma at hand. Each chapter closes around a series of engaging questions for school and district leaders that is followed by how to face the issue and pose a possible resolution.

In Chapter 1 we identify terminology present in the authorizations of the Elementary and Secondary Education Act and replace the federal terms with more assets-based ones. We continue by defining "multilingual learners" and their subgroups as well as describe a continuum of instructional models. Next, we offer research that supports bilingualism/multilingualism and underscores the social nature of learning, sociocultural language theory, and translanguaging as viable grounding for learning. Finally, we explore how to create language and assessment policies that make multilingualism and assessment in multiple languages integral to the functioning of schools and districts with multilingual learners.

Chapter 2 delves into research on effective leadership in dual language settings. It introduces the five-phase assessment cycle designed for multiple languages and addresses its purposes and first steps in planning at state, district, and school levels throughout the year. The chapter touches on initial identification of multilingual learners, annual and interim standardized testing, common assessment for districts and schools, and how combining data sources in multiple languages provides a comprehensive portrait of multilingual learners. Additionally, we introduce how linguistic and cultural sustainable assessment can evoke systemic change through social justice.

Chapters 3 through 7 describe in depth each phase of the assessment cycle, incorporating considerations for assessment in multiple languages: (1) planning, (2) collecting and organizing information, (3) interpreting information and providing feedback, (4) evaluating and reporting information, and (5) taking action. As does its companion, this book maintains a balance among assessment *as*, *for*, and *of* learning throughout each phase as an anchor for the design of a comprehensive and balanced assessment system. In addition, for each phase of assessment, we offer a variety of tools and resources for school and district leaders to apply to their individual contexts.

CONTRIBUTION TO SOCIAL JUSTICE AND EQUITY FOR MULTILINGUAL LEARNERS

Equity and social justice are on the minds of educators and educational organizations alike. The National School Boards Association states that "public schools should provide equitable access and ensure all students have the knowledge and skills to succeed as contributing members of a rapidly changing global society, regardless of factors such as race, gender, sexual orientation, ethnic background, English proficiency, immigration status, socioeconomic status, or disability" (cited in Center for Public Education, 2016, p. 2). Leadership for Educational Equity, a nonprofit leadership development organization, is devoted to ending the injustice of educational inequity (see educationalequity.org). One more instance is the Center for Education Equity where "equity, excellence, opportunity to learn, and social justice are at the heart of everything we do at MAEC" (Mid-Atlantic Equity Consortium, 2020). Indeed, the interplay of (in) equity and social (in)justice have become symbolic of our current crises that plague our minoritized students and communities.

Although we are thrilled that equity and multilingual learners have finally come into the limelight, we hope that educators view these turns as mandates with true sincerity and conviction rather than a passing fancy. There are some of us warriors who have been fighting this cause our entire professional careers—some of white privilege, others multiracial, and still others clinging to the identities of their ancestors. Together we have formed a mighty resistance to the status quo and have, in our own ways, forged uncharted territories on behalf of multilingual learners and their families.

Multilingual learners deserve relevant and fair assessment that generates useful information for improving teaching and learning in linguistically and culturally sustainable ways. Anything less is not equitable, just, or worthwhile. We assert that largely missing has been an educational system that embraces assessment in multiple languages. When multilingual learners can show their full linguistic and academic repertoires that are recognized across classrooms, schools, and districts, we enhance their opportunities for success in school and beyond.

SPECIAL FEATURES

There are some unique features of this book for school and district leaders to help them probe more deeply into assessment issues in multiple languages and engage multilingual learners. The opening scenarios, coupled with photographs, offer insight into assessment-related issues that educational leaders are grappling with. They may serve as stimuli for dialogue among school and district administrators along with First Impressions at the close of each scenario that pose questions for triggering action by leadership teams.

Throughout the chapters, you will see STARs, indicating time to Stop-Think-Act-React to how an issue applies to your setting or simply to get caught up on the latest theory or research. At the close of each chapter, there are further thought-provoking questions for school and district leaders. Lastly, there are an array of figures, many of which are duplicated as resources at the close of each chapter and posted to the book's website. These checklists, rating scales, and assorted activities are to share with all stakeholders who work with multilingual learners.

TIPS FOR DESIGNING AN ASSESSMENT SYSTEM IN MULTIPLE LANGUAGES

As shown in the photos that follow, multilingualism is a natural way of life around the globe; indeed, it is a worldwide phenomenon. What would it take for our schools and districts to adopt such a stance?

Stimulating systemic change in schools and districts with multilingual learners is a complex undertaking that takes time, much thought and deliberation, and coordination of effort. Here are some suggestions for leadership teams to consider in how to infuse assessment in multiple languages throughout an educational system, whether involving a strand of dual language/immersion classrooms within individual schools, a whole school, or an entire district devoted to multilingual education.

▶ Multilingual signs; a commonplace sight in Germany

To change the educational mindset through systemic assessment reform involving multilingual learners, school and district leaders must:

1. Ensure your proposed assessment system is compatible with principles of multilingualism and multiculturalism and is an expression of the school's or district's mission, vision, and values.

2. Develop, revisit, or revise your language and assessment philosophy and policy, seeking input and feedback from students, family members, teachers, and other school leaders.

3. Interact with the greater school and district community by connecting to multilingual families, organizations, and services. Leverage their linguistic, cultural, and experiential resources to promote assessment in multiple languages.

4. Rely on the community and multilingual learners' funds of knowledge (identified in #3) to help craft district/school curriculum with embedded assessment.

5. Foster school, community, and district participation in designing a framework that highlights multilingual learners' languages, cultures, and identities, the foundation of an equitable assessment system.

6. Guarantee that for local accountability purposes, the language(s) of assessment reflect the language(s) of instruction of each content area and exemplify the school's or district's language policy.

7. Provide educators sustained professional learning opportunities coupled with coaching around assessment literacy to further the understanding of the purposes for varying types of assessment, their link to content and language standards, and the use of data for making decisions.

8. Take action in advocating for multilingual learners and assessment in multiple languages and listen to the voices of students, families, and educational experts.

FACING THE ISSUE: TAKE TIME TO REFLECT ON INEQUITABLE PRACTICES

In this section, we revisit the central dilemma of the chapter and pose questions that recap important points for discussion among school and district leaders. In this preface, we confront two prominent inequities—racism and linguicism—and suggest that time be carved out of faculty meetings, professional learning, or intradistrict networking groups to confront this reality head-on. In other words, educators should be afforded time to be introspective and self-reflective in regard to their teaching practice.

In the case of outright discrimination occurring in schools or the district, leadership might wish to engage outside agencies, organizations, and families to help counsel and alleviate the situation. Professional learning opportunities, whether in person or online, or critical action research might be helpful in airing some of the inherent controversy surrounding these deep-seated issues. Here is a sampling of some questions to ask when facing discrimination against multilingual learners and their families as well as inequities in assessment in multiple languages.

For School Leaders

➢ Do you dare defy other school/district leaders who disagree with your school's or district's views toward and commitment to multilingualism? If so, what is your evidence to substantiate your stance? How might you convince your colleagues or educational community to change?

➢ How might you and other educators update your school's or district's mission and vision to be more representative and inclusive of multilingualism, multiculturalism, equity, and social justice?

➢ What actions might you and others suggest to counteract discrimination and social injustice of multilingual learners and their families?

➢ With whom might you collaborate to provide more equitable assessment opportunities for multilingual learners?

For District Leaders

➢ How might an assessment audit serve as a stimulus for change, and how might you share your position with the community, school leaders, and other educators?

➢ How might you promote viewing the languages and cultures of your students in a positive light?

➢ How might you inaugurate critical conversations as part of ongoing professional learning in your schools or district to explore discrimination associated with multilingualism and multiculturalism?

➢ How might you view assessment in multiple languages in a positive light? How do you plan to use data sources from multiple languages to create a full portrait of each student?

RESOLVING THE DILEMMA: FOCUS ON ASSESSMENT EQUITY FOR MULTILINGUAL LEARNERS!

At the conclusion of each chapter, there is a resolution to the dilemma that is introduced in the opening scenario. Here we see the commitment of Ana and her leadership team to eliminate the deleterious effects of discrimination in assessment of multilingual learners. The leadership team's endorsement of multiple-language use in assessment illuminates the need for additional evidence of learning besides the often dubious high-stakes data, which in most cases are in English. Also, Ana ensures that schools in her district document multilingual learners' social-emotional development through structured narratives that are tied to the students' multilingual and multicultural identities.

As you can see by this glimpse into the pages ahead, we try to capture the impact of crises that have ravaged the United States since 2020 on assessment for multilingual learners with the anticipation of changing the conditions for teaching and learning, not the students. First, the coronavirus has directly affected school environments, modes of learning, and school life of educators and families alike. Second, the cultural reckoning and awakening that have stemmed from racial and civil unrest have had a social-emotional impact on students and families. We can only hope that these life-changing watershed events provoke dual responses of equity and social justice for multilingual learners and other minoritized students, subsequently permeating education and society as a whole for years to come.

Acknowledgments

The assessment series, *Classroom Assessment in Multiple Languages: A Handbook for Teachers* (Corwin, 2021) and this companion book for school and district leaders, has been written during times of much anguish and consternation. The two books were born during the prolonged months of racial injustice, civil unrest, and the COVID-19 pandemic that indeed have impacted every facet of our professional and personal lives. The unforeseen consequences of these crises have spilled over onto its pages. If it wasn't for the amazing fortitude and support of some very special people at Corwin, I don't know if these books would have ever become reality; I thereby acknowledge their contributions. Thank you, Dan Alpert, Program Director of Equity and Publisher, a staunch believer and strongest of advocates, along with Lucas Schleicher and Mia Rodriguez, Senior and Associate Development Editors, who ensured compliance of every detail that goes into the final product. Thanks also goes to the Marketing Managers Maura Sullivan and Sharon Pendergast who helped shepherd these books postproduction to the marketplace. Lastly, appreciation goes to Amy Schroller, Project Editor for the assessment series, and to those persons responsible for the cover designs, editing the dual projects, copy editing, typesetting, proofreading, and indexing, who spent many an hour to ensure the quality of the end products.

About the Author

Margo Gottlieb, PhD, is Co-founder and Lead Developer for WIDA at the Wisconsin Center for Education Research, University of Wisconsin–Madison, having also served as Director, Assessment and Evaluation, for the Illinois Resource Center. She has contributed to the crafting of language proficiency/development standards for American Samoa, Commonwealth of the Northern Mariana Islands, Guam, TESOL International Association, and WIDA and has designed assessments, curricular frameworks, and instructional assessment systems for multilingual learners. Her professional experiences span from being an inner-city language teacher to working with thousands of educators across states, school districts, publishing companies, governments, universities, and educational organizations.

Highlights of Margo's career include being a Fulbright Senior Specialist in Chile and being appointed to the U.S. Department of Education's Inaugural National Technical Advisory Council. TESOL International Association honored Margo in 2016 "as an individual who has made a significant contribution to the TESOL profession within the past 50 years." Having presented in 20 countries and across the United States, she relishes having opportunities for extensive travel and cherishes her global friendships.

Margo's widespread publications include more than 90 chapters, technical reports, manuals, monographs, articles, and encyclopedia entries. Additionally she has authored, co-authored, and co-edited 21 books, her latest being *Classroom Assessment in Multiple Languages: A Handbook for Teachers* (2021), *Beyond Crises: Overcoming Linguistic and Cultural Inequities in Communities, Schools, and Classrooms* (with D. Zacarian and M. Calderón, 2021), *Language Power: Key Uses for Accessing Content* (with M. Castro, 2017), *Assessing Multilingual Learners: A Month-by-Month Guide* (2017), *Assessing English Language Learners: Bridges to Educational Equity* (2nd ed., 2016), *Academic Language in Diverse Classrooms: Definitions and Contexts* (with G. Ernst-Slavit, 2014), *Promoting Content and Language Learning* (a compendium of three mathematics and three English language arts volumes co-edited with G. Ernst-Slavit, 2013, 2014), and *Common Language Assessment for English Learners* (2012).

This book is dedicated to those persons who do not believe in the messenger who paradoxically has been labeled a person of white privilege and to those educators who do not believe in the message—that multilingualism shapes and defines the fastest-growing segment of the school population, our multilingual learners. The chapters before you will hopefully change your mindset by providing a convincing argument of the critical importance of assessment in multiple languages as a staple in the education of any and all students who choose to use multiple languages to carve out their identities and sense of belonging.

CHAPTER 1

Looking at Assessment Through the Lens of Multilingual Learners

▶ A most recognized worldwide multimodal resource (Queens, New York)

Sem um senso de identidade, não pode haver luta real.

Without a sense of identity, there can be no real struggle.

—Paulo Freire

The Dilemma

But English learners *isn't an appropriate term (or label), and initial screening only in English isn't an accurate depiction of who our multilingual learners are and what they can do!*

Neruda School in a K–12 unified school district in a sprawling suburb has a principal who is a strong advocate of multilingual learners and their families. Over the years, Carmen Hernández has supported the growth of dual language education in her building, which started with kindergarten six years ago, and has been an outspoken activist across the district network. Carmen speaks Spanish and English, and understanding the value of bilingualism, she encourages her students, teachers, and families to communicate in the languages they feel most comfortable using.

The same sentiment is not felt across the district; in fact, Carmen feels quite isolated in her leadership role. Her quest to promote the exclusive use of assets-driven language in referring to the students, their languages, and their cultures seems to be at a standstill. She realizes that these beliefs are a precursor to her goal of introducing common assessment in multiple languages to the other principals, and currently she doesn't know where to turn.

District administration insists on using the terminology of federal legislation and designated by the state—namely English learners, long-term English learners, *and* English learners with disabilities—*in part to be aligned with the intact system, but also because data are collected exclusively in English. Consequently, most of the schools have dutifully adopted these terms to be in accord with the district's accountability plan. Carmen believes that these rather pejorative labels have a negative impact on multilingual learners' identities. She wants to ensure that all students have positive self-images and are proud to represent the multilingual multicultural world in which we all live.*

*As Carmen refuses to perpetuate language that defines multilingual learners as a liability and the gathering of information only in one language, the principal has started suggesting changes in the terminology for students and language education programs at school and district meetings. The teachers at Neruda support their principal's action and have taken the initiative to delve into the literature on the social-emotional effects of categorizing and labeling **minoritized students** in negative ways, especially those from multilingual backgrounds. Additionally, they have had critical conversations with their multilingual learners to gain firsthand knowledge of the students' feelings and attitudes toward current labels.*

Bolstered by her faculty and community, Carmen decides to push district leadership a bit further. Using her building-level power, she initiates a campaign to update and transadapt enrollment forms and important communiqués with hopes the initiative will extend to collecting intake information in multiple languages for district screening measures. Based on the initial enthusiasm for the project, she requests to form a district task force to research how to capture the strengths of her multilingual learners through assessment in multiple languages.

- In what ways does this scenario resonate with you?
- What is the terminology you use in your school or district to represent multilingual learners, their languages, and language education programs?
- What has your district done in regard to having enrollment procedures and initial screening in multiple languages?
- What are the language and assessment policies that you currently have in place for your multilingual learners?

Let the truth be known. "When a bilingual individual confronts a monolingual test . . . both the test taker and the test are asked to do something they cannot. The bilingual test taker cannot perform like a monolingual. The monolingual test cannot 'measure' in the other language" (Valdés & Figueroa, 1994, p. 87). Today's reality reverberates this sentiment. Although increasing numbers of **multilingual learners** are immersed in grade-level content in multiple languages, **assessment** at school and district levels generally remains in the language of accountability—English. Participation in language education programs that are striving to meet the goals of bilingualism, biliteracy, biculturalism, cultural competence, and the most recent pillar, critical consciousness (Palmer, Cervantes-Soon, Dorner, & Heiman, 2019), is skyrocketing. Yet rather than having an assets-based orientation to education, reports from **large-scale assessment**, in particular, still tend to demoralize multilingual learners by emphasizing what these students lack, English language proficiency (Gándara, 2015).

In the pages before you, we attempt to overturn this negativity toward multilingual learners and their families that has prevailed in U.S. schools and districts. Rather than view these students as "disadvantaged" (who typically depress large-scale test scores), we take a more positive strengths-based stance where language and culture are viewed as a right and resource (Ruíz, 1988). In fact, we prioritize the term **bi/multilingual learners** (*bi* to accentuate *bilingual*) throughout this book to highlight an assets-based orientation toward languages, literacies, and learning. It comes with growing recognition of the richness of bi/multilingual learners' linguistic repertoires (Martínez, 2018; Ortega, 2014).

In this chapter, we offer a historical backdrop and rationale for assessment in multiple languages. We suggest how language and assessment policies pose ways in which school leaders and district administrators can agree on how to infuse multilingualism and multiculturalism into educational life. Finally, we explore how translanguaging and social-emotional learning from a multilingual perspective can shed some light on how we might envision assessment for multilingual learners in multiple languages.

Thinking about **linguistic equity** and **social justice** (e.g., as exemplified by the beliefs of Carmen and her staff), assessment for multilingual learners that is only in English fails to represent the whole child and tends to exacerbate the "achievement gap" mentality. Let's turn this perception around and follow Wong's

(2016) suggestion to use multilingualism as a tool for actually closing the achievement gap. Multilingual learners have the distinct advantage of having multiple languages and cultures at their disposal. School should be a place to nurture those resources; advance these students' language, conceptual, and social-emotional development; and assess more equitably.

This book is devoted to offering educators in leadership roles, including district administrators, principals, coaches, teachers, and other school leaders, ways to thoughtfully plan and execute assessment in multiple languages using an assessment cycle as a guide. In doing so, we offer ideas and strategies for documenting multilingual learners' growth over time. This ongoing process led by school and district leaders, with input from the community, will hopefully result in systemic educational change while making a difference in the lives of multilingual learners and their families.

FEDERAL INFLUENCE ON TERMINOLOGY AND ASSESSMENT

The United States has historically been and continues to be a multilingual multicultural mosaic with a long precedent of schooling in multiple languages that can be traced back to its colonization. In fact, by the late 17th century, at least 18 different languages were spoken by European ethnic groups (Crawford, 1987). Throughout American history, there have been waves of nativism and xenophobia followed by acceptance and promotion of multilingualism that have been reflected in our educational systems.

Fast-forward to the early 1960s. With the influx of Cubans post *la revolución cubana*, Coral Way Elementary School in Miami, Florida, was established as an exemplar for enrichment dual language education. For the first time in recent U.S. history, there was substantiation of assessment data that support bilingualism. As Crawford (1987) elaborates, "In English reading, both language groups did as well as, or better than, counterparts in monolingual English schools, and the Cuban children achieved equivalent levels in Spanish."

Since the mid-1960s, much of the terminology related to "bilingualism" and "bilingual learners" in kindergarten through twelfth-grade (K–12) settings has been influenced by legislation and litigation. The power of the precedent set by the courts and the federal government has come with deficit language and, in large part, emphasis on compensatory or remedial rather than enrichment education. Ironically, federal bilingual education policy was born as a legislative attempt to *remedy* the *inequities* experienced by **language minority students** in the educational system (Wiese & García, 1998); now, well into the 21st century, the goal of equity, especially as it applies to curriculum, instruction, and assessment, remains in question.

Federal Legislative Directives

The Elementary and Secondary Education Act (ESEA), a federal assistance and education reform package, was enacted in 1965 as part of Lyndon Johnson's

War on Poverty and Title VI of the Civil Rights Act of 1964. Reauthorizations of ESEA over the years have moved away from bilingual/multilingual acceptance to monolingual assimilationist perspectives and policies as the basis for educational reform.

As shown in Figure 1.1, in 2015, almost a half-century after the landmark Bilingual Education Act of 1968, references to bilingualism or multilingualism were nowhere to be seen in K–12 federal legislation. Consequently, states paid little heed to the possibility of developing or using **tests** or measures other than

FIGURE 1.1 Changing Terminology and Provisions for Language Assessment in Reauthorizations of the Elementary and Secondary Education Act (ESEA)

ESEA LEGISLATION	YEAR	TERMINOLOGY FOR MULTILINGUAL LEARNERS	PROVISIONS FOR ASSESSING ENGLISH LANGUAGE PROFICIENCY
Bilingual Education Act (BEA), Title VII of ESEA	1968	Students with limited English speaking ability (LESA)	None
Reauthorization of the BEA	1978	Children of limited English proficiency (LEP)	None
Improving America's Schools Act (IASA)	1994	Children and youth of limited English proficiency (LEP)	LEP students in state assessment systems but no mention of English language proficiency assessment
No Child Left Behind Act (NCLB)	2002	Limited English proficient (LEP) students	Annual English language proficiency testing required based on state- or consortium-wide K–12 English language proficiency/development standards aligned to state content standards
Every Student Succeeds Act (ESSA)	2015	English learners (ELs)	Requirements under NCLB, (although accountability moves from Title III to Title I), plus uniform statewide procedures to determine classification criteria for entrance (identification) and exit from language support

ones in English. This stripping of bilingualism has served as a national de facto language policy where English stands as the ultimate language of power (Menken, 2008), which, in turn, has tended to negate state acceptance of data from large-scale assessment in multiple languages as part of accountability provisions.

In 1994, assessment of "children and youth of **limited English proficiency (LEP)**" was first mentioned in federal legislation, the **Improving America's Schools Act (IASA)**, along with the introduction of state **academic content standards**, state testing, and **accountability**. The identical wording has been used in successive iterations of ESEA, notably the **No Child Left Behind Act (NCLB)** and **Every Student Succeeds Act (ESSA)**, with reference to assessment in the students' home language: "to the extent practicable, assessments [shall be] in the language and form most likely to yield accurate data on what such students know and can do in academic content areas, until such students have achieved English language proficiency." In other words, for over 25 years, the value-added nature of assessment in home languages for bi/multilingual learners has been part of federal policy, yet states have paid little attention to it (G. Solano-Flores & Hakuta, 2017).

Furthermore, both NCLB and ESSA call for:

- The inclusion of English learners (ELs) in annual state academic assessment (minimally in mathematics, reading/language arts, and now science)

- ELs to be assessed in a valid and reliable manner and provided with appropriate accommodations [Section 1111(b)(2)(B)(vii)(III)]

- States to exclude ELs from one administration of reading or language arts assessment (but not math) for those who have been enrolled in U.S. schools for less than a year

- States to name in their plans the languages other than English that are present to a "significant extent" in their participating student population, and to make "every effort" to develop such assessments [Section 1111(b)(2)(F)]

As of the 2013–2014 academic year, 13 states offered reading/language arts, mathematics, or science assessments in languages other than English (U.S. Department of Education, 2016). Under ESSA, states may assess students in their **"native" language** for three to five years on the state reading/language arts achievement tests with no limit to assessing mathematics and science in a student's "native" language. We italicize the term *native language* (students' home language) as it is a misnomer; today the majority of multilingual learners have been born and raised in the United States and are learning two or more languages simultaneously. Now is the time to seize the moment and for schools and districts to design "accountability systems [to] provide information that triangulate[s] with state and local English Learner plans and visions that have been developed to align with a state's theory of action" (Goldschmidt & Hakuta, 2017, p. 40).

Relax and Reflect: What does federal legislation tell us about assessment in multiple languages?

For almost two decades, the U.S. Department of Education has endorsed the development of state annual **achievement testing** in multiple languages. Are you in one of the states that offers a test in a language other than English for accountability purposes? If so, you may wish to investigate whether it is a translation (and, thus, not a truly valid representation of ELs' languages and cultures), whether it is a **transadaptation** (with considerations for linguistic and cultural nuances), or whether it has been developed specifically for multilingual student populations.

There are two provisions in ESSA that trigger state assessment in languages in addition to English. One is that ELs must be present in the student population to "a significant extent," and the second reference is to the fact that the state must make "every effort" to develop assessments in additional languages.

- How has your state interpreted these provisions?

- Do you believe that there is a fair representation of your multilingual student population in state assessment?

- How might you exert yourself to move conversations forward to bring equity to student assessment whether in one or multiple languages?

The deficit-ridden language in ESEA legislation tends to perpetuate educational inequity. At the federal level, what has prevailed over the years as the official definition of an EL is as follows:

> An individual, aged 3 through 21, who was not born in the United States or whose native language is a language other than English where difficulties in speaking, reading, writing, and understanding the English language may be sufficient to deny him or her the ability to meet challenging academic standards, the ability to meet the State's proficient level of achievement on State assessments, the ability to successfully achieve in classrooms where the language of instruction is English, or the opportunity to participate fully in society. (Sections 3201 and 8101 of ESSA, 2015)

The Name Game: Implications for Assessment

By now you should have noticed that we prefer the inclusive term *multilingual learners* to capture all students who are or have been exposed to and identify with multiple languages and cultures inside and outside of school. At times we add *bi/* in front of *multilingual* to represent bilingual learners within multilingual learning environments. We retain the label **English (language) learners (ELs)**, however, when referring to the legal term for the subset of multilingual learners who represent a protective class of students under federal legislation (i.e., ESSA) and accountability.

Carefully examine the federal definition of an EL, spelled out earlier, that shapes national and state educational policy. On a personal level, which words or phrases stand out to you? Perhaps you could highlight them.

Now go back and examine the wording more closely. Discuss its positive or negative connotations with other educators. Is it reflective of your personal belief system and that of your school or district? Why or why not? To what extent do you feel that this definition is a fair representation of your multilingual learners?

Think about crafting a more assets-based definition with your leadership team. How might you put your students in a more positive light? What are the implications of your definition for assessment?

To recap, ESSA requires states to create a uniform process for identifying ELs and a standard set of criteria for their "exiting" from language support programs. This directive, however, does not preclude screening of new students in languages other than English. As shown in Figure 1.2, according to Title I of ESSA, annual assessment results of ELs are to be disaggregated by specific designations.

There has been increasing focus on the accurate identification, assessment, and referral of multilingual learners with disabilities, especially those who qualify as ELs. Attention to this issue, in part, has been sparked from both the under- and overidentification of ELs, as compared to non-ELs, for special education services.

English learners with disabilities qualify for language support *and* services for their named disability; both are to be included in the students' **individualized**

FIGURE 1.2 English Learner Subgroups Recognized in ESSA

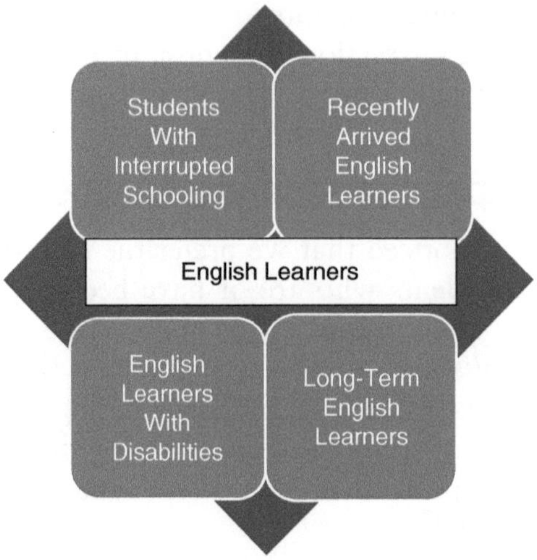

Students With Interrrupted Schooling

Recently Arrived English Learners

English Learners

English Learners With Disabilities

Long-Term English Learners

education programs (IEPs). This dual identification requires a multiphase assessment process that involves multiple measures in multiple languages. The type of disability also triggers permissible accommodations of these students in large-scale assessment and accountability systems for both English language proficiency and achievement (Burr, 2019).

Related Resources for Identifying Multilingual Learners With Disabilities

You might explore the following resources:

- Your state education agency should offer guidance for multilingual resources (or ELs) with disabilities consistent with the **Individuals with Disabilities Education Improvement Act** of 2004 (U.S. Department of Education, n.d.). This federal law states, "assessments and other evaluation materials are provided and administered in the language and form most likely to yield accurate information on what the child knows and can do academically, developmentally, and functionally, unless it is not feasible to so provide or administer" [Section 1414(b)(3)(A)(ii)].

- State frameworks inclusive of multilingual learners should have provisions for supporting assessment in the students' languages. Consider following the recommendation from the Council of Chief State School Officers' *English Learners with Disabilities Guide*—"State frameworks for identifying English learners with disabilities should include comprehensive evaluation measures" (Park, Martínez, & Chou, 2017, p. 17)—or check out the Minnesota Department of Education's Evaluation Lending Library with materials in Spanish and other languages (https://tinyurl.com/y3b4bh2x).

- There is a growing library of books dedicated to English learners with disabilities that treat assessment through a strengths-based lens, such as *Focus on Special Educational Needs* (Sánchez-López & Young, 2018) and *Special Education Considerations for English Language Learners: Delivering a Continuum of Services* (Hamayan, Marler, Sánchez-López, & Damico, 2013).

Long-term English learners (LTELs) are generally in middle and high schools, having attended U.S. schools for more than five years without having attained a threshold of academic language proficiency in English. Some LTELs are considered **students with interrupted formal education (SIFE)** while other SIFE are refugees or migrants, have inconsistent attendance records, are transient, or are the product of discontinuity in educational services. M. D. Brooks (2020) claims that these terms are problematic as they:

- Use single measures in English to judge students

- Undervalue the students' out-of-school interests, strengths, and abilities

- Overlook the context for learning (oftentimes these students are labeled "remedial")

- Do not consider languages and cultures as integral to student identity

- Do not represent students' opportunities to engage in grade-level content

- Do not value student input in decision making

Recently arrived English learners, also known as **newcomer students,** are a heterogeneous mix of multilingual learners. Some have been schooled outside the United States and have reached high levels of literacy and achievement in a language other than English. Others have had years of "English as a foreign language" and, while not yet commensurate with their peers, do communicate effectively in English. Still others, who know varying degrees of English, carry a SIFE label, and finally there are refugees who arrive at our shores, as in unaccompanied minors, without knowing a word in English.

Although not mentioned in federal legislation, historically there has been an underserving of multilingual learners as *gifted and talented* due to heavy reliance on test results in English. State and/or local policies determine **gifted and talented English learners** with identification criteria and assessment measures that, in large part, privilege **proficient English speakers**. Typically, identification involves the assessment of cognitive abilities in combination with achievement testing (Mun et al., 2016)—in English—with norms skewed toward proficient English students with little or no consideration for students' strengths in their other languages.

Absent in classifying ELs or other multilingual learners as gifted and talented is assessment in multiple languages. A recommendation from an exploratory study has suggested to "create alternative pathways to identification, allowing schools to use a variety of different assessment instruments (including native language ability and achievement assessments and reliable and valid nonverbal ability assessments) and apply flexible criteria to ensure that students' talents and abilities are recognized" (Gubbins et al., 2018). We must expand exceptionality for multilingual learners at the upper end to encompass multiple measures and data points to include a spectrum of cognitive, social and emotional, linguistic, and reasoning abilities expressed in multiple languages.

The Power of Labels

Most labels for English learners (and other multilingual learners) act as liabilities as they are based on monolingual constructs, standard English, and **high-stakes testing** data in English. As a result, educators tend to stigmatize rather than elevate the status of bilingualism and biliteracy. The dominant narrative that accompanies these labels is that these students are deficient linguistically and academically (M. D. Brooks, 2020). These negative labels become a deterrent to student learning, which, in turn, adversely impacts their self-esteem. This kind of framing essentializes students' abilities and masks their assets and educational experiences.

A growing number of researchers and educators question the pejorative labels applied to multilingual and other students who are marginalized by educational institutions (Flores & Rosa, 2015; Kibler & Valdés, 2016; Seltzer, 2019). Many educational leaders are aware of the destructive nature of these labels, yet blindly follow the language of legislation rather than challenge the status quo. There is no reason why schools and school districts cannot take on the entrenched system and create more meaningful designations while retaining separate terminology for state and federal accountability.

To summarize, there is a social stigma attached to the classification scheme designed to sort multilingual learners that has tangible and lasting effects on multilingual learners' opportunities in school (Umansky & Dumont, 2019) and their identity formation. Even though the vast majority of multilingual learners function in more than one language, large-scale assessment remains directly aligned to a **monoglossic language ideology**. Unfortunately, there is little attention to the worth of bilingualism in language testing practices (Shohamy, 2011).

Subgroups of Multilingual Learners, Specifically English Learners

Rarely is the heterogeneity of the student population considered, no matter the labels. For example, ELs, one of the many groups of multilingual learners, are identified based on mandated assessment data rather than their unique characteristics, histories, or contexts of learning. Given this cautionary note, Figure 1.3 is a table of subgroups of ELs with space to provide eligibility criteria, associated assessments, and the language(s) of data collection. It is partially completed here for gifted and talented multilingual learners with a blank duplicate as Resource 1.1.

FIGURE 1.3 Defining Subgroups of Multilingual Learners With Assessment Data

SUBGROUP OF MULTILINGUAL LEARNERS	TYPICAL ELIGIBILITY CRITERIA	APPLICABLE ASSESSMENT DATA	LANGUAGES OF ASSESSMENT
Gifted and talented	*Multiple measures (in English), including upper-end percentiles on achievement tests*	*Student oral, written, graphic, and visual samples; teacher recommendations; and a student interview*	*English and the student's other language(s)*
ELs with individualized education programs (IEPs)			
Students with interrupted formal education (SIFE)			
Long-term English learners (LTELs)			
Recently arrived English learners			

Relax and Reflect: Are eligibility criteria fair for defining subgroups of multilingual learners?

Based on the information you produce in Figure 1.3, would you consider assessment equitable for ELs in your state, district, or school? To what extent are there examples of assessment in multiple languages? Do these assessment measures contribute to fair identification of subgroups of multilingual learners? Why or why not?

What suggestions might you or a team of educational leaders make to improve assessment practices in multiple languages to more accurately shape the criteria for defining subgroups of multilingual learners? How might you consider changing current policy, and what would you provide as evidence?

More Subgroups of Multilingual Learners

Multilingual learners, by definition, possess a single linguistic repertoire composed of multiple languages; they are not to be considered two monolinguals in one (Grosjean, 1989). Just as there are terms for different subgroups of ELs, so, too, there are terms that are more strengths-based that have been gaining acceptance over the past decade. Besides multilingual learners, these include **bilingual/dual language learners**, and **emergent (or emerging) bilinguals** (Escamilla, 2006; García, 2009; García, Kleifgen, & Fachi, 2008; Menken, 2013).

There are other multilingual learners who have been exposed to multiple languages, or continue to be, besides the heterogeneous group of ELs. These students, considered multilingual learners due to their flexible use of two or more languages, are included in broad categories of "proficient English learners." Figure 1.4 offers the broad categorization scheme of multilingual learners, in addition to English learners, including the following.

1. *"Exited" English learners* (aka former ELs) are students who have previously participated in language support programs and have met state "exit" criteria; in most states after four years post-participation, their educational status as ELs is officially changed; however, they remain from multilingual multicultural homes.

2. **Heritage language learners** are students who come from home backgrounds with family connections to multiple languages and cultures, although the students may not be proficient in a language other than English, such as members of Indigenous communities (e.g., Navajo, Hawaiian, Arapaho) who are studying their heritage language for preservation, restoration, or maintenance (Kelleher, 2010). Some may have been ELs.

3. *Never English learners* may be **simultaneous bilinguals** who grow up proficient in multiple languages (one of which is English). Some of these multilingual learners are considered **balanced bilinguals** as,

FIGURE 1.4 Multilingual Learners in K–12 School Systems

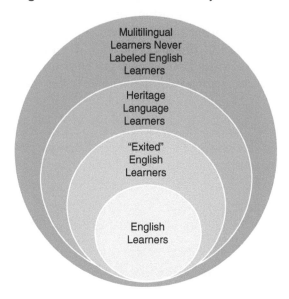

depending on the context, they are equally proficient in two languages. Additionally, there are learners from "upwardly mobile, highly educated, higher socio-economic status" families participating in language education programs in this category (de Mejía, 2002). In large part, for these **elite bilinguals** participating in immersion or dual language programs, English is the sole language at home.

Reframing Language Education Models

Besides a broad classification scheme for defining multilingual learners, there is an equally wide range of language education models for instructing these students. Currently, more and more multilingual learners are learning in English and a **partner language**. In 2000, there were an estimated 260 dual language education programs in the United States where K–8 students were learning in multiple languages for minimally half a day. By the 2012–2013 academic year, the number of programs had risen exponentially to over 2,000 in over 39 states (Boyle, August, Tabaku, Cole, & Simpson-Baird, 2015). Given the tremendous growth of dual language/multilingual programs, states and school districts should be open to the option of assessment in multiple languages. Not only could the assessment yield more valid inferences for multilingual learners; it could also serve as a response to the call for equity.

Notice the relationship between named instructional models and the language(s) for assessment shown in Figure 1.5, a continuum of language models for multilingual learners (see the Glossary for definitions of the models). It is a broad range of programs that begins with **submersion** (**"sink or swim"**), one with no built-in language support, and proceeds to **dual language, one-way** or **two-way immersion programs** with systematic inclusion of two languages to support learning. **Structured English immersion (SEI), English as a second language (ESL), sheltered English,** and **English language development (ELD)**

programs are almost exclusively in English. **Transitional bilingual** programs introduce two languages with a gradual movement to English. The goal of the last two categories of programs (and schooling) in the continuum is to develop and nurture bi/multilingual individuals minimally in two languages. Although there is mixed recognition of the value and use of multiple languages for instructional purposes, there is no reason to deny multilingual learners access to the languages of their choice for classroom assessment (Gottlieb, 2021).

Deficit-laden terminology related to multilingual learners serves as a gatekeeper to prevent their educational advancement. Remember, language is a resource,

FIGURE 1.5 A Continuum of Instructional Models for Multilingual Learners: Implications for Assessment in Multiple Languages

Deficit Orientation 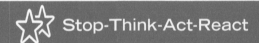 Assets Orientation

Language Education Models or Programs

Submersion in English	Structured English Immersion	English as a Second Language/ English Language Development	Sheltered English	Transitional Bilingual/ Early Exit	Maintenance/ Late Exit/ Developmental Bilingual	Dual Language/ Two-Way Immersion/ One-Way Immersion

Assessment Only in English ⟹ Assessment in Multiple Languages

---

☆ **Stop-Think-Act-React**

Relax and Reflect: What terminology prevails in your setting?

Educators tend to classify the many terms that refer to multilingual learners and multilingualism as either **additive (assets-based)**, impartial, or **subtractive (deficit-based)**. With other school leaders, take time to categorize the terms in Resource 1.2 (or others specific to your setting) as either positive, neutral, or negative in their messaging. Discuss any built-in **biases** you perceive, and determine where your school or district fits along the continuum.

Based on your findings from this activity, what message do you think your school or district sends to its multilingual learners, teachers, and community? What is the basis for or evidence of your thinking? What might be your rationale for change, and how might you involve multilingual learners, the community, and/or other educators?

What alternative language might you pose that is more equity-driven and representative of your students' assets? What are the implications for assessment in multiple languages?

not a barrier. Educators need to make the commitment to use more constructive affirmative language. There should be "enrichment" for multilingual learners, not "remediation." There should be **linguistically and culturally sustainable** resources that help empower and inspire multilingual learners rather than **"intervention" programs** that discourage their attempts to learn in creative ways. After all, it is equity, not equality, that should prevail throughout educational systems.

Equally distressing are some of the ways we describe and treat language education. Are our multilingual learners who are "submersed" in English going to sink or swim? What does "English as a second language" mean? Students should not be seen as "second language" learners if they are allowed to use their entire language repertoire to make meaning (Kleyn & García, 2019). The term *dual language*, referring to two distinct languages, is also being contested with preference for the descriptor *dual language bilingual education* to better attend to the sociolinguistic realities of acceptance of **translanguaging** as part of language learning of bi/multilinguals (M. T. Sánchez, García, & Solorza, 2017).

Examining Language Allocation in Immersion Models

Each program type or instructional model for multilingual learners represents a unique learning environment that has implications for assessment. Even within the same program type there can be varied language allocations that affect instruction and assessment. For example, in one-way or two-way dual language immersion programs there may be different configurations of language distribution, such as:

- Beginning with 90% of the day in a partner language and 10% in English (generally in kindergarten) and gradually decreasing 10% each year in the partner language with subsequently increasing English until reaching 50% in both languages (in fifth grade)

- Beginning with and maintaining a 50/50 division of languages

- Alternating languages each day

- Associating languages with specific content areas (e.g., math in one language, science in another)

- Not having a specified language allocation plan but allowing for the flow of two languages

There is simply no single program or pathway that addresses all the needs of the multifaceted group of students known as multilingual learners (California Department of Education, 2020). Nor is there necessarily a strict adherence to one or more languages when it comes to assessment for multilingual learners; it depends on the local context.

School leaders and administrators must be mindful of the inequities in policies that still prevail in the world of **multilingual education**. Hopefully the tide is

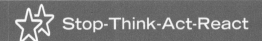

Relax and Reflect: How might you describe your language education program(s)?

How would you describe the language allocation of instructional models that involve two languages in your school and district? What is the corresponding assessment, and in which languages? Is there a 1:1 match between the percentage of language allocation and the languages of assessment? How might you strike a better balance of assessment between languages?

turning so that multilingual education is seen as an invitation for embracing multiple perspectives and a stimulus for deep thinking for all stakeholders. However, skepticism still remains, and when enacting assessment, there are many misconceptions to dispel. Let's take a look at our students through a multilingual lens and strive for educational programs that are linguistically and culturally sustainable.

Linguistically and Culturally Sustainable Schools

Any and all language education programs or models that embrace bilingualism or multilingualism should aim to operate within linguistically and culturally sustainable schools. These schools are ones where the climate, pedagogies, policies, and practices are responsive and representative of the language and cultural experiences of multilingual learners and their families. Everyone is

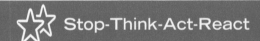

Relax and Reflect: How might you enhance the linguistic and cultural sustainability of your school or district?

In the introductory vignette, Carmen pushes her colleagues to initiate a districtwide campaign to update the terminology of its enrollment forms and the use of multiple languages to administer the initial screening of multilingual learners and interpret the results. What can you do personally or collectively (as a school, district, or community) to make terminology more descriptive of the students' multiple languages? What might you do, or whom can you contact, if there are no provisions for assessment in multiple languages upon students' initial entrée into your district?

committed to supporting students in enhancing the cultural and linguistic competence of their communities while simultaneously accessing the ways of other cultures.

THE RESURGENCE OF BILINGUAL AND DUAL LANGUAGE EDUCATION

The rise and fall of bilingual education in the United States has a long history. In recent times, there has been less emphasis on transitional bilingual education (where the goal is achievement in English with the "home" language gradually removed from instruction) in favor of models that recognize the strength of growing two languages (with the goals of bilingualism and biliteracy). In essence, dual language education has become the norm and gold standard (Palmer et al., 2019). However, there are also apprehensions that in "this neo-liberal multicultural era of dual language education, bilingualism and cultural diversity are too often commodified off the proverbial backs of [multilingual] Latinx youth" (García & Sung, 2018).

Multilingual Education

Multilingual education is an umbrella term that represents the infusion of linguistically and culturally relevant and sustainable practices into teaching and learning. Multicultural education operates within a sociocultural context under the umbrella of comprehensive school reform. At its heart is a critical pedagogy that represents social justice, which is important for all students (Nieto, 2018). Multilingualism and multiculturalism support culturally sustaining pedagogy that fosters and maintains linguistic, literate, and cultural pluralism as part of schooling (Paris, 2012).

In this book, the concepts of multilingualism and multilingual education are considered an extension of Cenoz and Gorter's 2015 definition: "multilingual education refers to the use of two or more languages in education, provided that schools aim at multilingualism and multiliteracy" (p. 2). In school, multilingualism is inclusive of multilingual learners' multiple languages and cultures as resources for curriculum, instruction, and assessment in their pursuit of deep and sustained learning in two or more languages. Like many educational concepts, multilingualism is not monolithic with one set way of being; in fact, it is so diversified within the multilingual population that it might be envisioned along a continuum (de Jong, 2019b).

Research That Supports Bilingualism/Multilingualism

A growing body of evidence worldwide favors bilingualism and the benefits of multilingual education. In the brief review of research in Figure 1.6, we see that multilingual learners, including those with special needs or "disorders," tend to possess a greater linguistic skill set than their monolingual counterparts. There is strong evidence that biliteracy development tends to be value added—that is, multilingual learners can simultaneously enhance their literacy in two languages. However, systematic assessment to document growth in multiple languages is absent.

FIGURE 1.6 Positive Effects of Bilingual and Multilingual Education: A Brief Synopsis of Recent Research

RESEARCHERS	SUMMARY OF FINDINGS USING THE AUTHORS' TERMINOLOGY
Bialystok (2011)	Bilingual individuals consistently outperform their monolingual counterparts on tasks involving executive control.
Collier & Thomas (2017)	High-quality, long-term bilingual programs "close the gap" in achievement between ELs and "native" English speakers after 5–6 years of schooling.
Cummins (2017)	There is overwhelming research evidence that languages interact in dynamic ways in the learning process and that literacy-related skills transfer across languages as learning progresses. Bilingual/multilingual instructional strategies acknowledge the reality of, and strongly promote, cross-language transfer.
Goldenberg & Coleman (2010)	Teaching ELs to read and develop literary skills in their "primary language" boosts their reading achievement in English; additionally, teaching ELs subject matter content in their "primary language" is a more efficient strategy than teaching content in a language students do not understand as well.
Hopewell & Escamilla (2013)	Applying two competing ideologies to interpret one data set—emergent bilinguals who are viewed as two monolinguals in one vs. those students who are seen as having a single integrated language repertoire—yields two interpretations. The same set of scores tells an entirely different story depending on the frame of reference, and these differences are statistically significant.
Paradis, Genesee, & Crago (2011)	Knowing two or more languages and using them, even with language or reading impairments, is a personal, social, professional, and societal asset.
Valentino & Reardon (2015)	The English language arts test scores of ELs in bilingual programs grow at least as fast as, if not faster than, those in English immersion programs.

Multilingual Theory: Cummins's Contributions

The theoretical contributions of Jim Cummins on the value of multilingualism as foundational for multilingual learning have been long lasting. Cummins (1979, 1981) describes the close relationship between languages as linguistic interdependence—that is, each language bolsters the other to optimize the academic performance and metalinguistic awareness of multilingual learners. Additionally, Cummins posits that multilingual learners' language learning is drawn from a common language proficiency, where knowledge acquired in one language is potentially available for the development of another. These theories have had direct relevance to the instruction and assessment of multilingual learners.

COMPETING THEORIES AND VIEWS OF ASSESSMENT

Two theories of language learning are competing for how we envision assessment in one or more languages. Both stem from linguistics (the study of language) and its related fields of applied linguistics, sociolinguistics, and psycholinguistics, which have strongly influenced the instruction and assessment of multilingual learners. Having these dueling language theories is causing angst for school leaders who, on one hand, must comply with federal mandates (a structuralist orientation) yet, on the other hand, understand the value of the social nature of learning that occurs in every classroom (a sociocultural orientation).

Structural linguistics, dominant for more than a half-century, has traditionally governed large-scale language assessment. In this theoretical approach, language is viewed as static, linear in development, and composed of underlying interrelated structures within a linguistic system. Language tests have been designed, in large part, to assess students' proficiency in different areas or language domains, such as listening, speaking, reading, and writing, in isolation. As an extension of this structuralist thinking, students' performance has been equated with the measurement of their language learning at a given point in time with results that fall within a predictable straightforward progression.

Another tenet of structuralist theory is equating the end point of a language proficiency scale with reaching the proficiency of an "idealized native speaker" (The Douglas Fir Group, 2016). However, fitting into a native-speaking norm does not necessarily imply superior or more effective language use. The bar of being "native" or native-like is not sufficient or necessary for becoming a successful and effective teacher or learner (Mahboob, 2019). The structural stance counters educational perspectives that see teaching and learning as cultural, social, and interactional (Hawkins, 2019).

Counterstructuralism language assessment, especially in the classroom, is seen as a socially embedded interactive process for improving teaching and learning (Bachman & Damböck, 2017; P. Moss, 2008). Here language development is seen as fluid, which is a function of students' familiarity with a topic, audience, and particular context. Consequently, there is tremendous variability in the pathways to language proficiency with no one trajectory. At the classroom level, assessment *as*, *for*, and *of* learning occurs within a sociocultural context that is student-centered where teachers act as facilitators.

Sociocultural theory sees language as a social activity with active student engagement and interaction. A sociocultural theoretical orientation takes on a more democratic approach that is open to the participation of stakeholders (Lynch, 2001; Shohamy, 2001). There is greater acceptance of bi/multilingual learners' use of multiple languages as instructional tools and acknowledgement of translanguaging as a classroom instructional and assessment practice (García, Johnson, & Seltzer, 2017).

Depending on a school's language policy, translanguaging may occur naturally, such as in the hallways, or in specified learning situations, such as engaging in cross-linguistic comparisons. The growing recognition of translanguaging as an expression of sociocultural theory has helped transform the acceptance of multiple languages and languaging as part of schooling (García & Wei, 2018). Translanguaging in school reflects the natural linguistic practices of bi/multilingual learners who have access to and use of their full linguistic repertoires, irrespective of the language(s) of instruction (García et al., 2017; Otheguy, García, & Reid, 2015).

In dual language and bilingual education classroom contexts that have a strong presence of two languages, assessment may be dynamic, inclusive of

▶ The use of translanguaging on a menu (in Spanish and English)

translanguaging, to show what multilingual learners can do with language(s) in different circumstances. Assessment of multilingual learners revolves around these students' competencies to make meaning to act as scientists, historians, or literary authors, for example (Kleyn & García, 2019). Although the notion of translanguaging has been proposed for large-scale language assessment, this more socially oriented way of languaging has yet to be accepted and operationalized by the language testing community (Chalhoub-Deville, 2019).

The challenge for educators is how to respond to the medical model and discrete-point or multiple-choice tests that exemplify structuralism when this model simply cannot relate the complexity of the interaction among multiple languages. To counter this long-standing precedent, there has been a push toward more socioconstructivist perspectives and social justice ideologies that are inclusive of the cultural and linguistic variety of multilingual learners (V. González, 2012). At the heart of the shift toward more student-centered learning and assessment is the social embedded nature of learning, which accounts for the broader communities where students live (Kaul, 2019).

So for now both theoretical orientations are alive and well in the world of multilingual education. Thus, the potential conflict between data from large-scale **standardized testing** (that are structuralistic in nature) and information from classroom assessment (that exemplifies socioculturalism) remains. Teachers, school leaders, and district leaders must navigate these dueling theories in supporting language development and assessment for multilingual learners whether in one or multiple languages.

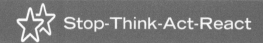

Stop-Think-Act-React

At times there is conflict between the theory that grounds large-scale testing and the theory that reflects classroom instructional assessment practices. Teachers and administrators alike feel this tension.

How can teachers, together with school and district leaders, reconcile the differences in these views in describing and determining approaches to assessment for multilingual learners? How might you balance these conflicting ways of understanding and using information from assessment in multiple languages? In professional learning communities or leadership teams, discuss how these different theoretical camps can both apply to multilingual assessment in your setting.

CREATING LANGUAGE AND ASSESSMENT POLICIES

Language policy is educational policy; language and assessment policy should help shape local accountability. To do so, programs for multilingual learners need to craft and maintain an infrastructure to support state and district accountability systems in ways that promote valid, appropriate, and useful assessment (Howard et al., 2018). Therefore, from the outset, a district's policy for incoming and ongoing information for multilingual learners should include multiple languages. Additionally, multilingual learners participating in dual language programs should be assessed in multiple languages to allow for measurement of student growth rather than absolute outcomes (Menken, 2008).

School Policy

School leaders, instructional leaders, school staff, community representatives, family members, and students should join in building consensus around how to portray their school as a haven for multilingualism and multiculturalism. A stunning example of how multilingualism has become engrained into the fabric of teaching and learning is Lincoln International School (Asociación Escuelas Lincoln) in Buenos Aires, Argentina. Led by a language coach, its teachers have crafted and adopted a set of belief statements and evidence-based practices to form a language philosophy that highlights the strength of multilingualism. Some of these language-centered, research-based principles have become engrained in the school's practices. As multilingualism and multiculturalism are critical to family communication, cultural identity, making meaning, and thinking, the school promotes and reinforces their continuous development. Equally important, in learning through multiple languages, students, through teacher facilitation:

- Construct understandings about interculturalism and global interdependence

- Develop competencies in conflict resolution in socially responsible ways

- Formulate insights to foster movement across cultural and linguistic boundaries

- Respect multiple perspective taking

Consequently, school-level assessment policy stems from language policy, reflecting consensus reached by multilingual learners, teachers, school leaders, and families.

District Policy

Districtwide policies should establish coherent K–12 language programming for multilingual learners, articulate the district's stance toward multilingualism and multiculturalism, and support families along with the greater community. A school district language policy should consist of a dynamic action statement that defines the positive role of language (and culture) in areas of each school's operation. It should include expectations for linguistic parity and pride of multilingualism. An effective district language policy should:

- Represent and be responsive to local community needs, interests, and issues

- Promote the development and implementation of educationally and theoretically sound programs for multilingual learners that deliver positive results with fidelity

- Be formulated and supported by all stakeholders (administrators, teachers, students, parents, community members)

- Exemplify or be embedded in the school's mission, vision, and values

- Comply with (and exceed) all federal, state, and local assessment and accountability requirements (August, Goldenberg, & Rueda, 2010)

A district language policy that embraces multiple languages sets precedent for establishing an assessment policy that is inclusive of multiple languages. Within the districtwide system, a multilingual assessment policy should include provisions for:

- Multiple sources of data among an array of stakeholders

- Linguistic and cultural equity

- Multiple languages reflective of teaching and learning

- Acceptance of multiple perspectives

- Balance of assessment approaches

- Validity of large-scale and interim measures

- Student and teacher voice

MULTILINGUAL LEARNERS AND SOCIAL-EMOTIONAL LEARNING

In this age of everyday stress filled with uncertainty for everyone that has been complicated by persistent worldwide crises, multilinguals' social and emotional development and well-being are as important as academics. Issues of health, economics (e.g., living in poverty or homelessness), fearing deportation of family members, and having students serve as the family spokesperson all factor into multilingual learners' social-emotional state. Administrators have to be sensitive to social and emotional issues that plague multilingual learners and their ties to the students' linguistic and cultural identities.

The state of Delaware defines **social-emotional learning** (SEL) as "a process through which students acquire and apply the knowledge, attitudes, and skills necessary to understand and manage emotions, set and achieve positive goals, feel and show empathy for others, establish and maintain positive relationships and make responsible decisions" (see Rodel Teacher Council, 2018). For multilingual learners, SEL should always reflect multicultural norms and traditions rather than those valued by a monoglossic society.

The Collaborative for Academic, Social, and Emotional Learning (CASEL) describes SEL as a lever of equity in creating inclusive school communities (see CASEL District Resource Center, 2021). As all learning is in fact social and emotional (Frey, Fisher, & Smith, 2019), it is critical for multilingual learners and their families to be part of that conversation. Equally important, school leaders need to have a pulse on documenting SEL as part of the core instructional program, and of course, for multilingual learners, that means collecting information in one or more languages.

TIPS FOR ASSESSMENT IN MULTIPLE LANGUAGES

Multilingual learners are talented individuals who deserve every opportunity to have language choice when engaged in learning with or without embedded assessment. Remember that there is much **intersectionality** or crossover in this student population with other groups—in particular, race. As we have mentioned before, one unique variable, language proficiency, is going to vary, not necessarily based on test scores, but according to multilingual learners' personal and educational experiences, social-emotional influences, the situation at hand, the audience, and the purpose of the task.

Assessing bi/multilingual learners in multiple languages is a complex undertaking. Therefore, school and district leaders need to formulate ground rules or policies with other educators. Here is some general advice for what to do to help form a community that values instruction and assessment in multiple languages.

1. Ensure that multilingual learners are comfortable using multiple languages by creating a warm, inviting, and safe school environment, whether in person or remote, that accentuates and supports their assets.

2. Maintain caring empathetic relationships with multilingual learners and their families whether online or in person; show compassion for stressful situations by supporting social-emotional development and learning in multiple languages.

3. Adopt assets-based terminology for students, families, programs, curriculum, instruction, and assessment that makes multilingual learners proud of who they are and strengthens their identities.

4. Create and disseminate a district and/or school language and assessment policy with leadership teams, other educators, and family members to help set parameters for multiple language use.

5. Insist that initial screening of new students is comprehensive, minimally with provisions for collecting information about multilingual learners' use of multiple languages, and, to the extent possible, includes language samples in the students' multiple languages.

6. If necessary, augment district or school policy on the assessment of multilingual learners to make provisions for treatment of data in one or more languages.

FACING THE ISSUE: RETHINK TERMINOLOGY AND LANGUAGE EDUCATION MODELS

Multilingualism is a worldwide norm. Gaining acceptance of a multilingual stance in U.S. educational circles when the power of English is irrefutable and xenophobia prevails in some circles is indeed a challenge. Federal terminology simply does not reflect multilingual learners' full linguistic repertoire, nor does it reflect students' strengths.

The educational future of today's children and youth rests in our hands. Take that privilege to maximize the potential of multilingual learners by cultivating their most enduring assets—their languages and cultures. Use these questions as a starting point to engage in ongoing discussion about how to make multilingualism and multiculturalism the new education normal in your setting with assessment central to maintaining linguistic and cultural sustainability of your district and schools.

➤ How might you amend the initial enrollment process to more accurately capture multilingual learners' abilities in multiple languages?

➤ What might you do to change terminology around multilingual learners to be more strengths-based (if warranted) and their participation in different instructional programs?

➤ Does current assessment in your school represent the whole student, including multilingual learners' full range of language use? If not, what might you do to ensure that the students' languages and cultures are fairly represented?

For District Leaders

➤ How might you enhance the initial enrollment and screening process to more accurately depict the languages and cultures of multilingual learners?

➤ What might you do to enhance terminology for multilingual learners, their participation in language education programs, and related assessment while adhering to state/federal regulations?

➤ Do you believe that assessment procedures adequately reflect your district's mission, vision, and values? Do they represent the students' and families' languages and cultures? Do assessment practices capture multilingual learners' full range of language use? How can you make assessment more equitable and just?

RESOLVING THE DILEMMA: ACCENTUATE EQUITABLE ASSESSMENT PRACTICES FOR MULTILINGUAL LEARNERS!

As the district task force that Carmen is chairing tackles issues of intersectionality of language, culture, race, and economics, on one level, the educators realize that they are applying a bandage to a deep wound and serious educational concern that deserves immediate attention. School leaders brainstorm how to enhance multilingualism and multiculturalism in schools. Here are some ideas that the group has generated:

• Have friendly and visually appealing signage around schools and the district office; welcome families in the languages of the students and the community

• Display original student work in multiple languages and murals that depict multiple cultures

• Encourage multilingual learners to use multiple languages per school language policies

- Ensure that all communication that touches families is in the languages they understand

- Insist that any instructional program with provision for multiple languages assesses multilingual learners in those languages

Specifically, in thinking about assessment in multiple languages, the task force makes the following recommendations:

- Pledge that school- and district-related technology, such as computers or handheld devices, has greetings, important information, and initial enrollment forms in the languages of the students and their families

- To obtain comprehensive and more equitable baseline data, give incoming students opportunities to record orally and respond in writing in languages of their choice in addition to English

- Urge multilingual learners to complete surveys on their use of multiple languages in a variety of contexts as well as their language choices for instruction and assessment

- Throughout the school year, revisit results from assessment in multiple languages to ensure a balanced representation of data for multilingual learners

How might classrooms, schools, and districts around the nation begin to recognize the moral imperative of promoting and infusing multilingualism and multiculturalism into educational practice? We suggest beginning with broadcasting the benefits of multilingualism and multiculturalism by adopting positive terminology to describe the learners and their educational programs. One clear-cut way to advance the assets of multilingual learners is to value and highlight their languages and cultures in curriculum, instruction, and assessment.

Assessment in multiple languages should be engrained into the psyche of school. Simply stated, federal language and assessment policy has generally overlooked a national resource and treasure—multilingual learners along with their languages and cultures. That's where districts and schools can make a difference.

Resources for School and District Leaders

RESOURCE 1.1
The Link Between Subgroups of Bi/Multilingual Learners and Assessment

Compare eligibility criteria including applicable assessment data in one or more languages for different groups of multilingual learners from the table that follows. Do you feel that the criteria accurately portray the strengths of the students? How might you make the criteria and assessment data more equitable?

SUBGROUP OF MULTILINGUAL LEARNERS	ELIGIBILITY CRITERIA	APPLICABLE ASSESSMENT DATA	LANGUAGES OF ASSESSMENT
Gifted and talented multilingual learners, including ELs			
Multilingual learners, including ELs with individualized education programs (IEPs)			
Students with interrupted formal education (SIFE)			
Long-term ELs (LTELs)			
Recently arrived English learners			

online resources ↳ Available for download at **resources.corwin.com/ assessingMLLs-LeadersEdition**

RESOURCE 1.2
Categorizing Terminology: References to Students, Languages, Teachers, and Programs

To what extent does asset or deficit terminology prevail in your setting?

First, select words and phrases from the following categories that *your school or district* uses: (1) multilingual learners, (2) multilingualism, (3) teachers of multilingual learners, and (4) instructional models or programs.

Next, revisit the lists that follow and select terms to describe *your personal stance* on multilingualism.

Finally, repeat the activity with *other educational leaders* to describe their stance. Through discussion, figure out how to reconcile the different visions and how together you might move forward to advance more assets-based terminology to make a positive lasting impact on communities, schools, classrooms, and multilingual learners.

1. Multilingual Learners: References to Students

   - Balanced bilinguals
   - Bi/multilingual learners
   - Dual language learners (DLLs)
   - Elite bilinguals
   - Emergent bilinguals (EBs)
   - **English as an additional language (EAL) learners**
   - English language learners (ELLs)
   - English learners (ELs)
   - Heritage language learners
   - Language learners
   - Language minority (majority) students
   - Limited English proficient (LEP) students
   - **Linguistically and culturally diverse students**
   - Long-term English learners (LTELs)
   - Minoritized students
   - Newcomer students
   - **Plurilingual learners**
   - Proficient English speakers (acquiring an additional language)
   - Second language learners
   - Sequential bilinguals
   - Simultaneous bilinguals
   - Students with interrupted formal education (SIFE)

2. Multilingualism: References to Language(s) of Multilingual Learners

   - Dynamic bilingualism
   - **English (or language X) dominant**

- **"First" language (L1)** vs. "second" language (L2)
- **"Foreign" language(s)**
- Heritage language(s)
- Home language(s)
- "Native" language
- Partner language
- **World languages**

3. Teachers of Multilingual Learners

- Bilingual teachers
- Content teachers
- Co-teachers (or cooperating teachers)
- Dual language teachers
- English (language) learner (EL or ELL) teachers
- English as a second language (ESL) teachers
- English language acquisition (ELA) teachers
- English language instructional coaches
- English language development (ELD) teachers
- English to speakers of other languages (ESOL) teachers
- General education teachers

4. Language Models for Multilingual Learners in English or Multiple Languages

- **Content and language integrated learning (CLIL)**
- Dual language (DL) programs
- English as an additional language (EAL) programs
- English as a second language (i.e., ESL, ESOL) programs
- English language acquisition (ELA) programs
- English language development (ELD) programs
- "Foreign" language education programs
- Global studies/world language programs
- Language "intervention" programs
- **Maintenance/late exit/developmental bilingual programs**
- One-way immersion programs
- Sheltered English programs
- Structured English immersion (SEI) programs
- Transitional bilingual education (TBE) programs
- Two-way immersion programs

 Available for download at **resources.corwin.com/ assessingMLLs-LeadersEdition**

CHAPTER 2

Getting Started with Assessment in Multiple Languages

▶ Mural of diverse faces

Apprendre une autre langue, c'est comme le commencement d'une autre vie.

Learning another language is like the beginning of another life.

—Michel Bouthot

The Dilemma

But I only speak English! How can I be expected to communicate in other languages?

Irene Tan, the principal of Serenity School, has been busy promoting multilingualism and multiculturalism within her K–8 complex and across the community. Students representing 15 languages have crafted murals around the school, such as the one displayed earlier, to symbolize pride in themselves and their cultural heritage. Everyone at the school who is multilingual, including office, paraprofessional, lunchroom, and other support staff, volunteers to serve in an ambassador role to incoming students. Older students are paired with younger ones with the same partner language to mentor, advise, and read to their buddies. As principal, Irene has recruited a community cadre, from family members to local business leaders, to help with translation, health, and social services for students and families. Additionally, cultural liaisons supplement teacher teams in bridging the school to the community and the community to the school.

During the first days of the new school year, as an extension of the initial intake process, teachers systematically collect extensive information on their students' language use practices as a first step in getting to know their multilingual learners. Some teachers connect with families through technology, and some pair up to make home visits, while others gather information from students during opening activities. Throughout the school, there are built-in opportunities for multilingual learners to share their linguistic expertise through assessment in multiple languages. As a result, school leaders have a sense of multilingual learners' language proficiencies, and teachers are able to ascertain patterns of language use by their students to help inform their craft.

As part of baseline data at the beginning of the school year, all hands are on deck to collect oral and written language samples in English and, for multilingual learners, students' additional languages, whether they participate in a language education program or not. It is a schoolwide policy to videotape students' initial oral language samples and scan their written language samples common for each grade. The curriculum and assessment teams facilitate professional learning around interpreting student samples using grade-level cluster literacy rubrics. Coaches devote time to recalibrate scoring of the student samples with teacher pairs. As student bilingual samples are deemed reliable, they become the first entries in schoolwide portfolios that serve as evidence for local accountability.

As an instructional leader, Irene wants to safeguard fair and equitable assessment for all students, even though she is monolingual in English. She especially advocates for her multilingual learners whose full potential is realized through their multiple languages, and strives to maximize their opportunities for success. Irene encourages monolingual teachers to partner with bilingual colleagues for joint planning time, understanding that planning assessment in multiple languages with a full complement of measures is advantageous in describing what multilingual learners can do.

FIRST IMPRESSIONS

- In what ways does this scenario resonate with you?

- What baseline data do you collect in multiple languages to help with initial placement and grouping of students?

- How might monolingual teachers pair with bilingual teachers to optimize opportunities for planning assessment in multiple languages?

- What do you consider the primary purposes for assessment, and how might they be inclusive of multiple languages?

Educational leadership cannot be tacit or complacent when it comes to policies and practices revolving around multilingual learners and assessment in multiple languages. The entire educational community must come to endorse and promote multilingualism as a schoolwide and societal value. Hopefully, its commitment will have a ripple effect. The greater the acceptance of multilingualism as a right and resource, the greater the probability of embracing the assets of multilingual learners as demonstrated by assessment in multiple languages.

The opening two chapters of this book urge educational leaders to engage in systemic transformation of their current policies and practices to instill multilingualism and assessment in multiple languages as twin educational goals. To begin this journey, we attend to the conditions for change as educators delve into language planning and language policy. Questions address how to (1) use languages for specific needs and contexts, (2) ensure equitable treatment of different populations, and (3) create resource-rich learning environments where students see worth in themselves and in what they are learning (Reynolds, 2019).

In this chapter, we draw from the body of research on effective leadership in multilingual contexts and its impact on creating an aligned assessment system among schools, districts, and states. We introduce a multiphase assessment cycle for multiple languages that serves as the organizing framework for the remaining chapters. Then we match the purposes for assessment to specific assessment tools for multilingual learners across the school year. After that, we describe assessment *as*, *for*, and *of* learning through the lens of stakeholders serving multilingual learners. We conclude with a peek into how assessment can stimulate systemic change through social justice.

HOW LANGUAGE POLICY INFORMS ASSESSMENT IN MULTIPLE LANGUAGES

Language planning and language policy are necessary precursors to assessment planning and assessment policy, especially when multilingual learners are involved. Creating a multilingual language policy at district and school levels, as introduced in the previous chapter, is the first step to having confidence in creating an assessment plan. In formulating these policies, each school and its community should take an honest and hard look at their stance toward multilingualism and multiculturalism.

In 1984, Richard Ruíz outlined three orientations of language planning where each presupposes a unique mindset for exploring educational opportunities for multilingual leaners. Each orientation has implications for assessment planning: (1) language-as-problem, (2) language-as-right, and (3) language-as-resource. In the first instance, language diversity (namely, the presence of any language other than English in a school) is conceived of as a social problem to be resolved. This problem or deficit view of language learning is often portrayed as a medical model in need of treatment. The second approach emphasizes the legal rights of multilingual learners, as in their civil right to receive education in languages other than English. The third orientation, language-as-resource, is viewed as an assets-based position and a possible solution for promoting the infusion of multilingualism (and multilingual education) into national language policy.

Applying Ruíz's model, a school's or district's language policy should be a window into its mission, vision, and values. We know that school leaders are critical players in catalyzing school change, serving either as positive change agents or as barriers to the process (Bryk, 2010; Robinson, 2008). Principals, in particular, have great control in the leveraging of language education policies in schools with multilingual populations; however, many are not prepared to do so (Menken, 2014). Research shows that moving language policies along a continuum from monolingualism to multilingualism is possible when bilingualism is treated as a resource in instruction and leadership is **distributed** (Ascenzi-Moreno, Hesson, & Menken, 2016). These findings directly impact schoolwide assessment practices in multiple languages.

 Stop-Think-Act-React

Relax and Reflect: How does your school and district envision or enact language planning?

Which of Ruíz's three orientations to language planning does your school or district assume, and is it present in your language policy? As an extension, to what extent is your language policy reflected in your school's or district's assessment policy? How might you and other educators bolster the status of language planning for multilingual learners and their families so that it is inclusive of assessment in multiple languages?

EFFECTIVE LEADERSHIP IN PROGRAMS CULTIVATING MULTIPLE LANGUAGES

Just as a strong research base supports bilingual development of multilingual learners in school, there is also a growing body of research that suggests characteristics of effective educational leaders in dual language contexts. Many factors contribute to their success as leaders; Figure 2.1 identifies the traits that have emerged in the research, as cited in Menken (2017).

FIGURE 2.1 Research on Educational Leaders in Dual Language Contexts

RESEARCHERS	FINDINGS ON EFFECTIVE LEADERSHIP IN DUAL LANGUAGE CONTEXTS
K. Brooks, Adams, & Morita-Mullaney (2010)	Leaders working with multilingual learners must be cognizant of and willing to act on systemic inequalities facing these students.
DeMatthews & Izquierdo (2016)	Effective school leadership practices value all stakeholders, accept a variety of language perspectives, implement a collective approach to programming, and build capacity.
Heineke, Coleman, Ferrell, & Kersemeier (2012)	School leaders are part of negotiating language policy, enacting mandates, setting ideological foundations, and fostering meaningful collaboration with families and communities.
Howard et al. (2018)	School-level leadership entails advocacy for dual language programs along with professional development, strong oversight of programs, communication with district administrators, and equitable funding.

(Continued)

FIGURE 2.1 (Continued)

RESEARCHERS	FINDINGS ON EFFECTIVE LEADERSHIP IN DUAL LANGUAGE CONTEXTS
Hunt (2011)	Success of dual language immersion is contingent on (1) a schoolwide commitment to its mission, (2) collaborative and shared leadership, (3) mutual trust between teachers and administrators, and (4) flexibility in structures that are responsive to students.
Menken & Solorza (2013)	School leaders, particularly principals, play a critical role in either sustaining or eliminating bilingual education, including the formal preparation of their teachers to work with emergent bilingual students.
Scanlan & López (2012)	Dynamic building- and system-level administrators' goals include (1) cultivating language proficiency of multilingual learners, (2) ensuring student access to high-quality curriculum, and (3) promoting sociocultural integration in schooling.
Souto-Manning, Madrigal, Malik, & Martell (2016)	A principal's leadership skills feature a philosophy that insists on language equity, includes bilingualism and biliteracy, supports school-generated assessment, endorses multiculturalism, and has close relationships with families and communities.
Spillane (2006)	Through distributed leadership, organizational structures are created in which decision making is based on interactions among leaders and followers, and their situations within a school climate are built on collaboration.

SUPPORTING MULTILINGUAL LEARNERS DURING DIFFICULT TIMES

Being an educational leader in times of international, national, or local crises poses a unique set of concerns. In particular, school leaders must be realistic, genuine, and empathic, finding the strength to reassure students and families when their life circumstances might be unstable or unbearable. In searching for talent to lead in a post-pandemic world, Baldoni (2020) suggests that the following character traits are essential during challenging times, whether dealing with a global pandemic or a pressing local injustice:

- Out-of-the-box thinking based on data from multiple disciplines

- Critical thinking in which reasoning is precise for posing solutions

- Confidence that triggers inspiration of others

- Team ethos where there is sensitivity to the impact of actions taken

- Trustworthiness and reliability in information sources

School leaders who work with multilingual learners and their families have to be exceptionally resilient, yet flexible, during difficult times as many multilingual learners tend to be quite vulnerable and their families unduly impacted. There are unique linguistic and cultural issues of multilingual communities that need to be addressed during stressful situations. The following is a partial list of the qualities that educational leaders must display during times of increased anxiety and insecurity:

- Ingenuity to ensure that multilingual learners and their families are safe

- Resourcefulness in securing help for medical/health/social services, preferably in the families' primary language, along with shelter, food, and supplies

- Empathy for the plight of multilingual learners and their families

- Advocacy in support of multilingualism and multiculturalism in light of xenophobia

- Inventiveness in maximizing multilingual learners' access to reliable technology

- Creativity in designing online instruction with comprehensible content that is developmentally appropriate, interesting, and relatable to multilingual learners

- Respect for multilingual learners and their families' languages and cultures

Educators must be aware of the uncomfortable situations and apprehensions of multilingual learners, who in many ways may be traumatized. In trying times, it is more important than ever that multilingual learners' voices are heard. Therefore, leaders must think about how to make connections between students' social-emotional well-being and their educational program, including the impact of assessment.

During the most recent pandemic, assessing multilingual learners should have been laser focused on the students' welfare, with consideration of the languages of communication at home. **Feedback** from teachers should have taken the context of learning into consideration before evaluating specific content learning. At the same time, districts and schools must have been aware of and complied with mandates by the U.S. Department of Education for screening and assessing multilingual learners' English **language proficiency** (such as the one issued in May 2020), as assessment for multilingual learners has always been and continues to be an issue of civil rights and equity.

THE ASSESSMENT CYCLE IN MULTIPLE LANGUAGES

Effective leaders are critical players in determining how assessment can enhance learning rather than distract from it. When multilingual learners are involved, this translates into having school leaders appreciate and act on students' strengths by allowing the use of multiple languages. Having district or school language and assessment policies that reflect this belief helps facilitate acceptance by leadership of multiple language use in instruction and assessment.

Understanding a school's or district's approach to language planning and language policy is requisite to establishing the pathway to assessment in multiple

FIGURE 2.2 The Levels of Data in an Aligned Assessment System

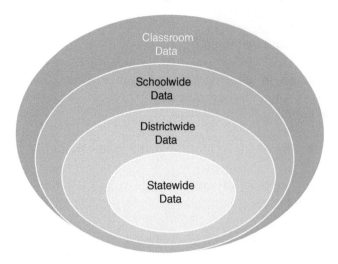

languages. Right now, however, a paradox is brewing. Generally, assessment practices in K–12 settings in the United States simply do not capture multilingual learners' language growth and achievement, which, in turn, leads to a distortion of the perceived capabilities of these students (S. V. Sánchez et al., 2013). Yet assessment in multiple languages is the cornerstone of growing numbers of instructional programs that value student-centered perspectives along with bilingualism, biliteracy, and sociocultural competence.

Assessment in multiple languages is most impacted at the classroom level as it is closest to teaching and learning (thus, the largest of the concentric circles in Figure 2.2). Ideally, the policies, practices, and information generated at the classroom level contribute to and are representative of the school as a whole. The school, in turn, shares assessment data with the district, and ultimately, districtwide data contribute to those at the state level. When one level of data readily dovetails and is compatible with the next higher one, we can say that there is an aligned assessment system.

To create an aligned system, assessment in multiple languages should be endorsed across educational levels, from the classroom to the state, but also the reverse, from the state to individual classrooms. According to provisions of the Every Student Succeeds Act (ESSA, 2015), states with sizeable multilingual populations of one language group are encouraged to provide achievement tests in that language. In turn, those states should incentivize districts to develop and use assessments in multiple languages, facilitating and supporting district dual language/bilingual education programs to demonstrate standards-based outcomes. Ultimately, schools should use assessment in multiple languages to more validly demonstrate multilingual learners' content learning (de Jong, 2019a).

An assessment cycle operates at each level of an educational system, ideally in a coordinated and coherent way. As shown in Figure 2.3, a five-phase cycle serves as the organizing feature for this book and its companion on classroom assessment in multiple languages (Gottlieb, 2021). When multiple languages are part of curriculum and instruction, then assessment must also be defined by multiple language use, always reflecting multilingual learners' understanding and expression in those languages.

The *planning* phase is critical as it sets the process in motion, first considering the characteristics of the students, in particular their languages and cultures, against

ASSESSMENT IN MULTIPLE LANGUAGES

FIGURE 2.3 A Multiphase Assessment Cycle for Inclusion of Multiple Languages

the context for assessment. The second phase, *collecting and organizing information*, identifies data in multiple languages to be gathered for making decisions. Next, the *interpreting information and providing feedback* phase examines the evidence generated from annual, interim, common, and classroom assessment in multiple languages. The fourth phase, *evaluating and reporting information*, explores dual language program effectiveness and **grading** policies for multilingual leaners. The final phase, *taking action based on results*, encourages educators to work together to advance teaching and learning across a school, district, or community.

PURPOSES FOR ASSESSMENT INVOLVING MULTILINGUAL LEARNERS

Administrators are responsible for assessment activities aimed at meeting state compliance; other activities are designed for district accountability, and still others are intended to determine the effectiveness of school- or districtwide initiatives or programs. Knowing the purpose for assessment determines the kinds of data that are most appropriate for a specific context. Figure 2.4 gives examples of purposes for assessment for states, districts, and schools. Resource 2.1 invites educators to match the purposes for assessment with specific measures and languages to determine to what extent large-scale assessment is equitable for multilingual learners.

The Role of Standards

State academic content and **language development/proficiency standards** are source documents for integrating language and content in curriculum, instruction, and assessment for multilingual learners. Spanish Language Arts and Spanish Language Development Standards coupled with English Language Arts and **English Language Development Standards,** when coordinated, provide the grounding for both school and district leaders in planning assessment for Latinx youth, who constitute approximately 75% of the multilingual learners in K–12 settings.

FIGURE 2.4 Matching Purposes for Assessment With Levels of Implementation for Multilingual Learners

LEVEL OF ENACTMENT	PURPOSES FOR ASSESSMENT
School	• Determine effectiveness of programs involving multilingual learners based on local goals • Ascertain multilingual learners' social-emotional, language, and conceptual growth in multiple languages • Make educational decisions based on linguistically and culturally relevant data from common and classroom assessment
District	• Evaluate effectiveness of district programs for multilingual learners • Provide evidence for meeting local and statewide initiatives • Determine trend data from common and interim assessment in one or more languages
State	• Determine impact of statewide programs for multilingual learners • Create procedures/policies to meet federal accountability and peer review requirements • Screen, identify, and classify multilingual learners according to uniform criteria for federal and state-supported services • Determine and apply uniform entry/exit criteria for language programs serving English learners

Figure 2.5 outlines some of the purposes and uses of these content and language standards. Although both sets of standards deal with language, there are distinct differences between language arts, a content area or discipline, and language development, the process of language learning across disciplines. As a general rule, whichever standards are used programmatically should be aligned with the large-scale assessment for accountability purposes. In Spanish dual language settings, all four sets of standards mentioned before should be interwoven into curriculum and assessment to provide a strong defensible educational program for Spanish–English bi/multilingual learners.

Initial Assessment for Multilingual Learners

Let's turn to a multilingual learner's first day of school. In Grades K–12, high-stakes assessment begins just as soon as a student walks in the school door (Gottlieb, 2017). As part of enrollment procedures, screening students for English language proficiency is a two-step process that determines which multilingual learners are English learners who qualify for language support services. The initial step generally consists of a short Home Language or Language Use Survey that includes items such as the following:

1. What is the primary language used in the home?

2. What is the language most often spoken by the student?

3. What is the language(s) that the student first acquired? (U.S. Department of Education, 2015)

FIGURE 2.5 Standards in English and Spanish for Curriculum, Instruction, and Assessment

STANDARDS	PURPOSES AND USES
English Language Development	• Inform curriculum, instruction, and assessment for multilingual learners • Provide pathways across levels of language proficiency and grade-level clusters for language learning in sociocultural contexts • Measure and interpret English language proficiency on an annual basis for federal accountability to report growth and contribute to reclassification criteria • Contextualize disciplinary content for learning in English
Spanish Language Development	• Inform curriculum, instruction, and classroom assessment in Spanish, and Spanish in conjunction with English, for Latinx students in dual language/immersion or developmental bilingual programs • Provide pathways across levels of language proficiency and grade-level clusters for language learning in sociocultural contexts • Determine and report Spanish language proficiency • Contextualize disciplinary content for learning in Spanish
Spanish Language Arts	• Inform curriculum, instruction, and assessment for Latinx students in dual language/immersion or developmental bilingual programs • Delineate Spanish language arts knowledge and skills for each grade level • Measure, report, and interpret student performance on reading/Spanish language arts on an annual basis for local or federal accountability • Set milestones for Spanish as a subject area
English Language Arts	• Inform curriculum, instruction, and assessment for all students • Delineate English language arts knowledge and skills for each grade level • Measure and report performance on reading/English language arts on an annual basis for Grades 3–8 and once in high school for federal accountability • Set milestones for English as a subject area

Answers to these questions specify whether there are languages in addition to English in the students' history and, if so, trigger an initial screening procedure.

In most school districts, the Home Language Survey (or Language Use Survey) and the English Language Proficiency Screener are the sole data sources for identifying and placing English learners (Kim, Molle, Kemp, & Cook, 2018). In response to the huge variability of criteria in these initial determinations, the U.S. Department of Education has come to require states participating in federally funded assessment consortia to have a common definition of English learners (Linquanti & Cook, 2013).

Although this tool is widely accepted and used, the trustworthiness of the Home Language Survey as a component of a statewide English-language proficiency assessment system remains at question (Bailey & Kelly, 2012). Overall, there is a lack of validity evidence of the procedure in determining English learner status (Linquanti & Bailey, 2014). The *Home Language Survey Data Quality Self-Assessment* (Henry, Mello, Avery, Parker, & Statford, 2017) may help diminish misidentification of students and improve the effectiveness of the data. Therefore, in addition to the survey, districts or schools should collect student self-reported background information (e.g., language and literacy use).

As suggested in the scenario, as part of the enrollment process or shortly thereafter, it is beneficial to collect baseline data on multilingual learners' access to and use of multiple languages, whether they are to participate in language education programs or not. Research has shown that multilingual learners who are literate, irrespective of the language, are advantaged and poised to become literate in an additional language. If students could simply respond to common oral and written prompts in multiple languages, teachers at least would have a sense of their literacy, and this evidence could be the first entries in their portfolio (see Resource 2.2 for guidelines).

 Stop-Think-Act-React

Relax and Reflect: How do definitions impact assessment for multilingual learners?

Review the Home Language Survey currently in place in your district or state to ascertain an initial determination of multilingual learner status. Then examine additional measures or criteria for identifying English learners and their placement in a language program.

Is there anything else you or your team might consider as part of multilingual learners' first assessment experience? How might assessment in multiple languages be helpful in making students welcome? How equitable is it to assess only in English knowing that multilingual learners are exposed to multiple languages and cultures at home?

Thinking about assessment means figuring out the data that will yield the optimal amount of useful information for decision making. Figure 2.6 illustrates how state, district, and school data can complement each other to offer a systemwide network of evidence for learning in multiple languages. It is replicated as Resource 2.3 with empty cells so that school leaders can supply specific measures across the school year—at the beginning, the middle, and the end—to gain a better sense of the distribution of data by type of assessment and language. In that way, everyone in a school or district can be apprised of the measures and languages for determining overall program, school, and district accountability.

At a State Level

The good news: Over half the states and the District of Columbia offer standardized achievement tests in languages other than English as part of their ESSA state accountability plans. The lion's share of these measures seems to be

FIGURE 2.6 Assessment Data for Multilingual Learners in Schools, Districts, and States Across the School Year

	STATE	DISTRICT	SCHOOL
Beginning-of-Year Data	Enrollment data, including demographic information; screening data for identification and placement	Initial diagnostic or baseline data in multiple languages; interim achievement data in one or more languages	Initial placement data based on language proficiency in multiple languages; baseline data in different content areas
Midyear Data	Annual English language proficiency data, K–12; achievement data, Grades 3–8 and once in high school	Interim achievement data; growth data in language proficiency in one or more languages from common assessment	Coordination of common data across classrooms in multiple languages; classroom assessment
End-of-Year Data	Performance data (results of language proficiency and achievement testing); exit and post-exit (monitoring) data plus data for other federal requirements	Interim achievement data; growth data from common assessment in multiple languages; language proficiency data	Data related to grouping of students; outcome achievement, language proficiency data in multiple languages based on common assessment along with social-emotional data

translations of state or consortium-led achievement tests for mathematics and science (Tabaku, Carbuccia-Abbott, & Saavedra, 2018). The bad news: Test translations have built-in biases and yield results with invalid inferences for multilingual learners. In other words, we cannot trust test scores from translated measures due to:

- Noncomparability of idioms or nuances that do not have translations

- Noncomparability of the language density of the tests—that is, translation yields different lengths of passages and literacy levels

- Noncomparability of cultural interpretations of the tests due to differing assumptions, perspectives, and traditions

- Noncomparability of student populations on which the measures have been normed

Put another way, "it [is] extremely difficult to create assessments in languages that are truly parallel, since each language has unique and distinct conceptual constructs with socially and culturally embedded meanings" (Abedi, 2011, p. 65). Another piece of cautionary advice on giving state tests in languages other than English (especially under high-stakes circumstances) is that research supports "native" language assessment only if the assessment matches the language of instruction (Abedi, 2011).

Assessment policies and practices that originate from federal legislation are generally based on monolingual constructs whereby multilingual learners are required to demonstrate their language proficiency in English without acknowledgement of their full linguistic potential (Escamilla et al., 2014; Menken, 2008; Shohamy, 2011). Additionally, there is a lack of cultural validity in large-scale assessment practices; that is, state tests generally do not address the sociocultural factors (beliefs, values, experiences) that impact the thinking of multilingual learners (W. Solano-Flores, 2011). As a result, measures often refer to experiences that are outside the socioeconomic realm of the students and lack reference to multicultural views; in essence, they are seen through a monolingual Anglocentric lens (Gottlieb & Honigsfeld, 2020).

At a District Level

Oftentimes, state-level policy and procedures are adopted by districts wholesale, without much thought for multilingual learners. For example, districts select **interim assessments**—for the most part, online commercial tests that are administered twice or three times during the school year—to serve as predictive measures for annual reading or mathematics tests in English. Little attention is paid to their likely impact on dual language classrooms where two languages have equal status. Although these data may provide a trajectory of student performance on state achievement tests in English, they do not necessarily reveal the true extent of multilingual learners' knowledge in their additional language.

District and school leaders should consider creating a districtwide council of multilingual educators to evaluate the appropriateness and usefulness of commercial interim measures for their context. Even though some interim tests may be available in multiple languages, their norming population could be the same as the test in English, thus invalidating the inferences from the results. Leadership must be aware of the caveats of tests that have been directly translated. Those that have been transadapted, on the other hand, contain modified test items to fit the cultural and linguistic backgrounds of the students and are considered more acceptable for multilingual learners.

At a School Level

With the rise of dual language programs across the nation, more and more schools are devoting resources to enrichment education for multilingual learners where content and language instruction co-occurs in two languages (Wilson, 2011). Any and all schools that house dual language programs should be held accountable for reaching their programmatic goals in multiple languages. School-level measures, such as common assessment, are (or should be) strongly tied to multilingual instructional practices.

Before embarking on the assessment cycle, schools should be knowledgeable of the linguistic, cultural, experiential, academic, and social-emotional makeup of their multilingual learners. Resource 2.4 at the close of the chapter lists a range of student variables with the hope that the information helps lead to fair and equitable assessment in one or more languages. Content and language teachers need to coordinate and co-plan assessment *as*, *for*, and *of* learning to offer a comprehensive data set that describes their multilingual learners.

DATA ASSOCIATED WITH ASSESSMENT *AS*, *FOR*, AND *OF* LEARNING

Three approaches—assessment *as*, *for*, and *of* learning—provide a range of potential data sources that complement each other for decision making from classrooms to districts. Together, the approaches offer a strong model of inclusion for multilingual learners, their teachers, and other educational leaders in one or multiple languages (Gottlieb, 2016, 2020, 2021; Gottlieb & Ernst-Slavit, 2019; Gottlieb & Katz, 2020). Put another way, the three approaches represent an ecosystem where assessment is constantly informed by and leads to better student learning (Jones & Saville, 2016).

As shown in Figure 2.7, assessment *as*, *for*, and *of* learning centers on stakeholders (people and their relationships with others) rather than assessment for formative or summative purposes that focuses on outcomes (scores reported as numbers or letters). **Summative** and **formative assessment** is a false dichotomy as "any assessment can be formative and summative at the same time" (Wiliam, 2020). Assessment *as* and *for* learning are broader in scope, living in and across classrooms and engaging students and teachers in the process; likewise, assessment *of* learning generally extends from classrooms to schools and districts to include leadership teams, principals, and superintendents.

Assessment *as* Learning

Assessment *as* learning is an approach that places students squarely in the center and substantiates the value of student engagement in learning (Christenson, Reschly, & Wylie, 2012; Dyer, 2015; Early, 2012). Assessment *as* learning offers opportunities for multilingual learners to become empowered through their multiple languages and cultures, thereby building agency and identity. School leaders must be sensitive to the unique qualities of multilingual learners that become visible through assessment *as* learning.

Data generated from assessment *as* learning are student driven. Student self-assessment offers school and district leaders an additional perspective on how students are faring. Assessment *as* learning enables multilingual learners to shine as they:

- Demonstrate **metacognitive, metalinguistic,** and **metacultural awareness**

- Use multiple languages as linguistic and conceptual resources

- Translanguage—that is, interact in two languages in natural settings with others of the partner language as they build their linguistic repertoire

FIGURE 2.7 Assessment *as*, *for*, and *of* Learning: An Outgrowth of Assessment for Formative and Summative Purposes

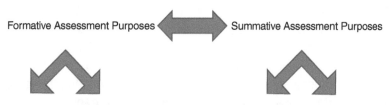

Formative Assessment Purposes		Summative Assessment Purposes	
Assessment *as* Learning by Students	Assessment *for* Learning by Students With Teachers or Teacher Groups	Assessment *of* Learning by Teachers or Teacher Groups With Students	Assessment *of* Learning by District and State Directors

SOURCE: Adapted from Gottlieb (2021).

Although assessment *as* learning is basically a classroom activity, there is no reason why it can't apply to a school or even district level. Here student self-reflection is incorporated into unit projects, performances, or products as well as common assessment. These data not only give students voice; they help guide instructional leadership teams to modify curriculum to be more inclusive of multilingual learners along with their linguistic and cultural perspectives.

Assessment *for* Learning

Distributive leadership is a most effective practice when it's shared among a team of individuals around a mutually agreed-upon mission to spark and sustain a schoolwide culture of learning. As a result, leadership teams consisting of teachers and coaches can drive positive change throughout a school. These teams of coaches or teachers who collaborate and interact with students for a common purpose—to advance learning—can spark **assessment *for* learning**.

Example activities that leadership teams can help organize on behalf of their multilingual learners might include:

- Having coaches and teachers engage in cycles of observation, feedback, and reflection on students' language use in content classes in order to adapt and refine instruction and instructional assessment

- Modeling criteria for success for projects or common assessment that apply to one or more languages

- Examining student-level data in multiple languages, whether digitally or in physical portfolios, on an interim basis to ensure movement toward meeting program goals

It is essential for school leaders, in conjunction with leadership teams, to schedule dedicated time for teachers to co-plan the why, what, how, and when for assessment. In assessment *for* learning, multilingual learners negotiate with their

---

Relevant Research on *Formative* Assessment

Today's educators often deal with the multiple, contradictory purposes of formative assessment or assessment *for* learning, which has led to misunderstanding of the use of data, especially for multilingual learners. In recent years, formative assessment has been viewed as an event, a test, or a tool (Shepard, 2005) rather than a transformative, iterative process or cycle between teachers and students (Heritage, 2010). Black and Wiliam's seminal research in 1998, confirmed by Hattie and Temperley (2007), unequivocally confirms the value of formative feedback within the instructional cycle as pivotal for improving student achievement. It is feedback—descriptive information that is goal-oriented, transparent, actionable, user-friendly for students, and timely—not test scores, that helps students move toward reaching their goals (Wiggins, 2012).

teachers on a variety of issues, such as what counts as evidence, in which languages, and how to interpret and use the information. Assessment *for* learning embraces increased decision-making power of teachers in their interaction with others.

Assessment *of* Learning

Assessment *of* learning, as depicted in Figure 2.7, serves two distinct purposes and audiences. The first purpose is for district or state accountability and stems from federal or state, and at times district, mandates. Here assessment *of* learning is externally imposed upon schools and is outside the control of teachers and, often, school leadership. It generally consists of standardized measures that are administered on annual and interim bases. In this case, assessment *of* learning is large-scale in nature, meaning that it occurs under standard conditions across a district or state.

At a district or school level, assessment *of* learning can also apply to internal accountability, such as in the use of common assessment data for making local decisions. Still considered large-scale as it crosses multiple classrooms, assessment *of* learning in this context represents democratized assessment in that it reflects what students have accomplished at the culmination of a period of instruction, such as a unit of learning. When determined by local leadership, in this case, assessment *of* learning is considered more authentic than test-driven (Sleeter & Carmona, 2017).

Common assessment is generally designed by a team of educators and occurs across classrooms in one or more grade levels, a school, or a district. As shown in Figure 2.8, this type of assessment *of* learning can vary from a mutually agreed-upon project, to a uniform writing or oral language prompt, to a unit test designed by teachers—all of which can and should have provisions for multiple languages. Common assessment, if based on a project, prompt, or end-of-unit test, has a uniform set of criteria or a descriptive rubric to interpret student work; if based on a prompt, it also has standard directions for administration.

Even if common measures are in English, there is no reason why multilingual learners cannot prepare for prompts or tests using another language, research their projects in multiple languages, or perhaps outline practice responses in

FIGURE 2.8 Features *of* Assessment of Learning for Common Projects, Prompts, and Tests in One or Multiple Languages

FEATURES OF ASSESSMENT *OF* LEARNING FOR LOCAL ACCOUNTABILITY	FOR PROJECTS	FOR PROMPTS	FOR TESTS
Standard directions for administration		X	X
Uniform criteria for success	X		
Interpretative rubric	X	X	
Inter-rater reliability in scoring	X	X	
Concrete timely feedback to students	X		
Linguistic and cultural relevance	X	X	

FIGURE 2.9 Types *of* Large-Scale Assessment of Learning

TYPES OF LARGE-SCALE ASSESSMENT	DESCRIPTION	LEVEL OF IMPLEMENTATION
Annual standardized tests	Measures required under federal legislation (i.e., reading/language arts, mathematics, and science achievement tests and English language proficiency tests); achievement tests in languages other than English; scored externally	States
Interim standardized tests	Off-the-shelf or online measures used for local accountability (e.g., reading/language arts, mathematics; English language proficiency tests) administered 2–3 times a year and scored externally	Districts
Common assessment with uniform prompts and procedures	Prompts (e.g., oral, written, multimodal) or performance tasks along with uniform procedures for collecting, analyzing, and interpreting information across multiple classrooms; locally designed and scored/interpreted	Schools or districts
Common assessment for projects, products, and performances	Projects, performances, or products at the end of an instructional cycle along with uniform procedures for collecting, analyzing, and interpreting information across multiple classrooms; locally designed and interpreted	Grade levels or departments within or across schools

their other language. If results contribute to school-level accountability, especially when multilingual learners are given the option of using more than one language, reliability of scoring and drawing inferences from the results are important. Figure 2.9 defines the differences in the types of large-scale assessment *of* learning that occurs at school, district, and state levels.

UNDERSTANDING THE BASICS OF ASSESSMENT *OF* LEARNING

One of the hallmarks associated with assessment *of* learning is basic psychometrics —validity and reliability. Test **validity** refers to the degree to which evidence supports the interpretations of test scores associated with annual and interim measures. **Reliability** is the overall consistency of a measure—the extent to which a test produces similar results under consistent or standard conditions—or consistency among teachers/raters in interpreting what students produce.

Validity for Large-Scale Testing

There are two primary purposes for educational large-scale testing: to inform educational policy and hold schools accountable for student learning (Sireci & Faulkner-Bond, 2015). The question at hand is to what extent can any monolingual test yield valid inferences for multilingual learners? If developers of language tests (or content tests) work from a monolingual lens, we lose sight of the totality of what multilingual learners can do. Therefore, we must insist that language testing operations be based on multilingual constructs (Chalhoub-Deville, 2019). To be valid for multilingual learners and multilingual learners with disabilities, large-scale assessment at a school, district, or state level must:

- Be based on principles of Universal Design for Learning with multiple means of engagement, representation, action, and expression

- Include an adequate sample of multilingual learners and multilingual learners with disabilities in trials, field testing, and norming

- Represent the experiences and perspectives of the student population

- Avoid **construct irrelevance** (e.g., multilingual learners' English language proficiency should not mask showing their content knowledge on content tests)

- Have minimal linguistic and cultural bias

 ## Stop-Think-Act-React

Relax and Reflect: How can construct irrelevance distort the validity of a test for multilingual learners?

The selection or development of large-scale assessment *of* learning generally has been decided by a district or state, outside the control of teachers and principals. The following is a list of potential construct-irrelevant factors when testing in English that skew the results for multilingual learners who are in the midst of developing that language. In testing content in English, multilingual learners may not be able to produce optimal results due to:

- Unfamiliarity with the context or situation of test items

- Idiomatic expressions

- Use of technical vocabulary outside of the content area being tested

- Complex and dense language

- Reliance on text without **scaffolding** (e.g., adding visual or graphic representation of the concept)

- Words that have multiple meanings (e.g., *table, arm*)

- Unfamiliar cultural references

Before selecting or administering an interim content test, the leadership team of a school or district should systematically review the items for these construct-irrelevant variables to ascertain the appropriateness of the measure for multilingual learners. Then the team should consider how assessment in multiple languages might counteract the ill effects of achievement measures only in English.

How can the validity of assessment be improved for multilingual learners? One way is to reduce the construct irrelevance of the items or tasks. Another way is to rely on more **performance assessment** as hands-on tasks are more authentic and can facilitate multiple language use. By allowing for variability in responses, students are not constrained by one correct answer, one way of expression, or one language. Ideally, these tasks have been designed based on theories that reflect multilingual or **heteroglossic language ideologies,** multilingual learners' funds of knowledge (N. González, Moll, & Amanti, 2005), and multilingual resources. By adopting a multilingual stance on assessment, we accentuate multilingual learners' personal, cultural, and linguistic assets.

Reliability

Reliability goes hand-in-hand with validity in assessment *of* learning. A multilingual assessment is considered reliable if it generates trustworthy and consistent results across various situations (Bisai & Singh, 2018). Reliability in assessment in multiple languages is also attributed to consistency in interpreting student-generated text in response to a prompt or a student project. To be reliable, samples from a prompt in each language generate the same degree of accuracy in scoring. For example, a common writing prompt in fourth- and fifth-grade dual language classrooms is based on a shared experience; multilingual learners then have an opportunity to respond in the language(s) of their choice. Reliability of results comes into play when the student samples are interpreted from comparable rubrics that are sensitive to each language and culture.

Together, assessment *as*, *for*, and *of* learning forms a comprehensive assessment system that is formulated by and seen through the eyes of different stakeholder groups. Resource 2.5 compares how different leadership teams at school and district levels might utilize these three approaches with an eye toward multilingual learners and assessment in multiple languages.

EVOKING SYSTEMIC CHANGE THROUGH SOCIAL JUSTICE

Effective leadership for multilingual learners, especially in dual language education contexts, advocates for social justice. When social justice is a tenet of teaching and learning practices, educators come to truly see students for who they are, where they come from, and what they can do. In fact, "improved student learning efforts are attributed to school efforts and structures that explicitly aim to reduce marginalizing conditions" in schools (Menken, 2017, p. 16). When assessment is introduced as a social justice issue, English-only measures serve to exacerbate inequities and undermine dual language programs (Californians Together, 2021).

Community organizations can be key players in effecting systemic change and meaningful power-sharing in issues of social justice. Case in point, Mujeres Unidas y Activas has identified four levers to spark change that has relevance to school and district leadership: (1) commit to fostering open discussion, (2) apply an equity lens, (3) agree on the pathway to change, and (4) dedicate resources to the transformation process (RoadMap, 2018).

When social justice permeates curriculum and assessment *as*, *for*, and *of* learning, it becomes a powerful driver of how and what students learn. When school and district leadership enact curriculum and accompanying assessment through a social justice lens, school and district culture can become transformed for educators, students, and families.

FACING THE ISSUE: ADVOCATE ON BEHALF OF YOUR MULTILINGUAL LEARNERS AND THEIR FAMILIES

School and district leaders do not necessarily have to be multilingual to support multilingualism and multiculturalism. However, they must have a deep understanding of and a steadfast commitment to multilingual education and its goals, as does the principal of Serenity School. Part of that conviction is the endorsement of assessment in multiple languages for multilingual learners.

Collaboration is paramount in enhancing the effectiveness of language education programs in schools and districts. Coordination of effort by leadership maximizes conditions for assessment in multiple languages. To cement the partnership among educational leaders, Cohan, Honigsfeld, and Dove (2020) suggest a collaboration framework based on four principles of teamwork: (1) common purpose, (2) shared mindset, (3) supportive environment, and (4) diverse team membership. These principles are foundational for moving the agenda of assessment in multiple languages forward. The following questions might be posed within that context.

For School Leaders

➢ How might common assessment in multiple languages help equalize the playing field for multilingual learners and their teachers at a school level?

➢ How do current school policies positively or negatively affect assessment in multiple languages?

➢ How might assessment *as* learning in multiple languages extend to the home and community?

For District Leaders

➢ How might you engage others in your district to help plan assessment for multilingual learners in multiple languages?

➢ How might you enlist multilingual adults in your community to help in initial screening and assessment in multiple languages?

➢ How might you create a network of administrators, school, and community leaders to answer difficult questions and issues revolving around instruction and assessment in multiple languages?

RESOLVING THE DILEMMA: ENLIST FAMILIES AND THE COMMUNITY IN THE ASSESSMENT PROCESS!

Just like Irene Tan, school and district leadership should think ahead about assessment in multiple languages. If you are in a setting with two or seventy-two languages, you can take steps to provide plentiful opportunities for multilingual learners to express themselves in their preferred languages to obtain a more comprehensive portrait of their conceptual, language, and social-emotional development. Here are some ideas for tapping multilingual resources in preparation for assessment activities.

- If you are a coach in a dual language or bilingual education setting, you have bilingual resources at your fingertips, starting with multilingual learners and their families. Their linguistic and cultural richness should be a source and inspiration for enhancing curriculum and assessment that are inclusive of linguistic and cultural perspectives.

- If you are a principal with multilingual learners of many different languages, or a program director, set up a schoolwide buddy system among multilingual learners. In addition, create a language resource bank of family and community members to assist in preparing for and proctoring during large-scale assessment.

- If you are a program coordinator or director, think of how you might involve the school's experts from the visual arts center, resource center, or technology center to form a multilingual literacy or coding club. Multilingual learners who participate in such activities could maintain a literacy log or a reflective journal in multiple languages to chronicle the impact of the club on their social-emotional development and achievement.

- If you are a district leader, consider how you might create a series of digital networks for different stakeholder groups around issues related to the assessment of multilingual learners in multiple languages. There might be one dedicated for principals and coordinators, one for school leaders, and one for the community. Have members of each network alternate monitoring the feed, posing questions, and offering ideas.

In this chapter, we have emphasized the value of school and district leaders as well as leadership teams' active participation and ongoing support for assessment in multiple languages. We have underscored the merit of having a balanced assessment system *as*, *for*, and *of* learning that touches on a variety of purposes, evidence, and stakeholders. Armed with resources from multilingual learners, we have illustrated how educational leaders might strategize how assessment in multiple languages might proceed to fortify connections among students, families, and the community.

Resources for School and District Leaders

RESOURCE 2.1
Conducting an Assessment Audit for Multilingual Learners

Starting with individual schools, complete the chart by answering the questions "Why assess?" (the school's purposes), "Which measures or types of assessment are used?" and "What are the languages of the assessment?" Analyze the responses to ascertain the equity of large-scale or common assessment practices for multilingual learners in schools, districts, and the state.

LEVEL OF ENACTMENT	PURPOSE FOR ASSESSMENT	MEASURES	LANGUAGES
School	• Provide evidence for and growth in learning grade-by-grade • Evaluate the extent to which programmatic goals are being met		
District	• Evaluate the effectiveness of programs serving multilingual learners • Screen and place new multilingual learners		
State	• Comply with peer review and federal requirements for assessment • Evaluate effectiveness of state initiatives for multilingual learners		

online resources 🔍 Available for download at **resources.corwin.com/assessingMLLs-LeadersEdition**

RESOURCE 2.2

Collecting Language Samples in Multiple Languages as Part of the Enrollment Process

Gathering oral and written language samples in multiple languages, if possible, should be part of overall data collection during the initial enrollment of K–12 students. Here are some suggestions for planning performance assessment that can readily be converted into a checklist.

In preparing for gathering performance data in multiple languages, have multilingual learners:

☐ Choose their preferred language, even if only available for instructions; then ease into the other language, if necessary

☐ Become familiar with the task

☐ Feel comfortable with the situation, to the extent feasible

☐ Select from multimodal resources such as action-packed, cross-disciplinary pictures, photos, or graphics

☐ Become acquainted with any equipment or technology

☐ Choose to use technology for keyboarding (for students in fourth grade and beyond) or paper and pencil for their written sample

☐ Listen to instructions in two languages or read instructions in two languages side by side to maximize comprehension

☐ Ask clarifying questions to each other in their preferred language

In addition, the following surveys may be helpful for districts and/or schools (see Gottlieb, 2016, 2021) as part of enrollment or during the beginning of the school year. Students respond as to whether they use English, their other language(s), or multiple languages in a variety of situations. The information from these surveys will help educators better understand the impact of multilingual learners' language practices on learning.

1. Language Use Survey

2. Oral Language Use Survey

3. Literacy Use Survey

4. Personal Interest Survey

 online resources Available for download at **resources.corwin.com/ assessingMLLs-LeadersEdition**

RESOURCE 2.3

Planning the Flow of Assessment Data for Multilingual Learners Throughout the School Year

Taking the information from Resource 2.1, think about how you might map assessment for your school, district, or state across the school year. Based on your measures, how might you better ensure fair representation of your multilingual learners in multiple languages?

	SCHOOL	DISTRICT	STATE
Beginning of Year			
Midyear			
End of Year			

RESOURCE 2.4
Gathering Information on Multilingual Learners for Planning Assessment in Multiple Languages

Data on multilingual learners are invaluable for many reasons, but the most important is knowing as much as you can about multilingual learners and their families. The information is also critical for ensuring equity in the design and enactment of curriculum, instruction, and assessment. Use these considerations as checklists for helping to craft assessment.

1. Linguistic considerations; multilingual learners'
   - ☐ language(s) at home
   - ☐ estimate of oral language proficiency in their home language(s)
   - ☐ estimate of literacy in their home language(s)
   - ☐ preferences and contexts (when and with whom) of language use at home
   - ☐ estimate of English language proficiency

2. Cultural considerations; multilingual learners'
   - ☐ cultural backgrounds
   - ☐ cultural traditions and perspectives
   - ☐ number of years and places educated outside the United States
   - ☐ estimate of familiarity with mainstream ways

3. Academic considerations; multilingual learners'
   - ☐ prior language(s) of instruction by content area or time allocation
   - ☐ opportunities to learn grade-level content (with and without language support)
   - ☐ opportunities to access and use technology
   - ☐ access and use of the home language at school

4. Experiential considerations; multilingual learners'
   - ☐ continuity of education within a year (mobility or interrupted education)
   - ☐ participation in and types of language education programs
   - ☐ allocation of language(s) by educational program (if applicable)
   - ☐ exposure to literacy experiences outside of school and in which languages

5. Social-emotional considerations; multilingual learners'
   - ☐ exposure to trauma from cultural or religious conflict or linguicism
   - ☐ exposure to trauma from separation (i.e., from parents, close relatives, classmates)
   - ☐ exposure to trauma from crises or pandemics
   - ☐ exposure to racial/ethnic discrimination
   - ☐ exposure to online or physical bullying
   - ☐ transiency/homelessness

 Available for download at **resources.corwin.com/ assessingMLLs-LeadersEdition**

RESOURCE 2.5
Thinking About Assessment *as, for,* and *of* Learning

How might assessment *as, for,* and *of* learning apply to different stakeholder groups? How might you and other educational leaders incorporate multiple languages into each of the approaches?

STAKEHOLDER GROUPS	ASSESSMENT *AS* LEARNING	ASSESSMENT *FOR* LEARNING	ASSESSMENT *OF* LEARNING
School leaders, including coaches, coordinators, and principals			
Leadership teams, including professional learning communities at a school or district level			
District leaders, including directors and assistant superintendents			

 Available for download at **resources.corwin.com/assessingMLLs-LeadersEdition**

CHAPTER 3

Planning Curriculum and Assessment In Multiple Languages

► Which languages do you relate to?

There once was a niña *who lived near the woods.*

She like to wear colorful capas *with hoods.*

"Roja" called Mom from her telenovelas . . .
—From *Little Roja Riding Hood*,
by Susan Middleton Elya

The Dilemma

The students are returning to school speaking a mix of languages!

It's been a tumultuous year across the nation for everyone, but the upheaval stemming from the novel coronavirus has brought the educational community to its knees. Consolidated School District #55 serves a K–12 suburban community with a dynamic superintendent, Dr. Ho, who oversees six schools—three elementary schools, two middle schools, and a high school. The district has prided itself on fellowship among staff and its congenial relationship with multilingual learners and their families. It has had everyone—including lunchroom staff, guards, and bus drivers—be part of a language immersion professional learning experience scheduled weekly throughout the school year. This ongoing activity has helped bind everyone across the district, with an astounding increase in empathy for language learning. In fact, people were beginning to spontaneously communicate with each other in languages other than English!

That hands-on experience came to a grinding halt in March 2020 when teaching and learning became remote and virtual. The joy of interacting and practicing a new language with colleagues disappeared, and was replaced with much concern and worry. The ability to use multiple modalities to show evidence of learning (e.g., through tactile, visual, and kinesthetic means), which had been central in reinforcing language learning, also vanished instantaneously.

Dr. Ho himself became apprehensive of how self-motivation on the part of administration, teachers, and students could carry everyone through the crisis with so much at stake. Many "experts warn[ed] that the loss of learning time would be catastrophic for kids in historically underserved communities" (Williams, 2020). Others were quick to paint a doomsday scenario of a severe academic slide for the "disadvantaged" or "underserved" students. All the strides that had been made in understanding the intrinsic value of interacting in multiple languages and cultures seemed to evaporate into thin air.

When it comes to disasters or crises, education leaders need to focus on their multilingual learners and other minoritized students, redoubling their efforts to use the time as an opportunity—but how might that happen? As Williams (2020) goes on to say, "as administrators and policymakers seek ways to help [English learners] succeed, they should use this moment to reassess some of the most pernicious misconceptions about what these students lack and need, but more importantly, [they should refocus on] what they already have."

That change of mindset makes all the difference in the outlook on multilingual learners. Recognizing how Dr. Ho and other district leaders can leverage the advantages of multiple language use by multilingual learners and their families is the first step toward creating a "can do" philosophy for learning and living. Administrators who have come to rely on families to champion multilingual learners in their distance learning must understand that, when these same students return to school, challenging educational goals can best be realized in multiple languages. Also, district leaders can support the notion that family engagement reinforces multilingual learners' continuous social-emotional development and that the language and culture of families create an inextricable bond that is foundational to the identity of multilingual learners.

With schools starting to resume a new normal with in-person learning, Dr. Ho has been astonished at how many multilingual learners have been conversing in multiple languages. Although he is familiar with the concept of translanguaging, as Dr. Ho himself often has conversed with friends and coworkers in multiple languages, the superintendent has never seen the simultaneous use of two languages being so pervasive among students. With assessment more important than ever to ascertain where and how teachers are positioned to renew in-school learning, Dr. Ho is perplexed as to where and how to begin the process. Surely the district's language and assessment policy has to be revisited. Perhaps now, more than ever, the opportunity is ripe for assessment in multiple languages to gain acceptance and become a commonplace practice.

FIRST IMPRESSIONS

- In what ways does this scenario resonate with you?

- What changes have you witnessed, or are you making, in your school's or district's assessment post-pandemic?

- In planning assessment in multiple languages, how might you engage your multilingual learners and their families?

- How might your school's or district's assessment policy change in the aftermath of the pandemic?

Multilingual learners process, think in, and use multiple languages; it is incumbent upon educational leaders who push for equity and excellence to leverage these students' strengths at all costs. We have organized this book around assessment in multiple languages so that it becomes a vehicle for social justice and an advocacy tool for school and district leadership. The assessment cycle serves as a resource for educators to plan and enact assessment in multiple languages through the linguistic and cultural assets of multilingual learners.

This chapter focuses on the preliminary phase of the cycle, *planning*, shown in Figure 3.1. It views the purposes for assessment (*the why*) for school and district leadership (*the who*) as central in proposing multiple language use (*the what*) that is realized through curriculum (*the how*). In addition, we pose considerations for an assessment-embedded curriculum that is linguistically and culturally sustainable. Finally, we refine the notion of common assessment to fit today's classrooms with multilingual learners and describe **portfolio assessment** as a body of evidence that highlights students' development and growth in multiple languages.

FIGURE 3.1 The First Phase of the Assessment Cycle: Planning Assessment in Multiple Languages

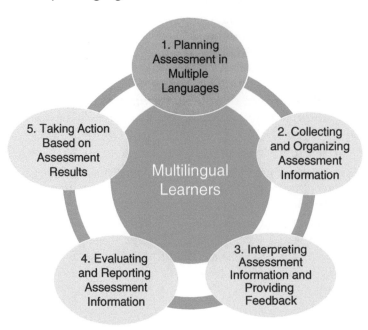

STIMULATING ASSESSMENT IN MULTIPLE LANGUAGES THROUGH DISTRIBUTIVE LEADERSHIP

Distributive leadership involves conversations among district administrators, school leaders, and other educators to drive systemic improvement; it is not necessarily the sharing of responsibility, as the term implies. A goal of distributive leadership is the development and maintenance of a high-quality educational system and a culture where all educators and students can thrive. Principals, assistant principals, and other school leaders, such as coaches, are critical to enabling and supporting distributive leadership teams. This work can be accomplished by building the leadership capacity in districts and schools and creating the conditions where expertise can be extended across educational systems (Smith, Mihalakis, & Slamp, 2017). It is in this context that we introduce assessment in multiple languages.

Building leadership teams through collaborative planning is a challenge, yet it is also essential to understanding assessment data, especially in multiple languages. Collaborative planning time between or among educators needs to include methods for collecting and analyzing classroom, grade-level, and schoolwide data to (a) inform policy, (b) apply to curriculum, (c) prepare for teaching, and (d) report to different stakeholders, including students, families, and the community. In planning assessment within and across classrooms, there also has to be attention to those multilingual learners with disabilities along with accessibility and accommodation guidance (and in which languages) as stipulated in their individualized education programs, or IEPs (Honigsfeld & Dove, 2015).

Sociocracy, a system of school governance of harmonious and deep solutions that values the ideas of all stakeholders, is an extension of distributive leadership. It is a model of decision making where teachers and staff have a more active role. Informed decisions stem from the expertise of teachers, the experience of parents and students, and the wisdom of enlightened administrators (Martell, 2020). Assessment, in crossing over to curriculum and instruction, plays an active role within the sociocracy of school.

ASSESSMENT AS AN EXPRESSION OF CURRICULUM DESIGN

The leadership of principals can have a substantial impact on the responsiveness of their schools to multilingual learners and their families. One area that can make a difference for schools and districts is the design of curriculum, or modification of extant curriculum, to ensure equitable representation and expression of multilingualism and multiculturalism. Multilingual learners deserve a rich, compelling, and challenging curriculum in which sound assessment is infused, not one that has been watered down (Ward Singer & Staehr Fenner, 2020).

Designing curriculum in which assessment is seamlessly wrapped helps define what's important to learning, what's needed to succeed, and how it is to be articulated. As Sleeter and Carmona (2017) say, we must think of "students as curriculum" first, tapping the knowledge that they bring to school rather than subject matter or standards. In crafting or adapting curriculum to fit multilingual students, we can instill multicultural perspectives and values rather than perpetuate normative cultural patterns that tend to marginalize these learners. Those principles directly carry over to assessment.

Curriculum may support backward design, also known as backward mapping or backward planning, where educators start with the end in mind, or it may be standards-referenced, tied to state academic content standards and language development/proficiency standards. Curriculum may be home grown by leadership teams where the focus is on relationships and "funds of knowledge" among students, families, and community (N. González, Moll, & Amanti, 2005). It may be dependent on the scope and sequence of textbooks or crafted from a combination of resources. No matter the source or format, when the time comes for planning assessment, especially in dual language settings, careful thought must go into how curriculum best represents multilingual learners' languages and cultures.

Relevant Literature on Curriculum

Three areas of research converge when speaking of **curriculum design** for multilingual learners. First, **Understanding by Design (UbD)** is a framework and planning process that considers **learning goals** as the starting point for curriculum, instruction, and assessment. Its three stages—(1) identify desired results, (2) determine assessment evidence, and (3) plan learning experiences—clearly align to each other and standards (Wiggins & McTighe, 2005). UbD has spurred an avalanche of resources; most recently, we see its relation to neuroscience (McTighe & Willis, 2019). The principles for UbD have also been addressed within the context of language development of English language learners (Heineke & McTighe, 2018); however, absent is their applicability to learning and assessment in multiple languages.

Second, planning curriculum, instruction, and assessment for multilingual learners should be linguistically and culturally sustainable (Paris, 2012). Part of linguistically and culturally sustainable pedagogy is the preservation of languages, literacies,

(Continued)

and other cultural practices of students and communities. Exemplifying linguistic and cultural sustainability, UNESCO (2014) recommends that school curricula be based on local cultures and themes reflecting the daily life and activities familiar to the learner. Most importantly, it states that in school "it is not a question of using one or the other language, but [a question] of using both languages."

A third area of literature that is unique to curriculum for multilingual learners is the intentional integration of language and content. In the 1980s, Mohan (1986) introduced the concept of learning language through content while Snow, Met, and Genesee (1989) proposed a conceptual framework for integrating these two constructs. Later, Gibbons (2015) situated language teaching within curriculum to support language and content integration. Most recently, educators and researchers of multilingual learners encourage the simultaneous building of disciplinary knowledge of the content areas, conceptual understanding, and language competencies (Cheuk, 2016; Davison & Williams, 2013; Gottlieb, 2016; Pimentel, 2018).

A powerful body of research suggests that content-rich standards-aligned curricula exert a powerful influence on student achievement. There is also early evidence that switching to high-quality curricula may be a more cost-effective way to raise student achievement than other school-level interventions (The Institute, 2017). High-quality curricula for multilingual learners are not a patchwork quilt with add-ons from mainstream content; rather, these curricula have a unique set of attributes.

Features of Effective Curricula for Multilingual Learners

More than any other feature, curricula should be designed to optimize students' potential for achieving the learning goals that have been carefully crafted by educators and students together. Maximizing multilingual learners' potential to accomplish their goals means having the flexibility for them to use one or more languages. The curriculum, as assessment embedded within it, should address linguistic and cultural dimensions of multilingual learners in its design; however, it is also feasible to retrofit an extant curriculum to improve its linguistic, cultural, and experiential accessibility.

Within a curriculum, the goals for assessment *of* learning at the close of a unit are matched to **learning targets** depicted in assessment *as* and *for* learning within and across lessons. Adapted from Suskie (2018), the following features illustrate the important role of assessment in multiple languages within effective linguistically and culturally sustainable curricula. Resource 3.1 at the end of the chapter converts these features into a **rating scale** for district and school leaders to determine the extent that multiple languages and cultures have been integrated into assessment.

- Every learning target and goal potentially sets up the context for assessment in multiple languages that invites multiple cultural perspectives.

- Ample and diverse opportunities are afforded multilingual learners so that they can capitalize on their full linguistic and cultural repertoires during assessment.

- **Cross-linguistic** and **cross-cultural considerations** are threaded throughout a set of related lessons in assessment *as* and *for* learning and the culminating event or project in assessment *of* learning.

- Research-informed strategies on bilingualism and biliteracy push multilingual learners to achieve their goals through assessment in multiple languages.

- Some challenging learning expectations are apparent in assessment for all multilingual learners regardless of their experiences and education status.

- Assessment captures the depth and breadth of a rich and meaningful culminating experience (i.e., performance, project, or product) with accompanying evidence.

- Assessment invites student voice that can be heard in multiple languages.

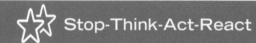

Stop-Think-Act-React

Relax and Reflect: What does your curriculum look like for multilingual learners?

Curricula can be represented in many forms. How would you describe the curriculum in your setting? Is it predetermined, packaged, or designed by teachers and leadership teams at the district or school level? How might you augment your current curriculum to ensure its linguistic and cultural sustainability and assessment in multiple languages for its multilingual learners?

To what extent:

- Do educators have input in curriculum design?

- Is it inclusive of multilingual learners, reflecting their languages, cultures, and perspectives?

- Is your curriculum socially just; that is, is it relevant and equitable for all students?

- Is your curriculum amenable to assessment in multiple languages?

- Is assessment in multiple languages seamlessly infused?

Purposes for Assessment in Multiple Languages for Units of Learning

The first consideration in planning or co-planning assessment in multiple languages is to determine its purpose and the use of information in decision making. As all assessment can simultaneously serve both formative and summative purposes, we use the trilogy assessment *as*, *for*, and *of* learning to highlight the stakeholders involved in the process. When planning curricula and units of learning, assessment *as* learning (student input and reflection or **self-assessment**) and assessment *for* learning (teacher and student co-construction and teacher feedback) are evident throughout the range of activities in individual lessons. Assessment *of* learning (teacher judgment of the final product) comes into play at the culminating of a unit coupled with assessment *as* learning (student reflection or self- and **peer assessment**) based on established criteria for success.

Expanding on the overall purposes for assessment reported in Chapter 2, there are purposes for assessment that specifically apply to the curriculum and units of learning. These purposes consider multiple language use and might include:

- Providing accumulated evidence of language and content learning

- Showing growth in multilingual learners' linguistic repertoire within and across content areas

- Informing instruction in each language

- Reflecting on learning goals and targets

- Supporting decisions based on multilingual evidence

- Fostering student agency, confidence, pride, and autonomy

Designing the curriculum is a dynamic and ever-changing way of organizing for learning. Why is there constant movement in curricula, you might ask? Because every year there are unique groups of students with different languages, cultures, histories, and understandings of the world; there are different configurations of classrooms with new and veteran teachers; and there are always new school, district, and state policies and practices to implement. Lest we forget the disruption caused by unexpected extenuating circumstances, such as a pandemic. School and instructional leaders have to be sensitive to the here and now of curriculum design in order to maximize opportunities for all students to learn.

More recently, curricula have been seen through a sociocultural lens where "enactment" has replaced "implementation" to reflect the agency of teachers and learners in the process. The heart of curriculum enactment is the classroom—the learning community—where the teacher is the catalyst for change (Graves, 2008). In classrooms with multilingual learners in which instruction is occurring in two languages, the curriculum cannot rely on prepackaged sets of materials, but rather relies on a series of related tasks around a central issue or theme that stems from integrated content and language targets where assessment is naturally embedded.

Sometimes the purpose for assessment for multilingual learners calls for use of two languages, especially in dual language contexts. At other times, assessment begs the use of a single language. Still other times, translanguaging is acceptable and encouraged. Sometimes the target for assessment will be content-related knowledge and skills where one or more languages serve as the modalities for expression; at other times, language will be the vehicle of targeted instruction within content. Within classroom assessment, translanguaging can be a vehicle for building metalinguistic, metacognitive, and metacultural awareness in multilingual learners.

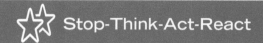
Relax and Reflect: How has the curriculum evolved in your school or district?

Has there been an influx of multilingual learners to your district and schools? How has the curriculum embraced this shift in student population? Is the curriculum suited for multilingual learners by being linguistically and culturally relevant, or is it a patchwork quilt? Are multiple languages, cultures, and perspectives present in units of learning? What have you done to ensure the best representation of multilingual learners' assets in curriculum design? How has technology helped improve multilingual learners' accessibility to multiple languages? How has assessment adapted to reflect these new realities?

Universal Design for Learning: Maximizing Accessibility for Multilingual Learners

Universal Design for Learning (UDL) defines accessibility for all students, especially multilingual learners and multilingual learners with disabilities. Aimed at optimizing students' learning experiences, UDL should be a non-negotiable feature of curriculum and assessment. Its historical backdrop rests in federal legislation—in particular, the Individuals with Disabilities Education Act (IDEA)—drawing its definition from the Assistive Technology Act, which states that UDL should apply to the design and delivery of products and services with the widest possible range of functional capabilities for people.

The Every Student Succeeds Act of 2015, Section 4104, urges states to adopt principles of UDL for their annual assessments. It also obliges schools to use the principles of UDL to support learning of all students, including English learners. Thus, for multilingual learners and for dually identified multilingual learners with IEPs, UDL translates into increased accessibility to grade-level content during learning and in assessment of that learning.

UDL is framed around three principles: (1) multiple means of engagement, (2) multiple means of representation, and (3) multiple means of action and expression. The intent of UDL is to reduce barriers in the learning environment such as "the design of curricular goals, assessments, methods, and materials" (Posey, 2020). Notice that *multiple* is the operative word in UDL principles, meaning that there should not be a single pathway to learning, but rather a variety of choices should be available for students. For multilingual learners and dually identified students, opportunities to learn and accessibility are improved by expanding their use of languages and accepting translanguaging as a communication mode.

The watchwords to remember when it comes to accessibility to learning are the student's *rights* and the *law*. As assessment in multiple languages is receiving increased attention at school and district levels, leadership should discuss how to thread accessibility throughout curriculum and instruction. When planning assessment in multiple languages, there are many questions for leadership teams, such as:

- How are our district and schools treating accessibility for all students, especially multilingual learners and multilingual learners with disabilities?

- To what extent is there a presence of multiliteracies, multimodalities, and translanguaging as multiple means of expression in curriculum, instruction, and assessment?

- If you have a dual language or developmental bilingual program that relies on a specific language allocation (e.g., 50/50, 80/20, 90/10), how might you apply the principles of UDL to instruction and assessment?

RESOURCES FOR CURRICULUM AND ASSESSMENT IN MULTIPLE LANGUAGES

As stated in the last section, all students can reach the same high bar set by state academic content standards if they have ample opportunities to interact and learn with others and have accessibility to an array of useful resources; these affordances can be maximized through UDL. Introduced here and elaborated in Chapter 4, multiliteracies and multimodalities are especially beneficial resources for multilingual learners and multilingual learners with disabilities when incorporated into planning curriculum, instruction, and assessment.

Multiliteracies and Multimodal Resources

Multiliteracies is an interesting concept that has been gaining ground in multilingual educational circles. Conceptualized by the New London Group in a groundbreaking 1996 white paper, the restrictive notion of literacy was reimagined as multiliteracies in a global context. It also became a counternarrative to the understanding of literacy as the text-bound tradition of reading and writing.

There are two important tenets of this vision. First, multiliteracies expand the teaching of literacy to account for the context of linguistic and cultural societies worldwide. Second, the teaching of multiliteracies acknowledges the expansion of text forms that are inclusive of the informational (**digital**) age in which we live and its multimedia technologies.

Multiliteracies are rooted in and have grown from both the local and international presence of multiculturalism. As a result, pedagogies have come to embrace technologies and social change (Early, Cummins, & Willinsky, 2002). In essence, multiliteracies recognize the variety of communication channels and media supports, such as visual design on computer screens, that contribute to constructing, interpreting, and expressing meaning. Multiliteracies rely on the interaction among different modalities in addition to text, such as the simultaneous interpretation of visual, audio, digital, and spatial representation. These new modes of communication are reshaping the way and the forms in which we use language.

Multimodal resources are related to multiliteracies in that they offer multilingual learners expanded resources for making meaning across content areas. In school, **multimodalities** encompass the use of textual, aural, linguistic, spatial, and visual materials for students to creatively show their learning. Multimodalities become seamless for students in leveraging their learning through multiple channels—for example, "to produce and interpret texts that incorporate graphs (science), formulas (mathematics), and multimedia (English language arts)" (Grapin, 2018, p. 32). Multiliteracies exemplified through multimodal strategies and translanguaging offer new pedagogical strategies for multilingual learners to make meaning. Together these resources challenge the dominant monolingual or monoglossic orientation in favor of multilingual or heteroglossic approaches to students' languaging in school (Guzula, McKinney, & Tyler, 2016).

Translanguaging

Translanguaging is a linguistic resource of bi/multilingual learners that enhances their accessibility and ability to meaningfully communicate with others of the same languages. Together, as shown in Figure 3.2, multiliteracies, multimodalities, and translanguaging, when incorporated into curriculum, instruction, and assessment, optimize opportunities for multilingual learners to engage in learning. A topic of interest to a growing number of educational stakeholders, including policy makers, practitioners, researchers, and scholars, it is most advantageous for schools and districts to formulate and implement a language policy that accounts for the treatment of translanguaging between and among bi/multilinguals in school—that is, for both teachers and students.

The act of translanguaging can be spontaneous among bi/multilinguals of shared languages or planned within an instructional sequence. However, when it comes to curriculum and assessment, the use of translanguaging should be intentional, such as in building multilingual learners' metalinguistic and metacultural awareness (through a comparative analysis of languages and cultures). Therefore, educators responsible for curriculum design at a school or district level must define and apply translanguaging to their own contexts. Teachers, in turn, should be encouraged to negotiate a language and assessment policy inclusive of translanguaging for individual classes that is reflective of their student population and language practices.

FIGURE 3.2   The Interaction Among Resources to Maximize Multilingual Learners' Access to Learning

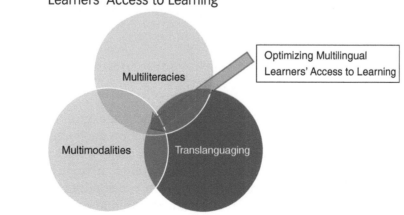

Photo by Il Vagabiondo on Unsplash, https://unsplash.com/photos/3B5ODR6ddpQ

▶ A multilanguage sign in Bangkok, Thailand

When assessment is planned and seamlessly interwoven into rich curriculum, it can be more coherently articulated. Having **integrated goals for learning** and an aligned planning process for curriculum, instruction, and assessment is a stepping-stone to effective enactment (Graves, 2016). One principle for curriculum design for multilingual learners is to "adopt a positive, welcoming mindset and culture of learning . . . by advanc[ing] bilingualism and bi-literacy as assets to learning and capitalizing on [English learners'] home language(s), cultural assets, and prior knowledge" (Pimentel, 2018, p. 3). Let's see how school and district leaders might envision a linguistically and culturally sustainable curriculum.

A MULTILINGUAL CURRICULUM FRAMEWORK WITH EMBEDDED ASSESSMENT

In planning for learning, whether in one or multiple languages, there should be a direct relationship between curriculum and instruction anchored in standards that is mediated by assessment. Figure 3.3 is an example of such a framework that is specifically designed for teaching and learning in multiple languages. Mirrored components reflect parallelisms between curriculum at the unit level and instruction at the lesson level. Assessment *as*, *for*, and *of* learning cements curriculum to instruction and brings cohesion, alignment, and continuity into the teaching and learning experience.

FIGURE 3.3 EL ESPEJO: Mirrored Components for Planning and Assessing Learning for Multilingual Learners

A Unit Plan Aimed at Multiple Languages and Perspectives: Planning for Learning Matched to a Compelling Question, Theme, or Issue and the Overall Purpose(s) for Assessment

Classroom/Grade-Level Products, Projects, or Performances With Use of Multimodalities	Community and Environmental Resources for Learning (Funds of Knowledge)	Coordinated Language and Content Standards, Including Disciplinary Practices	Integrated Learning Goals/Targets for Content and Language With Cross-Linguistic and Transcultural Considerations	Language Use Associated With the Compelling Question, Theme, or Issue

Considerations for Assessment *As*, *For*, and *Of* Learning

Classroom Learning Tasks and Activities With Multimodal Resources	Student and Family Resources for Learning (Funds of Identity)	Coordinated Language and Content Standards	Integrated Learning Targets/Objectives for Content and Language With Cross-Linguistic/Cross-Cultural Application	Oral, Written, Visual, and Digital Response to the Compelling Question, Theme, or Issue

A Lesson Plan Aimed at Multiple Languages and Perspectives: Documenting Learning Based on Feedback From Assessment

SOURCE: Adapted from Gottlieb & Hilliard (2019); Hilliard & Gottlieb (2018).

Embedded Language Expectations for Systemic Planning, Enacting and Justifying Outcomes (EL ESPEJO)—the mirror—is a linguistically and culturally sustainable curricular framework that is designed for multilingual learning inclusive of assessment. The sociocultural context for this curriculum framework is drawn from multilingual learners' resources: their "funds of knowledge" or household, community, and classroom practices (N. González et al., 2005), which, in turn, influence individual students' "funds of identity," a set of resources shaped by lived experiences essential for self-definition, self-expression, and self-understanding (Esteban-Guitart & Moll, 2014).

Starting with the purpose for assessment, EL ESPEJO is built from backward design as it first considers assessment *of* learning with its end product, performance, or project. A compelling or essential question leads to integrated learning targets that reflect multilingual multicultural realities. The other components address available resources (including standards) to draw from as part of the curricular and assessment experience (Gottlieb, 2021).

At a curriculum level, the top three rows of EL ESPEJO can readily be converted into a step-by-step process for contemplating and designing units of learning. As shown here and duplicated in Resource 3.2 as a startup outline, leadership teams can engage in assessment planning for multilingual learners as they:

Step 1: Identify the overall purpose(s) for assessment in multiple languages.

Step 2: Negotiate a final product, project, or performance with students.

Step 3: Name community and home resources to contribute to the unit.

Step 4: Identify corresponding content and language standards that exemplify the overall purpose.

Step 5: Design integrated content and language targets for learning with cross-linguistic and cross-cultural considerations.

Step 6: Generate a compelling question or issue that invites multicultural perspectives.

Step 7: Embed assessment *as, for,* and *of* learning.

Integrated Learning Goals/Targets

We emphasize Step 5 here in curriculum design as integrated learning goals/targets delineate the course of assessment in one or multiple languages. In essence, they encompass the expectations for language and content learning. Put another way, integrated learning goals/targets describe a pathway for multilingual learners' language development in conjunction with their conceptual development within and across the content areas (Cheuk, 2016).

Learning goals/targets at the unit level provide tangible and mutually agreed-upon expectations for teaching and learning. We use the term *learning targets* for student-generated ideas that are facilitated by teachers so that students can become leaders of their own learning. In contrast, *learning objectives* for individual lessons are perceived as teacher directives to meet district or school compliance (Berger, Rugen, & Woodfin, 2014).

Integrated learning goals/targets for curriculum and its associated assessment for multilingual learners who are engaging in learning in multiple languages should center on:

- Ideas or concepts rather than vocabulary or grammatical forms

- Effectiveness of communication rather than correctness

- Richness in comparing languages and cultures (i.e., metalinguistic and metacultural awareness) rather than blanket acceptance of only one

- A variety of linguistic and cultural perspectives

- Building students' bilingual identities

Learning targets should reflect both content and language expectations for the languages of instruction. For example, if striving for biliteracy in a dual language setting, multilingual learners, along with their teachers, should co-construct learning targets that apply to both English and the partner language. Cross-linguistic and cross-cultural considerations are part of integrated learning targets that can lead to translanguaging as a viable tool in curriculum design.

The following is an example of a multistep integrated learning goal/target from middle school multilingual learners and their teachers for a unit of learning.

We will:

- *Compare and contrast the language of familiar narratives (i.e., legends, fairytales) in two languages (e.g., How is the opening paragraph expressed in different languages, and how does it set the stage for action?)*

- *Reflect on the differences in cultural and linguistic perspectives in narratives*

- *Co-produce an original narrative (i.e., fairytale or legend) as an oral performance or a written product (with translanguaging)*

- *Perform/act out a narrative (with peers) or create an illustrated children's book*

There is a fully fleshed-out unit of learning based on the EL ESPEJO framework for third graders on a similar theme in the companion book on classroom assessment in multiple languages (Gottlieb, 2021).

COMMON ASSESSMENT FOR SCHOOLS AND DISTRICTS

Curriculum planning can lead to either individual classroom or common assessment across classrooms. Common assessment is a curriculum-based form of assessment *of* learning as it represents a culminating point in the learning process. When it is a district- or school-level initiative, common assessment usually consists of mutually agreed-upon activities, tasks, or projects across classrooms (often at a grade level or department), at times with input by students, teacher leadership teams, and professional learning communities or networks. In planning common assessment, school or district leadership can be supportive of teachers by:

- Creating and maintaining joint planning time for teacher pairs or teams

- Building in a feedback loop across different grade levels or departments to ensure spiraling of content and language

- Forging consensus of a language and assessment policy across classrooms or grade levels

- Scheduling educator-led professional learning for ongoing curriculum and assessment design

- Attending and contributing to grade-level and team meetings

Common Assessment

Students will work in cooperative groups to create a presentation that demonstrates their knowledge of the staff and their roles in schools.

Instructional Assessment

| Students will complete a Venn diagram comparing two roles. | Students will match staff pictures to roles. Students will orally present the roles. |

▶ A common assessment task built from a series of instructional assessment activities

The poster on common assessment *of* learning shows a culminating task for all Grade 2 students, their group presentations. In preparation for this final task on different school roles, students have engaged in assessment *as* and *for* learning, where they have devised questions and interviewed different school personnel, taken their photos, and compared their different roles using a Venn diagram.

A mark of common assessment is a uniform set of procedures for collecting, analyzing, and interpreting information across classrooms, even though the ways of showing evidence of learning do not have to be identical. For example, although the common assessment is identical across second-grade classrooms, some students obtain information on school roles by researching websites, others by listening to books on tape, and still others through questioning adults before comparing the information to the people in their own school. Students are given choices to demonstrate their learning through a variety of multiliteracies and multimodalities as long as they meet the same set of criteria for success as all students. As shown in Figure 3.4, the purpose for common assessment influences the potential number of classrooms, the time span, and its frequency.

FIGURE 3.4 Purposes, Classrooms Involved, Time Span, Frequency, and Examples of Common Assessment

PURPOSE FOR COMMON ASSESSMENT	CLASSROOMS INVOLVED	TIME SPAN	FREQUENCY	EXAMPLE
Document attainment of specified skills or concepts	Two or more classrooms	Within a unit of learning (e.g., for a series of lessons)	Every couple of weeks	Students compare elements of different mentor texts (e.g., claims, evidence, and reasoning in arguments) in one or more languages
Provide evidence of meeting grade-level learning targets or standards	Classrooms across a grade level or department	At the close of a unit of learning	Every couple of weeks to several months	Students exhibit their robotics project or present their multimedia research to a panel
Contribute to schoolwide or districtwide accountability	Classrooms across a school or district	A class period or two	Every three to four months	Students produce a first-draft response to a common writing prompt with visual or graphic scaffolds

Having consistent procedures for common assessment allows for increased reliability or consistency in interpreting what multilingual learners can do; using reliable procedures also improves validity in the inferences made that, in turn, bolsters claims of the effectiveness of multiple language use. In dual language settings where biliteracy is an expected programmatic outcome, common assessment can help fortify goal attainment. Common assessment that honors the integrity and uniqueness of each language while acknowledging the value of translanguaging is a natural outgrowth of schools that uphold multilingual language policies and practices.

Supported by school leadership, common assessment can serve as a form of local accountability that can lead to systemic transformation of teaching and learning. It is based on "classroom assessment, created and scored by classroom teachers, [which] is the gold standard in educational accountability" (Reeves, 2004, p. 114). When teachers are acknowledged and accepted as contributors to accountability, they become empowered, and with empowerment, teachers can change educational practice. When students are part of the assessment process, they, too, can develop a sense of efficacy and become motivated to succeed academically. In addition, such students can demonstrate greater ownership over their learning, persist longer on their tasks, and show higher levels of motivation than students who engage in similar but more traditionally structured classroom activities (Stiggins, 2008).

It is rare that common assessment is planned for and initiated in multiple languages unless it is designed for a dual language context. At best, prompts in English are translated into the language(s) of the multilingual learners, which lessens the integrity of the assessment. The inherent linguistic and cultural biases of translation simply do not yield accurate useful information for making instructional decisions. Resource 3.3 at the close of the chapter is a rating scale to prepare schools and districts for designing common assessment in multiple languages; Resource 3.4 is a checklist for leadership teams to jumpstart the planning process.

In planning common assessment, school and district leadership should account for every student. To be inclusive of linguistic and cultural sustainability and promote educational equity for multilingual learners, common assessment at a grade, department, or school level should be:

- A commitment to the use of multiple languages (including translanguaging if part of the school's or department's language policy)

- A tool for empowering multilingual learners and their teachers

- A planned activity in multiple languages that consists of:

  o Integrated learning target(s)

  o Challenging engaging tasks that draw on students' experiences and perspectives

  o Clear criteria for success

  o Minimal cultural bias and sensitivity

  o A planned feedback loop to inform teaching and learning

Planning common assessment that contributes to school or district accountability requires specific guidelines and preparation. If planned carefully and systematically, steps for building common assessment may take an entire year. Listed as follows are some quarterly milestones to help teams think about designing common assessment in multiple languages whose data that are generated will point to the effectiveness of a school's or district's multilingual program.

A Suggested Timeline for Developing and Enacting Common Assessment of Content-Based Prompts Throughout the School Year

Quarter 1:

- Choose the team: teacher and school leadership, multilingual learners, and other stakeholders

- Determine roles and responsibilities for team members

- Investigate types of common assessment that typify different content areas

- Determine the amount of time to devote to (schoolwide or districtwide) common assessment

Quarter 2:

- Survey students and colleagues for interesting themes, topics, or issues to pursue

- Select relevant language development and state academic achievement standards

- Propose specific ideas for common assessment for designated content areas

- Suggest multimodal resources as part of the common assessment prompt or task

Quarter 3:

- Draft a timetable along with project milestones, resource materials, and instructions

- Craft criteria for success in one or more languages

- Pilot test the common assessment on a few multilingual learners in the grade above or below to ensure minimal linguistic and cultural bias and maximum accessibility

- Have students self-reflect on the pilot task

Quarter 4:

- Analyze the results from the pilot study and revise the task, as necessary

- Finalize directions, visuals and/or graphs, and criteria for success

- Administer the common assessment (if a prompt)

- Select anchor student samples from multilingual learners in multiple languages that exemplify the full range of criteria for success

- Conduct professional learning around determining inter-rater agreement among teachers

- Provide concrete feedback to students based on their results in relation to the criteria for success

Co-planning Common Assessment in Multiple Languages

If we are to engage in common assessment, by definition it has to be a co-planning process as multiple classrooms participate. Planning common assessment among educators may take longer than anticipated as it is as much a relationship-building exercise among individuals (e.g., between coaches and teachers, teachers and teachers, teachers and multilingual learners) as it is a professional learning experience in **assessment literacy**. It can begin with as few as two teachers and then hopefully spread across a grade level or department, until the entire school embraces having consistent ways of collecting, analyzing, and interpreting evidence of student learning.

Consistent with different time spans (as those in Figure 3.4), common assessment may be a single activity (such as a response to a prompt), a series of activities that form a task, or a long-term project. One of its primary features of common assessment is that it should be performance-based, with students interacting with each other around significant issues to produce original work. Common assessment activities, tasks, or projects for multilingual learners in one or more languages should also be:

- Salient—meaningful for students and teachers alike

- Relevant—containing real-world applicability for students that draws from their lived experiences as well as their linguistic and cultural resources

- Valid—realistic and authentic with minimal bias, suitable for their given purpose and audience

- Reliable—capable of generating data with consistency of interpretation and reporting

- Robust—deliberate and mindful of the depth and breadth of the activity, and, for multilingual learners, where language connects with content and there is a provision for (multiple) language use

- Explicit and clear—containing and sharing specified expectations or criteria

- Enacted with fidelity—with understandable and replicable procedures, as in always allowing multilingual learners to use their language of choice at strategic points in the process

 Stop-Think-Act-React

Relax and Reflect: How do you rate common assessment for multilingual learners?

To what extent do you consider common grade-level, schoolwide, or district assessment presently effective for your multilingual learners? How might you use the features of common assessment as a checklist or simply as a guide as you plan common activities, tasks, and projects?

A Fifth-Grade Example

What does common assessment look like? The following mini-scenario illustrates how a pair of teachers in a midsize school with a growing multilingual student population in a northeastern metropolitan suburb co-plan and enact common assessment in Spanish and English.

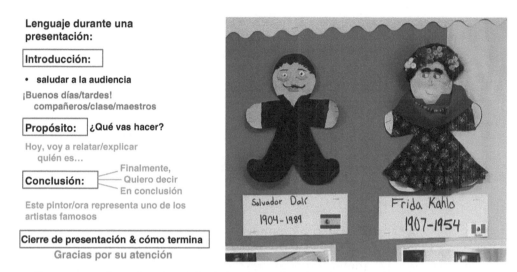

▶ The poster outlines directions/criteria for the students' oral presentation. The puppets are part of a hallway display of two classes' chronology of Hispanic artists.

Sara and Sofia are Spanish dual language teachers with contiguous rooms filled with enthusiastic 10-year-olds, the majority of Mexican and Central American descent, some with intense learning needs. These multilingual learners bring tremendous strengths to the classroom. In fact, one student from Guatemala reads stories in Spanish with family members, communicates in English at school, and speaks K'iche' with her grandparents.

At first the two teachers are rather apprehensive about co-planning instruction and assessment, but their mutual respect and pride of Spanish languages and cultures draw them together. In co-planning a unit on biography, the teachers center on a question of interest to their students: "How have Hispanic artists contributed to the beauty of the world?" They present this idea to their classes, which, knowing that they will be going to an art museum, even if it has to be virtually, embrace it enthusiastically.

Little by little a plan brews—the teachers decide to combine their classrooms to share the news about investigating artists from the Hispanic world (*los artistas del mundo hispano*). After the groups take a joint field trip to the nearby city's fine arts museum (it was open!), each student chooses an Hispanic artist of personal interest to research.

Next, students create an overall string timeline of all the selected artists for their multimedia project. As shown, the chart paper delineates the agreed-upon elements of their presentation: (1) introduction, (2) purpose, (3) conclusion, and (4) closure. The photo is a partial display of the multilingual learners' artist puppets in chronological order to advertise their biography fest.

The series of common classroom assessment tasks leads to the final project; in it, multilingual learners are invited to:

1. Portray their chosen Hispanic artist as a puppet for display, following a model

2. Digitally research and take notes on the life of their artist in their preferred language

3. Produce a timeline of the artist's most salient life events

4. Create an oral report using the puppet or multimedia, such as a PowerPoint presentation or a video

5. Orally present the biography of their artist to the combined classes

6. Check their performance against the agreed-upon criteria

Planning Interim Assessment

Interim assessment is a form of common assessment in that it occurs across classrooms; however, it differs in its purpose in that it is (1) a school- or district-level decision, (2) administered in prescheduled windows across the school year, and (3) generally a commercial standardized, often online, test. Interim tests of mathematics and language arts/reading are generally administered two to three times per year as the data serve as measures of local accountability and predictors for state annual achievement tests. Being more high-stakes in nature, interim measures adhere to stricter psychometric standards of reliability and validity. If there happens to be availability of these tests in multiple languages, school leaders need to check the:

- Technical manual for student demographics to ensure there is a match with the school or district population and that bias and sensitivity panels have been enlisted to ensure fairness in item selection

- Size and breakdown of the norming population by subgroups and languages

- Scoring tables to verify their applicability and usefulness in other languages

Common and interim assessment data may be included in a student, school, or district portfolio as contributors to local accountability. Culminating capstone projects (another form of common assessment) are also ideal candidates for portfolios, especially for dual language programs. Assessment portfolios, by being systematic collections of student work, provide authentic commonly agreed-upon evidence of student learning over time (Gottlieb & Nguyen, 2007).

STUDENT ASSESSMENT PORTFOLIOS IN MULTIPLE LANGUAGES

Portfolios are compilations of student work that aim at showing student growth in learning over time. When assessment encompasses multiple languages and the interaction between those languages through translanguaging, student portfolios boost relevance and authenticity of learning as entries are near and dear to students and more reflective of the whole child. Multilingual learners, as all students, can take on increased responsibility for learning as they participate in the selection of their portfolio entries.

Portfolios may be built around classroom performance assessment tasks or schoolwide projects, either with or without other forms of assessment information, such as common, interim, and annual test results. Ideally, school or district culminating capstone products are the final entries for elementary, middle, and high school; these passionate projects illustrate student voice and decision-making power. If the primary purpose for portfolios is for local assessment and accountability, then the portfolio as a whole must be a reliable and valid measure of learning (Gottlieb, 1995). By amassing a variety of different approaches to assessment in student portfolios (i.e., assessment *as, for,* and *of* learning), teachers gain a comprehensive view of each student's accomplishments.

Assessment portfolios for multilingual learners should be sensitive to and reflective of the goals of local multilingual education programs. By definition, portfolios of multilingual learners in dual language or two-way immersion classrooms have to be characterized by a balanced set of entries in two languages. To maximize their practicality and usefulness for students, teachers, and administrators, student portfolios that center on bilingual development should have the following features:

- Representation of students' original work in multiple languages

- Evidence of students' bilingual language development in relation to their achievement

- Ample assessment results or feedback in multiple languages that inform stakeholders, including students, family members, and teachers

- Strong reliability that shows consistency in scoring or evaluation in multiple languages from project to project and comparability from year to year (if applicable)

- Validity that expresses the extent of meeting the multilingual education program's mission and vision in conjunction with student learning goals and targets

- Provision of a rich and comprehensive portrait of overall learning that reflect students' access to their full linguistic repertoires

- Enough entries to inform local accountability for a school's or district's multilingual program and the stakeholders involved

Figure 3.5 is intended as a checklist of potential kinds of evidence for multilanguage development, academic achievement, and special projects for multilingual learners' assessment portfolios that makes provision for the languages in which evidence is produced. It has been filled in as to whether the entry represents assessment *as, for,* or *of* learning. In this example, note a place for fine arts, technology, and community service for students to demonstrate learning through multiple venues inside and outside of school.

FIGURE 3.5 A Checklist for Planning Multilingual Portfolios Across Assessment *as*, *for*, and *of* Learning

INCLUDED IN THE PORTFOLIO (CHECK ALL THAT APPLY):	ASSESSMENT INFORMATION GATHERED FROM:	AS, *FOR*, OR *OF* LEARNING	EVIDENCE		
			LANGUAGE(S)		
			LANGUAGES OTHER THAN ENGLISH	ENGLISH	TRANSLANGUAGING
	Classroom projects with specific feedback on the criteria for success	*For* and *of* learning			
	Student reflection on overall projects	*As* learning			
	Common tasks accompanied by rubrics	*Of* learning			
	Student self-assessment on tasks or prompts	*As* learning			
	School- or districtwide interim achievement testing	*Of* learning			
	School- or districtwide interim language proficiency testing	*Of* learning			
	Apprenticeship in community or school service-learning projects (with a learning log, summary of the experience, and lessons learned)	*As, for,* and *of* learning			
	Peer and self-assessment on projects	*As* learning			
	Technology (digital) projects with ongoing feedback from teachers and peers	*For* and *of* learning			
	Fine arts projects (including drama, dance, and arts options)	*Of* learning			
	Annual assessment data from state academic achievement and language proficiency testing	*Of* learning			

Relax and Reflect: How might you plan a student portfolio with a balance of assessment as, for, and of learning?

As part of the planning process, grade-level and leadership teams should think about the value of student assessment portfolios as a record of multilingual learners' personal growth and attainment in multiple languages. Data from portfolios can elevate the status of learning in multiple languages for local accountability purposes. Take Figure 3.5 (duplicated in Resource 3.5) to determine the feasibility of designing a programwide or schoolwide portfolio in multiple languages with strong evidence of learning.

A portfolio is an ideal archive for students to organize and maintain data on their preset learning goals over a semester or academic year, but it can also be a logistical challenge. Planning ahead—for example, for what might be required and optional entries for a grade or department—will minimize some of the hassle. Here are some tips to follow:

- Consider beginning with one content area (e.g., language arts), one language domain (e.g., writing), or one communication mode (e.g., writing and multimedia), and gradually introduce others throughout the year

- Proportion the range and languages of entries within and across content areas

- Decide a realistic time frame to submit entries, such as for each final project or at the close of a quarter; always build in extra time as everyone will need it!

- Co-plan with others to select software to support digital portfolios and how entries are to be uploaded, coded, scanned, organized, and stored

FACING THE ISSUE: UTILIZE MULTILINGUAL LEARNERS' RESOURCES TO MAXIMIZE THEIR LANGUAGE LEARNING

Inclusion of multilingual learners' linguistic and cultural strengths in schooling includes their comfort with and use of multiliteracies, multimodal means of communication, and translanguaging. Schools might leverage these assets of multilingual learners as an entrée to or a consideration in planning instruction and assessment in multiple languages. The following questions prompt some ideas for connecting these resources to assessment.

For School Leaders

➢ How might you create a schoolwide advocacy plan to highlight multilingual learners' strengths through assessment in multiple languages (that also acknowledges translanguaging)?

➢ How might you design a professional learning plan to provide educators with opportunities to design linguistically and culturally sustainable curriculum, instruction, and assessment or revisit and revise what is currently in place through a multilingual lens?

➢ How might you plan a survey with teachers or leadership teams that asks students to pair their preferences for language use with showing what they know, working with peers or independently, or displaying their work?

For District Leaders

➢ How might you plan professional learning across the district to promote assessment literacy with special attention to multilingual learners?

➢ How might a school or district team of dual language teachers and coaches plan for collecting data on multilingual learners' use of translanguaging during instruction and assessment as evidence for learning?

➢ How might you plan common assessment in one or more languages that is fair for multilingual learners and multilingual learners with disabilities?

RESOLVING THE DILEMMA: PUT TRUST IN YOUR MULTILINGUAL LEARNERS' LANGUAGE USE!

The educational landscape as we knew it prior to March 2020 is forever changed. When returning to brick-and-mortar buildings on a permanent basis, everyone—from the district superintendent to cafeteria workers—will, or will have had to, adjust to work in unfamiliar environments with different norms, policies, and procedures. The watchwords for educational leaders for how to navigate in this new era are *be compassionate*, *be nimble*, and *be strong*. Be empathic, as every human being has been negatively impacted by multiple crises in some way and we must all be humane to one another. Be flexible, as it is hard to imagine what our students and their families have endured, and we must adjust accordingly. Be resilient, and stay strong for the sake of others. Only then can we start thinking about how assessment fits into this new world order.

Planning for school and district assessment while acclimating to a new normal for life and for education is going to be challenging for a long time to come. Changes to teaching and learning will be compounded by a perpetual uneasiness about how to cope with the present and worry about what might be looming ahead. Hopefully, some semblance of teaming and scheduling is already in place to facilitate adjustments to common and interim assessment that will enhance, not disrupt, learning. Dr. Ho and his team are constantly working and reworking plans to care for students and optimize conditions to seamlessly embed assessment into curriculum and instruction.

The message for this chapter is clear: accept all forms of languaging and language-related resources as the basis for teaching and learning as well as expressions of curriculum and assessment. This openness extends to the use of multiliteracies, multimodal communication, and translanguaging as part of a school's language and assessment policy. Ultimately, if we indeed strive for linguistic and cultural equity in our schools and districts, we have to be resilient so that our students become compassionate, nimble, and strong.

Resources for School and District Leaders

RESOURCE 3.1
A Rating Scale: Integrating Assessment into Curriculum Design for Multilingual Learners

How would you evaluate the integration of assessment into curriculum for multilingual learners in your school or district? Use this rating scale to express the extent to which assessment-embedded curriculum is effective for multilingual learners in one or more languages.

CRITERIA FOR INTEGRATING ASSESSMENT INTO CURRICULUM	VERY EVIDENT	EVIDENT	SOMEWHAT EVIDENT	NOT YET ON THE RADAR
1. Every learning target sets up the context for assessment in multiple languages that invites multiple cultural perspectives.				
2. Ample and diverse opportunities are afforded students so that they can capitalize on their full linguistic and cultural repertoires during assessment.				
3. Cross-linguistic and cross-cultural considerations are threaded throughout the unit in assessment *as* and *for* learning and the culminating event or project in assessment *of* learning.				
4. Research-informed strategies on bilingualism and biliteracy push multilingual learners to achieve their goals through assessment in multiple languages.				
5. There are consistent challenging learning expectations for all multilingual learners regardless of their backgrounds and education status, as is apparent in assessment.				

6. Assessment captures the depth and breadth of a rich culminating experience (i.e., performance, project, or product).			
7. The synthesizing summative assessment experience at the close of a unit represents the learning targets along with evidence.			
8. Assessment offers student voice to be heard in multiple languages.			

online resources ⟋ Available for download at **resources.corwin.com/ assessingMLLs-LeadersEdition**

RESOURCE 3.2
Planning Assessment in Multiple Languages for a Unit of Learning

As part of the planning phase, use the following steps with colleagues to help frame your multilingual units or as a checklist to guide the development of linguistically and culturally relevant units of learning.

Step 1: Identify the overall purpose(s) for assessment in multiple languages.

Step 2: Negotiate a final product, project, or performance with students.

Step 3: Name community and home resources to contribute to the unit.

Step 4: Identify relevant content and language standards.

Step 5: Design integrated content and language targets for learning with cross-linguistic and cross-cultural considerations.

Step 6: Generate a compelling question or issue that invites multicultural perspectives.

Step 7: Embed assessment *as*, *for*, and *of* learning.

 Available for download at resources.corwin.com/assessingMLLs-LeadersEdition

RESOURCE 3.3

A Rating Scale for Planning Common Assessment in Multiple Languages

To what extent is common assessment designed for multilingual learners in your setting?

Use this rating scale to determine the presence of multilingual learners in common assessment. Discuss with leadership teams how you might begin to co-plan common assessment for units of learning in multiple languages. Individually and then with collaborators, mark the extent that you agree with the following statements about common assessment. Discuss any discrepancies in your thinking and how you might reconcile your differences.

COMMON ASSESSMENT FOR MULTILINGUAL LEARNERS IN MULTIPLE LANGUAGES	YES!	TO SOME EXTENT	WE'RE CONSIDERING IT	NOT ON OUR RADAR YET
1. Considers the integration of language and content as a schoolwide, program, or districtwide commitment				
2. Is a tool for empowerment of multilingual learners and their teachers who collaborate and share responsibility for student learning				
3. Is a planned process that accentuates what multilingual learners *can* do				
4. Is based on instructionally embedded tasks that multilingual learners have been prepared to engage with clear criteria for success				
5. Uses results to document student growth, provide feedback for instruction, assist in educational decision making, and improve teaching and learning				
6. Attempts to minimize issues of bias and sensitivity				

online resources

Available for download at **resources.corwin.com/ assessingMLLs-LeadersEdition**

RESOURCE 3.4
A Checklist for Planning Common Assessment in Multiple Languages

Who's involved in your school and district? Which languages are represented? Use this checklist to help plan common assessment for multilingual learners.

1. The Role of the Educator Design Team(s)

   ☐ The majority of the members are proficient in the languages of instruction for multilingual learners and are certified in language education or multilingual/bilingual education.

   ☐ Both language and content teachers contribute resources and ideas to projects.

   ☐ School leaders participate in the team or serve as team coaches or advisors.

   ☐ Every team member makes a commitment, has a role, and shares responsibility for each project.

   ☐ The team is knowledgeable of the students' linguistic, cultural, historical, and experiential backgrounds.

2. The Role of Other Stakeholders

   ☐ Staff and school leaders have been informed of and endorse the assessment plan.

   ☐ Family members have been consulted or are involved in the planning process.

   ☐ The school's local council or the district's Board of Education has been informed and approves the overall assessment plan.

3. The Role of Multilingual Learners

   ☐ Multilingual learners have been identified by grade and by language proficiency levels in English and their other language(s).

   ☐ The features of the instructional programs for multilingual learners, including language allocation, are carefully considered in planning assessment.

   ☐ Provisions for the languages of assessment are synchronized with the languages of instruction for multilingual learners.

 Available for download at **resources.corwin.com/** assessingMLLs-LeadersEdition

RESOURCE 3.5

Planning Multilingual Portfolios to Represent Assessment *as,* *for,* or *of* Learning

Student assessment portfolios should represent an even distribution of assessment approaches along with languages of instruction for multilingual learners. If assessment portfolios are a schoolwide initiative, grade or department teachers should have input in its contents. Complete the chart for potential entries in the portfolio by indicating the type of evidence and associated language(s) in each column.

ASSESSMENT INFORMATION GATHERED FROM:	EVIDENCE			
	AS, FOR, OR *OF* LEARNING	LANGUAGE(S)		
		LANGUAGES OTHER THAN ENGLISH	ENGLISH	TRANSLANGUAGING
Individual classroom projects with specific criteria for success				
Ongoing teacher and peer feedback for projects along with subsequent action				
Common tasks and rubrics				
Student reflection on tasks or projects				
School- or districtwide interim achievement testing				
School- or districtwide interim language proficiency testing				

(Continued)

(Continued)

ASSESSMENT INFORMATION GATHERED FROM:	EVIDENCE			
	AS, FOR, OR OF LEARNING	LANGUAGE(S)		
		LANGUAGES OTHER THAN ENGLISH	ENGLISH	TRANSLANGUAGING
Community or school service-learning projects (with a learning log, summary of the experience, and lessons learned)				
Technology projects (including digital and multimedia options), with teacher and peer assessment				
Fine arts projects (including drama, dance, and arts options)				
Student reports for annual assessment data from state academic achievement and language proficiency testing				

 Available for download at **resources.corwin.com/assessingMLLs-LeadersEdition**

CHAPTER 4

Collecting and Organizing Assessment Information in Multiple Languages

▶ A multimodal sign in Hanno, Saitama, Japan

Il existe une beauté particulière qui naît dans la langue, de la langue, et pour la langue.

A special kind of beauty exists which is born in language, of language, and for language.

—Gaston Bachelard

The Dilemma

Discrimination abounds against multilingualism and multiculturalism . . . What can we do?

Black lives matter. The lives of multilingual learners—including African, Afro-Asian, and Afro-Latinx immigrants from around the world—matter. Racism, classism, and **linguicism** *cannot be tolerated. As marginalized children and youth, multilingual learners (and their families) have historically been subjected to discrimination and racism. It is not a new phenomenon, but rather since the birth of the United States, these attitudes have prevailed and have been inculcated into the American psyche. As Flores (2020a) states, "The only way to ensure that bilingual education is a tool for social change is to ensure that it is situated within a broader project that seeks to dismantle anti-Blackness. Anything less than this is tantamount to treating Black lives as if they don't matter."*

Conflict theorists believe that it is not public schools but rather educational systems that tend to reinforce and perpetuate social inequalities that arise from differences in class, gender, race, and ethnicity. The question then becomes, "How can the staples of an educational system—namely, curriculum, instruction, and assessment—be conduits of systemic change for schools and districts with multilingual learners?" In a midsize metropolitan school district, Dra. Ramírez-Olson was specifically hired as an assistant superintendent to inaugurate a diversity initiative to mitigate racial and cultural tensions and to strengthen ties internally within the district and between schools and the community.

During their initial meetings, la doctora and the leadership team created a districtwide theory of action, an evidence-based plan to explain the changes intended to improve teaching and learning across the year through a

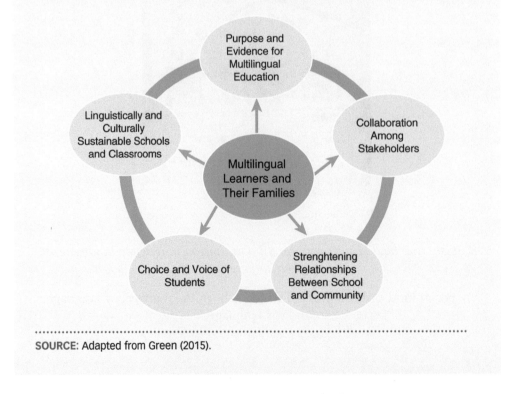

SOURCE: Adapted from Green (2015).

linguistically and culturally sustainable curriculum with embedded assessment. It was built around collaborative leadership with engagement of multilingual learners and their families at its center. In essence, the district's theory of action is as follows: "Linguistically and culturally sustainable schools and classrooms offer students choice and voice that draw from their identities and relationships, fostering collaboration among stakeholders and advocacy for multilingualism and assessment in multiple languages." Above is the graphic of the major tenets of the action plan that was shared with all schools in the district during the opening professional learning activity.

Based on the district's theory of action and its distributive leadership philosophy, representatives from each school, including principals, coaches, teachers, community members, and students, formed a multicultural council. First, the council conducted an investigation into the research on multilingualism to dispel the myths that tended to pervade the district. Then, based on overwhelming evidence and after much discussion, the council decided the district's focus for the year would be to infuse multimodalities through multiliteracies throughout the curriculum. The reasons were twofold: (1) to help improve accessibility for multilingual learners, multilingual learners with individualized education programs, and other minoritized students, and (2) to generate more equitable assessment practices.

Now during the collection and organization phase of the assessment cycle, Mozart School is taking the district's theory of action and applying it directly to instruction and assessment in multiple languages. Unlike other schools in the district, Mozart has long realized that multilingual learners' identities are wrapped in their languages and cultures. Additionally, the school is aware that multiliteracies along with multimodal communication underscore the strength in diversity that enables multilingualism to prevail and thrive inside and outside of school. The faculty of Mozart and its community hope that the district's multicultural campaign can convert into a sound and enduring educational practice for all its schools to counter racism and root it out.

FIRST IMPRESSIONS

- In what ways does this scenario resonate with you?

- How might your district or school develop a theory of action around multilingualism and multiculturalism?

- In collecting information during assessment in multiple languages, how do you ensure equity of language representation?

- What resources are available during the data collection phase of assessment for multilingual learners in multiple languages?

In classrooms, every moment is an opportunity for assessment and the collection of information. As we have seen in Chapter 3, however, for schools and districts, common assessment across classrooms is generally a planned event several times a year.

The more time and careful consideration that go into the planning or co-planning of common assessment, the more reliable the data collection. As shown in Figure 4.1, this chapter focuses on the second phase of the assessment cycle, *collecting and organizing information.* As part of data collection, educators of multilingual learners have to determine, especially when instruction is in multiple languages:

1. Which language(s) students can use to examine content, explore options, and express themselves

2. How to incorporate multiliteracies and multimodalities into performance tasks

3. Which modes of communication are most appropriate for the task at hand

4. When to consider and how to incorporate scaffolding as part of assessment

In this chapter, school and district leaders are presented as drivers of data collection, and we see how proactive and supportive leadership can make a difference in assessment in multiple languages for multilingual learners. First, we show how a theory of action can be a stimulus to spark change in school and district assessment practices. Next, we examine how Universal Design for Learning helps enhance opportunities for all students to access content and make meaning during instruction and assessment. Under that umbrella, we further define three resources for improving the quality of data collection for multilingual learners—namely, multiliteracies, multimodal communication, and translanguaging. In addition, we touch on strategies for scaffolding learning during data collection to assist multilingual learners, especially newcomers. Finally, we contextualize the data collection phase within the assessment trilogy *as*, *for*, and *of* learning and its applicability to portfolios as a frame for organizing and managing data.

FIGURE 4.1 The Second Phase of the Assessment Cycle: Collecting and Organizing Assessment Information in Multiple Languages

ASSESSMENT IN MULTIPLE LANGUAGES

THE ROLE OF LEADERSHIP IN COLLECTING DATA IN MULTIPLE LANGUAGES

District and school leaders hold the key to successful data collection in multiple languages as it is their responsibility to create the architecture to be inclusive of multilingual learners and their families through integrated service delivery (Scanlan & López, 2012). In other words, educational leaders hold equity and social justice for students in their hands. Without their insight, assistance, and support, the viability of language education is in jeopardy.

School leaders often have to negotiate with district leadership and at times resist top-down policies that promote English-only instruction (Menken, 2017). Wherever there are multilingual learners, data collection is hampered if it is limited to one language: Multilingual learners' voices are silenced, their social-emotional development is stunted, and their academic potential is stifled. Although multiple measures should always be part of an effective assessment plan, when examining a dual language or any bilingual education program with multilingual learners, it is nonsensical if the measures and subsequent evidence are only in a single language.

Creating and Applying a Theory of Action Tool for Assessment in Multiple Languages

Before jumping into collecting data, school and district leaders need to have a plan that expands assessment to encompass multiple languages. Let's elaborate on the theory of action graphic introduced in the opening scenario of this chapter as a stimulus for change in assessment. One way of looking at a theory of action is by connecting a set of propositions with a logical chain of reasoning that explains how change will lead to improved or transformed practices.

In the example theory of action, we start with the purpose for change (e.g., improving school and district accountability for multilingual learners through linguistically and culturally sustainable assessment) that is matched to research-based evidence (the cognitive, linguistic, cultural, and social-emotional benefits of multilingual education for bi/multilingual learners). We move clockwise around the proposition wheel until we reach linguistically and culturally sustainable schools and classrooms (with aligned curriculum, instruction, and classroom assessment in one or more languages).

 Stop-Think-Act-React

Reflecting on Research: What is the relevant evidence to support multilingual education?

Revisit the research base for bilingualism and multiculturalism presented in Chapter 1. What evidence might you draw from the research to support your theory of action for assessment in multiple languages? What additional evidence is necessary to strengthen your claim? The research evidence that you gather should form a strong rationale for your theory of action.

FIGURE 4.2 Creating a Theory of Action for Assessment in Multiple Languages

EXAMPLE PROPOSITIONS IN A THEORY OF ACTION FOR ADMINISTRATORS	APPLIED TO ASSESSMENT IN MULTIPLE LANGUAGES
Identify purposes for assessment in multiple languages and attach them to evidence by . . .	Determining and defending local accountability for learning in multiple languages and program effectiveness
Foster collaboration among stakeholders by . . .	Creating networks of educators dedicated to co-planning and enacting the assessment cycle in multiple languages
Build relationships and networks between schools and their communities by . . .	Co-planning collection of ethnographic data in the community to help inform and contextualize school-based data
Give students choice and voice by . . .	Inviting multilingual learners to participate in assessment *as*, *for*, and *of* learning in multiple languages
Transform schools and classrooms into linguistically and culturally sustainable environments by . . .	Offering professional learning and action research opportunities on assessment literacy through a multilingual multicultural lens

As a precursor to collecting school or district data, setting up a framework or template for a theory of action provides a pathway for initiating change, such as the one in Resource 4.1. It is a powerful tool for a leadership team to design and use to challenge assumptions and support consensus building through critical thinking and reflection. Figure 4.2 takes the propositions suggested for a theory of action pertaining to multilingual education and illustrates how they might be applied to assessment in multiple languages. It is suggested that leadership begin this journey by stating the intended outcome, as in *"Ultimately, our educational program can achieve its goal of multilingualism through embedded assessment in multiple languages if school or district administrators . . ."*

ADVICE FOR COLLECTING DATA IN A POST-PANDEMIC WORLD

Although it is advisable to have a theory of action, administrators must also attend to emergencies that spring up. To say that the global pandemic impacted absolutely everyone in the world of K–12 education is an understatement. Within a matter of hours in mid-March 2020, the ecology of school as we all knew it, along with its intricacies of relationships, was totally dismantled. It surely will have lasting effects on our institutions and stakeholders; assessment is one of those areas in which there will be reverberations for years to come.

A report from a prestigious panel issued in the midst of the pandemic offers sage advice based on principles of assessment appropriate for schools and districts (Lake & Olson, 2020). The overarching message is that assessment still matters. Purposes may shift, types of assessment may shift, timelines may shift, and modes of data collection may shift, but at its core, assessment provides valuable information about students, is inextricably tied to teaching and learning, and must be taken to heart.

In this era of uncertainty and instability, we have to be vigilant and have a plan about what kinds of information to collect, how to gather it, and, ultimately, its usefulness. Overall, any assessment strategy cannot be isolated but rather must align with and contribute to that of the broader educational system. The following recommendations from the consensus panel lay out principles for assessment to contemplate as we slowly move past our educational crises:

1. "First ask why—or why not—to assess." It is paramount to have a clearly defined rational purpose for assessment. Policy makers must exert care in ensuring that the *why* for assessment matches the *how* for data collection, analysis, and use.

2. "Do no harm." As assessments can be powerful tools for equity and informing curriculum and instruction, districts and educators must be proactive in their use, relying on information for only its designated purpose. For example, do not collect assessment data to make high-stakes decisions knowing their possible negative effect on students, such as repeating a grade or tracking. Rather, think about how to take that information to build on students' strengths.

3. "Take the first two or three weeks to focus on students' physical and emotional well-being and to strengthen relationships as foundational to learning." During these difficult and not-so-difficult times, getting a pulse on students' social-emotional development is just as important, if not more so, as taking a barometer of their achievement. For multilingual learners, there are added stressors to their lives. Schools need to reach out to the community to form a network of partnerships among social and medical agencies. Additionally, cross-agency data-sharing agreements should be formulated to protect families, not to instill fear.

4. "Prioritize measures closest to classroom instruction to help teachers know what to do next." District and school leadership should make use of existing large-scale data. Assessment data that are collected throughout the year should directly relate to subject matter curriculum, and for multilingual learners, data should be aligned with academic content and language development standards.

5. "Be cautious about using interim assessments" for school and district decision making. School and district decision makers should be aware that data from these commercial measures most probably are not comparable to those in the past, as there may be:

   • Unequal intervals between administrations of the measures, thus hampering making comparisons and determining growth

   • Different contexts (remote vs. face-to-face) and conditions (home vs. school) for data collection

   • Intervening variables (e.g., illness, family dynamics) that skew the results

- Teachers who have not had professional learning opportunities to become familiar with the measures

- Students who have experienced or are undergoing trauma and stress

6. "Engage parents as partners." Parents/family members/guardians are going to be apprehensive on many fronts with regard to school reentry, whenever it occurs. Teachers should gather information, to the extent feasible, on the stressors of family members during crises, what they have observed about their children during their time at home, their languages of interaction, and how these factors may have impacted learning grade-level content. To the extent possible, data should be transparent, understandable, and in the languages of multilingual families.

7. "Don't use assessments for accountability unless they were designed and validated for that purpose." First and foremost, whenever the new normal falls upon us, school and district leadership must have a plan and a clear-cut strategy for moving forward. Attention should be given to individual students' emotional and learning needs. Consideration should also be given to resetting of baseline data for school and district accountability along with a strong rationale for doing so.

IMPROVING ACCESSIBILITY IN DATA COLLECTION

Interestingly, districts and schools have become more vigilant in attending to the idea of accessibility for students and understanding its close ties with equity. At the same time, the pandemic has underscored the lack of access and equity for so many of our multilingual learners, especially in the area of technology. Multilingual learners' opportunity and accessibility must also extend to their freedom of expression. To increase participation in school and engagement in learning, these students must feel safe to tap and use their entire linguistic repertoires. "Researchers argue that restricting language use in the classroom to one language or another stigmatizes minoritized languages and limits speakers' ability to make meaning. Students need to be able to suppress what they know how to do in more than one language in contexts where others will not understand them, but they also should be able to demonstrate freely linguistic abilities not tied to a single language, such as locating information, structuring an argument and creating multilingual texts" (Reynolds, 2019, p. xii).

Revisiting Universal Design for Learning

The principles of Universal Design for Learning (UDL), introduced in Chapter 3, should guide the design of learning experiences to maximize opportunities of all students—in particular, multilingual learners and multilingual learners with individualized education programs (IEPs)—throughout the assessment cycle. Compatible with assessment *as* learning in its student centeredness, the goal of UDL is for all learners to become motivated, resourceful, strategic, and goal-directed about learning.

When examining UDL in relation to assessment in multiple languages, however, there are issues of bias and sensitivity to consider (Lea & Dame, 2020). What is reasonable in one language may not make sense in another. What is commonplace in one language may be a rarity, if present at all, in another. When thinking about developing common assessment for a grade level or school, for example, we have to attend to multilingual learners' languages and cultures as part of UDL and make sure that its principles extend across the assessment cycle.

Accessibility in and of itself is not a panacea. Here is a partial list of issues that can potentially impede UDL for bi/multilingual learners when assessment occurs in multiple languages. The examples are ones in English, but can readily occur in other languages as well:

- Idiomatic expressions (e.g., *think outside the box*)

- Regionalisms (e.g., *stand on line* vs. *stand in line*)

- False cognates (e.g., *embarrassed* vs. *embarazada*)

- Cultural nuances of language use (e.g., *the Underground Railroad*)

- Topics that evoke distress or anxiety caused by hardship or disaster (e.g., tsunamis, pandemics, typhoons)

- Culturally specific proper names (e.g., *Beauregard*, *Sashenka*)

- Extraneous information that confounds the message

UDL, when integrated into assessment at school and district levels, can also attenuate some of the potentially damaging effects of assessment designed for multilingual learners. As shown in Figure 4.3, UDL can be envisioned as an umbrella for a set of nested resources that expand possibilities for how multilingual learners can access and express their learning—namely, through multiliteracies, multimodal channels of communication, and translanguaging. These resources optimize and legitimize multilingual learners' multiple language use in school. For educational leaders, it is important to acknowledge and endorse these resources as part of a compendium of effective assessment practices in multiple languages.

FIGURE 4.3   Resources for Increasing Accessibility in Assessment in Multiple Languages

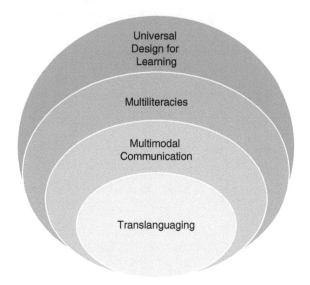

REVISITING RESOURCES FOR ASSESSMENT IN MULTIPLE LANGUAGES

As mentioned in Chapter 3, we need to be sensitive to the role of multiliteracies and multimodalities in fostering learning, starting with planning assessment within curriculum design. These resources underscore the shift from traditional definitions of literacy that are focused on print, primarily reading and writing, to more expanded forms through additional modes of communication. In this section, we turn our focus to the use of multiliteracies, along with multimodalities, as integral to data collection in classroom or common assessment designed for multilingual learners.

▶ A sign in Thessaloniki, Greece, that draws on multiliteracies

Using Multiliteracies in Data Collection

Multiple languages are wrapped up in the notion of multiliteracies; "effective citizenship and productive work now require that we interact effectively using multiple languages, multiple Englishes, and communication patterns that more frequently cross cultural, community, and national boundaries" (The New London Group, 1996, p. 64). If in fact multiliteracy is to become the new normal for all students, educators must be cognizant of its role in assessment. When coupled with translanguaging, multiliteracy provides more equitable and meaningful avenues to learning for bi/multilingual learners. Figure 4.4 suggests how multiliteracies, with or without translanguaging, can be incorporated into data collection during assessment.

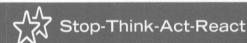 Stop-Think-Act-React

Relax and Reflect: As an educational leader, how might you transform literacy practices to practices of multiliteracies?

Teachers, especially those of multilingual learners and students with disabilities, tend to gravitate toward multimodal communication, often coupled with or integrated into multiliteracies to support student learning in inclusionary classroom environments. Yet, unfortunately, assessment is often heavily dependent on text. How might you as an educational leader work with others to formulate an assessment policy that is accepting of these resources and encourages teachers to use these resources as characteristic of strengths-based assessment?

FIGURE 4.4 Capturing Multiliteracies (and Multimodalities) During Data Collection

COLLECTING DATA WITH EMBEDDED MULTILITERACIES	
Oral text, combined with visual, graphic, and digital representation in one or more languages	Written text, combined with visual, graphic, and digital representation in one or more languages
Oral or written bilingual text exhibiting translanguaging with visual, graphic, and digital representation	

Using Multimodalities in Data Collection

Many modes of communication have always existed; however, they have not always been acknowledged as a socially and culturally accepted form of expression in school. The use of multiple languages as a bona fide means of transmitting information, ideas, and concepts is still being contested in some educational circles, yet it is readily accepted as a multimodal resource. The blending of modes, such as images, words, sounds, gestures, and movement, can occur simultaneously through either **interpretive** (listening and reading) or **expressive** (speaking and writing) channels (Walsh, 2011).

Think about it. If someone says or reads the word *corn*, it generally conjures up a single image. Coupling the word with a visual representation, however, illustrates how the mode of visualization can enhance its meaning. The following photo of a real-life representation of its many varieties expands the notion of corn from a single image to one of a cultural symbol and a way of Mexican life.

▶ Itanoní, a restaurant in Oaxaca, México, devoted to Indigenous varieties of corn

Images can serve as engaging stimuli for students to produce authentic text whether in oral, written, or multimodal forms for instruction and assessment. Multimodal imagery—photography, cartoons, animation, or illustration—especially if interesting, can raise different feelings, meanings, interpretations, and perspectives. As depicted in Resource 4.2, photos or other visuals can readily jumpstart ideas for recording impressions, generating feelings, or remembering a personal experience. For common assessment, the same prompt and image could be given across grades, such as "What do you think of when you look at this photo? Describe a time when you did something special at sunrise or sunset. Whom were you with? What did you do? How did you feel? You may choose one or more languages

▶ Relying on a visual stimulus for assessment: a photo of sunset over the Gulf of México

to express yourself orally, in writing, or even by drawing yourself in the photo."

Data collection for common assessment across a grade-level cluster or even for an entire K–8 building can revolve around the use of a single image as a stimulus, as exemplified by the photo; it's not necessary to have a text-dependent prompt. Students can be part of the assessment process by taking photos themselves and nominating different images from books or other media for use as common assessment prompts.

 Stop-Think-Act-React

Relax and Reflect: Which modes of communication best supplement language samples in multiple languages?

Multimodal channels of communication can be readily embedded in interpretative (listening and reading) and expressive (speaking and writing) common assessment activities or prompts. The leadership team crafting the common assessment should also simultaneously be considering ideas for incorporating multimodalities. For example, students might preview creating a personal narrative by first listening to a podcast, watching a video, or examining a set of illustrations. Have your team revisit common assessment for applicable grade levels or departments, the school or district and add multimodal resources to increase accessibility and enrich the experience for the students.

Multimodal Resources in Multiple Languages for Assessment as, for, and of Learning

Multimodal resources are the tools of the disciplines or content areas, not supplemental but rather serving as scaffolds for the more traditional language-centric means of communicating. In the classroom, multilingual learners' access to multimodalities should be directly connected to everyday instruction and expressions of assessment *as* and *for* learning. Multimodalities, when wrapped into projects, products, or performances at the close of units of learning, also serve as expressions of assessment *of* learning. An end product with embedded multimodalities, coupled with criteria or descriptors for success, can serve as common assessment across classrooms. Multilingual multimodal products can be displayed, performed, or captured throughout the year; in addition, they make ideal candidates for student assessment portfolios. Such products might include:

- Multilingual class videos, such as students reporting or reenacting events

- Multilingual performances or demonstrations, where multilingual learners create raps, recite original poetry, or explain a unique use of technology

- Multilingual schoolwide or district fairs or exhibitions, such as robotics

- Multilingual presentations, such as PowerPoint presentations

- Multilingual galleries around the school of murals or displays open to the community

- Multilingual community outreach events

- Multilingual audio or video broadcasts

- Multilingual classroom or school websites or newsletters

Stop-Think-Act-React

Relax and Reflect: How are multimodal resources connected to assessment?

The use of multimodalities increases students' opportunities to learn, enhances ways of communicating that learning, and simultaneously serves as a passage to equity. How might you envision infusing multimodal resources in common assessment for all students? How might you use exemplars of common assessment for grade-level teams or departments to be more sensitive to and inclusive of multimodal communication in instruction?

Multimodal channels of communication involve the complex interweaving of word, image, gesture/movement, and sound, including speech, and are presented through a range of media (Kress, 2010). Together, multiliteracies and multimodal resources have the potential of enhancing teaching and learning by providing students with greater accessibility to meaning, thus contributing to instructional and assessment equity. Figure 4.5, with a blank form in Resource 4.3, illustrates how multilingual learners might express their learning using these resources across assessment *as*, *for*, and *of* learning with one or more languages as an option.

Using Translanguaging in Data Collection

Before launching into a teaching and assessment policy for translanguaging for schools or districts, school leaders should take time to observe multilingual learners interact with each other in different settings throughout the school day—for example, in lunchrooms, in chat rooms, in hallways, and in study halls. The topic of translanguaging should also be investigated as part of school leaders' professional learning. Here is a poster that was created by teachers and coaches as a professional learning activity that shows their thinking around translanguaging.

FIGURE 4.5 Using Multiliteracies and Multimodal Resources in Assessment *as*, *for*, and *of* Learning

	ASSESSMENT *AS* LEARNING IN ONE OR MORE LANGUAGES	ASSESSMENT *FOR* LEARNING IN ONE OR MORE LANGUAGES	ASSESSMENT *OF* LEARNING IN ONE OR MORE LANGUAGES
Through Which Multiliteracies	Incorporating personal multiliteracy preferences (e.g., technology and its audio and visual presence) into final projects	Explaining how multiliteracies enhance multimedia exhibits	Presenting capstone research projects through multiliteracies to a school or community panel
With Which Multimodalities	Including self-reflection on use of an array of resources (e.g., graphic, auditory, digital) in gathering evidence for projects	Describing multimodal resources in multimedia exhibits	Summarizing content for capstone projects with one or more multimodal resources

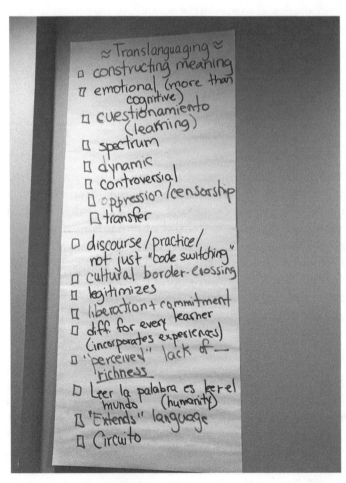

▶ Brainstorm on features of translanguaging from participants in a dual language workshop

The practice of translanguaging has a divided camp—it is deemed either acceptable or not. Hornberger (2004) introduced continua of biliteracy "to break down the binary oppositions so characteristic of the fields of bilingualism and literacy and instead draw attention to the continuity of experiences, skills, practices, and knowledge stretching from one end of any particular continuum to the other" (p. 156; see also Hornberger, 2003). The same analogy applies to translanguaging.

Biliteracy continua, as described by Hornberger (2003, 2004), are fluid rather than fixed and are dependent on the context, the content, and the language development of the multilingual learner, as is translanguaging. Additionally, for translanguaging, the persons with whom one is interacting play a sizeable role. Figure 4.6 envisions translanguaging along a continuum of instructional and assessment practices.

 Stop-Think-Act-React

M. T. Sánchez, García, and Solorza (2017) contest the rigid policies of dual language education programs that impose strict separation of languages during the day or across days, such as 90/10, 80/20, and 50/50 models. Instead of focusing on two independent languages, they suggest flexibility of bilingualism and translanguaging use. Their proposal for reframing language policy to one of **dynamic bilingualism** has huge implications for assessment in multiple languages.

Do you agree or disagree that there should be a space for translanguaging as part of assessment across dual language classrooms? If you agree, how does the policy impact your collection of assessment data in multiple languages whether at a classroom, school, or district level?

"Student learning is at the center of translanguaging pedagogy and students must be involved in assessing their own learning" (García, Johnson, & Seltzer, 2017, p. 92). This statement epitomizes assessment *as* learning as it exemplifies how multilingual learners are valued as self-assessors. In assessment *as* learning,

FIGURE 4.6 A Continuum of Translanguaging Practices in Instruction and Assessment Among Multilingual Learners Who Share a Language

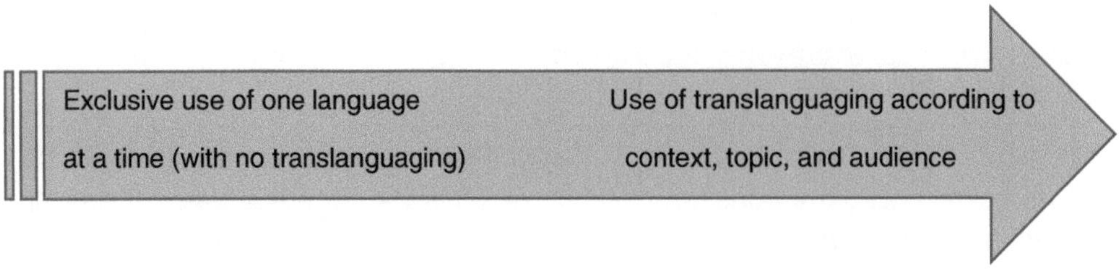

| Exclusive use of one language at a time (with no translanguaging) | Use of translanguaging according to context, topic, and audience |

translanguaging is recognized as an idiolect (the speech habits peculiar to an individual), as each multilingual learner has:

- A unique exposure to an array of languages

- An individual linguistic history

- Different positions on the continua of biliteracy and bilingualism

- Personalized ways of expression

- Distinct lived cultural experiences

- A singular set of opportunities for languaging

Whereas assessment *as* and *for* learning might be classroom-specific, assessment *of* learning across classrooms might readily encourage translanguaging as well. We have seen how translanguaging can be incorporated into assessment *of* learning in curriculum design, in particular, in bilingual units of learning. As translanguaging for units is intentional and planned, there should be specific provisions for data collection based on preset integrated learning goals or targets. Acceptance and use of translanguaging in curriculum design should automatically be part of assessment.

CO-PLANNING DATA COLLECTION IN MULTIPLE LANGUAGES

Co-planning, co-teaching, and co-assessing have been gaining momentum in educational circles as there are advantages for having a partner to collaborate with, whether remote or in person. Benefits of this instructional and assessment partnership when working with multilingual learners include:

1. Sharing a positive vision for teaching and learning

2. Increasing responsiveness to students who use multiple languages

3. Enhancing teacher capacity to problem-solve around issues of multilingualism

Relax and Reflect: What are different teacher configurations for co-planning, co-teaching, and co-assessing in one or more languages?

We have mentioned how district and school leadership can facilitate co-planning for common assessment across a grade level, department, or even school. Co-planning assessment can occur between many different educator partners. Think about which educators might pair up to provide the most effective educational opportunities for the multilingual learners in your school or district and what role each might play:

- Monolingual classroom teachers

- Monolingual classroom teachers endorsed or certified in English as an additional language

- Special education teachers

- Special education teachers endorsed or certified in English as an additional language

- Language education teachers endorsed or certified in English as an additional language

- Bilingual/dual language classroom teachers

- Bilingual special education teachers with dual certifications

- Monolingual coaches

- Bilingual/dual language coaches

4. Envisioning collaboration as mutually empowering for co-teachers and students

5. Serving as models for promoting student interaction and respect (Honigsfeld & Dove, 2015; Villa, Thousand, & Nevin, 2008)

Leadership teams should work with teacher pairs in co-planning assessment prior to data collection. Figure 4.7, replicated in Resource 4.4, is a helpful tool to enhance the assessment experience for multilingual learners in multiple languages. It outlines resources for co-teachers to use, points to consider, and ideas for co-constructing assessment.

COLLECTING AND ORGANIZING COMMON ASSESSMENT IN MULTIPLE LANGUAGES

Students should be active participants in data collection as they are the ones producing the data. Equally important, students should be made aware of how data are to be used. Collecting oral, written, and multimodal language samples

FIGURE 4.7 A Checklist to Facilitate Co-assessment in Multiple Languages

Teacher Team: _____

In co-planning assessment and collecting data from multilingual learners . . .

We have used . . .
☐ Academic content standards
☐ Language development standards (i.e., English Language Development and Spanish Language Development Standards, as applicable)
☐ Spanish Language Arts Standards (for Latinx students)
☐ IEP goals for dually identified multilingual learners
☐ Linguistically and culturally relevant curricular, instructional, and assessment resources

We have considered/determined . . .
☐ The purpose for assessment in one or more languages
☐ Learning goals for units of learning tied to standards
☐ Language choice(s) for multilingual learners
☐ Multimodal channels of communication/multiliteracies
☐ Accommodations/accessibility as stipulated in multilingual learners' IEPs
☐ Built-in time for student self- and peer reflection
☐ Time for scoring of prompts or interpretation of projects by co-teachers
☐ How we are going to use the assessment data in multiple languages

We have we thought about/conceptualized . . .
☐ A menu of products, performances, and projects along with models or exemplars
☐ Timelines/windows for projects or a schedule for common assessment prompts
☐ Product/project descriptors, rubrics, or criteria for success
☐ A set of instructions for common assessment prompts
☐ Multimodalities within the assessment

in multiple languages should be a classroom practice embedded in instruction so that when similar data are gathered during common assessment, students are familiar with the routine.

At the beginning of a school year, schools should arrange for the collection of baseline data with common or uniform prompts for each mode of communication (i.e., expressive and interpretive) and each language. Subsequently, multilingual learners and teachers may wish to design the parameters for language use in their individual classrooms in accordance with the district, school, and classroom language policies. Initial data collection, whether for individual classrooms, grade levels, or departments, may also be useful in forming flexible groups.

During the year, common assessment across grades should be planned at regular intervals, such as once a quarter, to establish a schoolwide data source for accountability of learning in multiple languages. Even if remote instruction is the norm and students are engaged in online learning, common assessment within instructional activities can easily be shared among teachers.

Students can submit files of their oral, written, or multimodal responses for storage in an individual e-portfolio or a designated space in a classroom collection. Common assessment across classrooms for local accountability purposes should be archived and password protected on the school or district server.

Relax and Reflect: Why is it important to have literacy data in multiple languages?

Cummins's 1979 hypothesis—that in bilingual development, language and literacy skills can be transferred from one language to another—has been confirmed many times over. Research is clear that the stronger the literacy development in the students' home language, the greater the trajectory for English language literacy (Arellano, Liu, Stoker, & Slama, 2018; Relyea & Amendum, 2019). How might you apply these findings to your data collection efforts for multilingual learners in multiple languages?

Common assessment involves mutually agreed-upon measures or a set of uniform procedures that apply throughout the assessment cycle—planning, collecting, interpreting, evaluating and reporting data, and taking action—across multiple classrooms (Gottlieb, 2012). District-, school-, or grade-level goals for learning can trigger common assessment in one or more languages.

Figure 4.8 (replicated in Resource 4.5) offers a general timeline for collecting common assessment in multiple languages three times a year. A district leadership team of directors, coaches, teachers, and older multilingual learners might convene on a monthly basis to generate themes, refine ideas, and develop resources for common assessment prompts or activities. For example, in the fall, the prompt might be a chart (shown in Resource 4.6) in which students select/provide a topic of interest for each content area and write/draw (1) why they chose the topic, (2) what they know about the topic, and (3) what more they wish to learn. In that way, teachers gain insight into students and their language use while collecting baseline data.

Another way to organize data on interpretive and expressive language is according to the contributions of different stakeholders, as each stakeholder group represents a different approach to assessment—those enacted by students (assessment *as* learning), by teachers and students (assessment *for* learning), and by teachers in collaboration with administrators (assessment *of* learning). Figure 4.9 offers educators ideas for collecting information in one or more languages across assessment approaches and modes of communication for a student-centered research project.

FIGURE 4.8 A Sampling of Data Collection From Common Assessment Prompts

	AUTUMN DATE: GRADE LEVELS:	WINTER DATE: GRADE LEVELS:	SPRING DATE: GRADE LEVELS:
Common Multimodal Assessment in English	Baseline oral language prompt Baseline writing prompt	Oral language prompt	Integrated oral language and writing prompt
Common Multimodal Assessment in Other Languages	Baseline oral language prompt Baseline writing prompt	Writing prompt	Integrated oral language and writing prompt

FIGURE 4.9   Ideas for Collecting Student Samples During Assessment *as, for,* and *of* Learning

	ASSESSMENT *AS* LEARNING IN ONE OR MORE LANGUAGES	ASSESSMENT *FOR* LEARNING IN ONE OR MORE LANGUAGES	ASSESSMENT *OF* LEARNING IN ONE OR MORE LANGUAGES
Interpretative Language: Listening/ Reading/ Viewing	Students reflect on connecting oral, written, or visual text to their own experiences to pose research questions	Teachers help students select multilingual resources to examine their research questions	Leadership team members set a timetable for data collection (e.g., for the school's cultural fair) based on input from teachers and the community
Expressive Language: Speaking/ Writing/ Illustrating	Students interact with each other to investigate ideas to research and then design a graphic organizer of their plan	Teachers give actionable feedback to students on their research projects based on agreed-upon criteria	Leadership team members serve as the school's ambassadors in collecting classroom data (e.g., during the cultural fair)

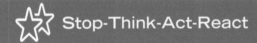

Stop-Think-Act-React

Relax and Reflect: How does district and school leadership facilitate data collection?

District and school leadership can readily carve a bit of time into teacher schedules to facilitate co-planning, which is essential for uniformity in data collection, especially for common assessment across a grade level or department. Teachers should agree on *what* (the theme or essential question and type of evidence), *how* (the overall procedure), and *when* (the length of time of an activity or timeline/window for an extended project) before collecting data. What suggestions might you make to improve data collection for common assessment in your school or district?

One last thought when it comes to this phase of the assessment cycle is the role of technology. Data can be collected and organized digitally, electronically, or manually with paper copies. Once data are in hand, information can be stored in individual student e-portfolios, uploaded to a database that is time stamped, or scanned and stored in a designated place. There are a lot of options and decisions to make! Remember to return to the purpose for assessment; if, in fact, assessment in multiple languages serves as school or district accountability, then there must be extra care in ensuring uniformity in data collection efforts.

ORGANIZING AND ASSEMBLING ASSESSMENT PORTFOLIOS IN MULTIPLE LANGUAGES

Portfolios can offer multilingual learners insight into their language, conceptual, and social-emotional development over time, helping students see learning as an ongoing process of inquiry, exploration, and reflection. In part, assessment portfolios should help students self-assess in systematic and comprehensive ways. For multilingual learners, portfolio assessment can and should incorporate multiliteracies and multimodal communication channels and, of course, entries in multiple languages to witness their growth over time.

All students should assume responsibility for their portfolio entries, starting in the early grades. In today's learning environment, it is quite easy to scan and upload files with one click or even a QR code to preserve the contents. Additionally, multilingual learners, in collaboration with their teachers, should ensure that there is a balanced representation of languages based on the purpose and approach to assessment. Individual student portfolios are perfect stimuli for **student-led conferences** with teachers and family members.

Assessment portfolios can be organized in a number of ways. The easiest strategy for collecting assessment data for portfolios is to maintain all entries in chronological order. Of course, students (and teachers) have to remember to consistently date each entry, which is often easier said than done. If the portfolio is treated more like a collection of entries than tied to specific purposes for assessment, it should be culled every quarter (usually before report cards are issued), or it might tend to get unwieldy. Taking class time to have students relive, reflect on, and evaluate the merit of each entry is an effective management strategy and a beneficial learning experience in and of itself.

One way to configure assessment portfolios is to maintain common classroom, school, or program entries throughout a student's life in a language education program. We call this type of portfolio a pivotal one as it is a systematic collection of agreed-upon student work that offers authentic evidence of learning over time (Gottlieb & Nguyen, 2007). If the purpose of the assessment portfolio is to provide evidence of student learning that contributes to program effectiveness, then interim and annual standardized test data in multiple languages (required by the district or state) should also be included. If, on the other hand, the purpose of the portfolio is to document an individual multilingual learner's journey in developing multiple languages, then perhaps a standards-referenced organizational scheme might be more useful. Resource 4.7 is a checklist for educators to use in selecting (and adding) entries for multilingual learners' assessment portfolios.

Another way to organize portfolios is for students to create personal narratives over the course of a semester based on their individual goals for learning, content that is facilitated by their teacher, and choice in the selection of individual entries. The introduction to the narrative may be multimodal where students have an opportunity to express their learning, for example, through multimedia or even a rap. It may also be produced in segments, as in a series of chapters, and include multilingual learners' reflections on their conceptual, language, and social-emotional development.

The portfolio suggested as follows is an aspirational one for secondary students, but it could be readily amended to be more developmentally appropriate for younger multilingual learners. Here the portfolio is treated as an entity unto itself to be judged as a whole. Its contents highlight different aspects of multilingual learners that are important to their overall development and identity. The following list offers some suggestions for entries to include in assessment portfolios in multiple languages.

Suggested Components of a Multilingual Assessment Portfolio for Middle and High Schools

☐ Introduction: My Portfolio Experience (My Personal Narrative)

☐ Table of Contents

☐ My Thoughts as a Multilingual Learner

☐ My Learning Goals and Ambitions

☐ Evidence of My Learning in Multiple Languages

- My annotated reading list by language

- Description of bilingual materials and documents I used for investigation

- My final work products (or their artifacts) along with teacher and student feedback

- Classroom tests or quizzes, if relevant

- Notes on how I have collaborated in small group activities

- Self-evaluation on how I have improved as a multilingual learner

☐ Electronic Assessment Portfolio (e-Portfolio) Entries

- Artifacts of my multimedia projects with related documents

- Video or audio recording of discussions, conversations, or interviews in multiple languages

- Recording of oral presentations in multiple languages

- My contribution to our classroom website, newsletter, or blog

- Description of my service-learning project and how it helped me grow as a person

- Annotations and photos from my service-learning project or a summary and self-evaluation of my community service

☐ Reflection on My Portfolio as a Body of My (Bi/Multilingual) Work

☐ My Final Thoughts, Hopes, and Dreams

Relax and Reflect: How might you organize an assessment portfolio?

Given the many different ways for organizing assessment portfolios, what types of entries might you consider with your teachers as part of data collection? Which entries would you designate for multilingual learners to submit in the language(s) of their choice? What role might students play in arranging and presenting their portfolios?

FACING THE ISSUE: COLLECT DATA IN MULTIPLE LANGUAGES USING MULTIPLE RESOURCES TO FORM A CONVINCING BODY OF EVIDENCE

Dra. Ramírez-Olson's strengths-based educational practices are intended to accentuate the assets of students. In *Breakthrough Leadership*, Blankstein and Newsome (2021) propose six principles for guiding schools where inequity is not an option. In following their advice, assessment should embody resources for accessibility, such as multiliteracies, multimodalities, and translanguaging, and be balanced among three approaches—assessment *as*, *for*, and *of* learning—with the goal of empowering minoritized students. To promote equity and social justice, district and school leadership, teachers, and multilingual learners need to leverage assessment evidence. Here are some questions to stimulate discussion.

For School Leaders

➢ How is collecting and organizing data in multiple languages a question of equity for multilingual learners?

➢ How does approval, tacit approval, or disapproval of translanguaging as a schoolwide policy affect instruction and assessment? Which is your preference, and why?

➢ What do you deem to be the most effective data in multiple languages, and what suggestions do you have for data collection?

➢ How do you organize schoolwide data from multilingual learners in dual language or other language programs to form a body of evidence in multiple languages?

For District Leaders

➢ What is your district's theory of action to advance multilingualism and multiculturalism as a contributor to an agenda of equity and social justice?

➢ What do you do as an educational leader to combat discrimination against your minoritized student populations?

> ➤ How might you craft, schedule, and collect data on common assessment in multiple languages so that it complements other assessment approaches?

> ➤ How might leadership teams design assessment portfolios to high-light a school's or district's commitment to multilingualism along with evidence for achieving that goal?

RESOLVING THE DILEMMA: TAKE RESPONSIBILITY FOR DIMINISHING DISCRIMINATION FOR MULTILINGUAL LEARNERS AND THEIR FAMILIES!

District and school leaders must counteract discrimination against multilingualism and multiculturalism that continues to run rampant in our society. As a nation, we have to come to understand that racism has no place in our schools nor our society. In response, Mozart School has taken the district's theory of action and has added the value of social justice to educate its community and teach its students to fight against discrimination and the injustices of society. It honors and celebrates multilingualism and multiculturalism as ways of life for multilingual learners and their families.

Following the district's theory of action—"linguistically and culturally sustaina-ble schools and classrooms offer students choice and voice that draw from their identities and relationships, fostering collaboration among stakeholders and advocacy for multilingualism and assessment in multiple languages"—Mozart School has formed its own multicultural council. It realizes that assessment in multiple languages requires careful planning on the part of school leadership and the collection of data must be comprehensive, including multilingual learn-ers' conceptual, language, and social-emotional learning. Provisions must be made to capture multilingual learners' use of languages in a variety of contexts with resources that improve their accessibility to learning.

Data collection that captures common assessment for a program, school, or even district should represent full coverage of assessment *as*, *for*, and *of* learning. In essence, assessment must cast an equity lens to ensure that multilingual learners are afforded the opportunities they deserve. Said another way, multilingual learners bring tremendous value to the institution known as school and to soci-ety as a whole. Their bilingualism and multiculturalism should be central to schooling in today's multilingual world. School and district leaders have the responsibility of warding off discrimination and securing evidence of excellence and equity that marks quality education for every student.

Resources for School and District Leaders

RESOURCE 4.1
Creating a Theory of Action Tool for Assessment in Multiple Languages

EXAMPLE PROPOSITIONS FOR A THEORY OF ACTION

Sample starter: *Ultimately our educational program can achieve its goal of multilingualism through embedded assessment in multiple languages . . .*

IF ADMINISTRATORS . . .	AND IF TEACHERS AND OTHER SCHOOL LEADERS . . .	THEN MULTILINGUAL LEARNERS AND THEIR FAMILIES . . .
Identify purposes for assessment and attach them to student evidence for multilingual development		
Foster collaboration among stakeholders		
Build relationships and networks between schools and their communities		
Give students choice and voice		
Transform schools and classrooms into linguistically and culturally sustainable environments		

 Available for download at **resources.corwin.com/ assessingMLLs-LeadersEdition**

RESOURCE 4.2
Using Images in Collecting Common Assessment Data

Select an image that represents a universal experience and appeals to a wide range of students. Or better yet, have students nominate photos that perhaps they have taken or have viewed in social media (that match a set of agreed-upon criteria). Make sure that the image does not have any inherent bias or sensitivity issues. Then invite multilingual learners to respond to these suggested prompts in the language(s) of their choice.

What do you see? Describe what stands out to you, using details.	What are your feelings when you see this image? What does the image remind you of?

What are you thinking? What might you be doing in this image? What might happen next?

RESOURCE 4.3

Using Multiliteracies and Multimodal Resources in Assessment *as*, *for*, and *of* Learning

Using Figure 4.5 as a model, leadership teams in schools or districts can generate ideas for incorporating multiliteracies and multimodalities into assessment *as*, *for*, and *of* learning. It might be useful to replicate this model in planning and collecting data for each unit of learning across the curriculum.

When using multiple languages, through which multiliteracies and with which multimodalities can multilingual learners maximize their engagement in assessment as, for, *and* of *learning?*

Unit of Learning: _____

	ASSESSMENT *AS* LEARNING	ASSESSMENT *FOR* LEARNING	ASSESSMENT *OF* LEARNING
Through Which Multiliteracies			
With Which Multimodalities			

online resources

Available for download at **resources.corwin.com/ assessingMLLs-LeadersEdition**

RESOURCE 4.4

A Checklist for Co-planning Data Collection in Multiple Languages

Whether remote or in person, school leadership or co-teachers should work together to consider different facets of assessment in one or more languages for multilingual learners in anticipation of data collection.

Teacher Team: _____

1. Have we used . . .

   a. academic content standards?

   b. language development standards?

   c. Spanish language arts standards (for Latinx students)?

   d. Spanish language development standards (for Latinx students)?

   e. IEP goals for dually identified multilingual learners?

   f. linguistically and culturally relevant curricular, instructional, and assessment resources?

2. Have we determined . . .

   a. the purpose for assessment in one or more languages?

   b. learning goals for units of learning tied to standards?

   c. language choice(s) for multilingual learners?

   d. multimodal channels of communication/multiliteracies?

   e. accommodations/accessibility as stipulated in multilingual learners' IEPs?

   f. built-in time for student self- and peer reflection?

   g. time for scoring of prompts or interpretation of projects by co-teachers?

   h. how we are going to use assessment data in multiple languages?

3. Have we designed . . .

   a. a menu of products, performances, and projects along with models or exemplars?

   b. timelines/windows for projects or a schedule for common assessment prompts?

   c. product/project descriptors, rubrics, or criteria for success?

   d. a set of instructions for common assessment prompts?

   e. multimodalities within the assessment?

 Available for download at **resources.corwin.com/** assessingMLLs-LeadersEdition

ASSESSMENT IN MULTIPLE LANGUAGES

RESOURCE 4.5
Adding Multimodal Communication Channels to Common Assessment

Multimodal channels of communication should be integral to and seamlessly embedded into common assessment. The following is a template for school leaders to plan and collect samples in multiple languages, with or without provisions for translanguaging, across the school year.

	AUTUMN DATE: GRADE LEVELS:	WINTER DATE: GRADE LEVELS:	SPRING DATE: GRADE LEVELS:
Student multimodal samples in English	Baseline common oral language and writing assessment Prompt or activity for oral language: Prompt or activity for writing:	Common oral language assessment Prompt or activity:	Common oral language/writing assessment Prompt or activity:
Student multimodal samples in other languages	Baseline common oral language and writing assessment Prompt or activity for oral language: Prompt or activity for writing:	Common writing assessment Prompt or activity:	Common oral language/writing assessment Prompt or activity:

 Available for download at **resources.corwin.com/ assessingMLLs-LeadersEdition**

RESOURCE 4.6

Collecting Initial Common Assessment Data (for Students in Grade 3 and Beyond)

For each subject area, think about what you'd like to learn this year. Fill in the boxes.

	SOMETHING I'M INTERESTED IN	SOMETHING I KNOW ABOUT THIS TOPIC	SOMETHING ELSE I'D LIKE TO LEARN ABOUT THIS TOPIC
Language arts			
Mathematics			
Science			
Social studies			

 Available for download at **resources.corwin.com/ assessingMLLs-LeadersEdition**

ASSESSMENT IN MULTIPLE LANGUAGES

RESOURCE 4.7
Assessment Portfolio Considerations

Leadership teams might respond to each question to determine the appropriateness of entries in multiple languages for a school or district assessment portfolio.

ARE ASSESSMENT PORTFOLIO ENTRIES . . .	YES	NO
1. Representative of best assessment practices for multilingual learners?		
2. Reflective of multilingual learners' full linguistic repertoire?		
3. Tied to student learning in multiple languages?		
4. Helpful to educators in making timely decisions?		
5. Useful in providing information about student growth and achievement in one or more languages?		
6. Examples of authentic performance assessment tied to learning goals and standards?		
7. Developmentally, culturally, and linguistically relevant?		
8. Applicable for providing evidence of school, district, or state initiatives?		

SOURCE: Adapted from Gottlieb & Nguyen (2007), p. 200.

Available for download at **resources.corwin.com/ assessingMLLs-LeadersEdition**

CHAPTER 5

Interpreting Information and Providing Feedback in Multiple Languages

▶ An outdoor mural in Amsterdam, Netherlands (notice the unique style of each character)

Photo by Alp Ancel on Unsplash, https://unsplash.com/photos/WKQt_X-SKFI

Una lingua diversa è una diversa vision della vita.

A different language is a different vision of life.

—Federico Fellini

The Dilemma

There simply aren't enough qualified language teachers, so let's place multilingual learners in "special education" classes for support.

Report after report on data from the National Assessment of Educational Progress (NAEP), dubbed The Nation's Report Card, indicates that there is a persistent gap in the academic performance between "Hispanic and White" students (Hemphill, Vanneman, & Rahman, 2011). The National Education Association (2020) speaks of "achievement gaps between English language learners (ELLs) and non-ELL students" as "deeply rooted, pervasive, complex, and challenging," with ELLs facing some of the most pronounced achievement gaps of any student groups. The Center for Education Policy Analysis (n.d.) at Stanford University claims that "achievement gaps are one way of monitoring the equality of educational outcomes." As a nation, we are measuring racial equality (or inequality as the case may be) by examining discrepancies in racial achievement gaps. What these reports and others like them do is perpetuate the negativity of the status quo. Thus educators and policy makers alike continue to hinge interpretation of high-stakes standardized test scores for multilingual learners based on a single language, English.

These pronouncements of national achievement gaps in mathematics and language arts/reading in groups of students that are inclusive of multilingual learners in Grades 4, 8, and 12 appear every four years with every round of NAEP testing. These data are often cited by district superintendents, at times as substantiation of differences in subgroup academic performance. Yet no one seems to question the test—the sole data source that is being interpreted and reinterpreted, yielding practically identical results about our students, time after time. These test data, often exacerbated by those of annual state academic achievement tests, tend to portray multilingual learners in a negative light. And with this verified achievement "gap"—in English, that is—we wonder why there is an overrepresentation of multilingual learners in special education classes.

So, what are we to do? By definition, English learners have not yet reached academic parity with their peers who are proficient in English. A special education placement in and of itself is not warranted, nor is it an appropriate strategy, to help multilingual learners succeed. In fact, unless there is sound documentation and a body of evidence from multiple sources and in multiple languages (as is required by law), special education should never be an option for normally developing multilingual learners. Multilingual learners must have the same rigorous grade-level expectations as their peers, with hopefully added wealth of opportunities to develop in multiple languages. Superintendents should make every effort to ensure that teachers, all teachers, are qualified to instruct multilingual learners.

When national and state data are misinterpreted or misused, there can be grave consequences for multilingual learners, their teachers, and schools. For example, researchers note that more targeted skill-based interventions that help students with language-based learning disabilities often are not beneficial to multilingual learners as these students require rich and varied language development (Newhall, 2012). In fact, constricting language usage can make it challenging for multilingual learners to understand and retain information. Using special education as a legitimate placement for multilingual learners when qualified language teachers are not available is irresponsible, unethical, and misguided.

As an educational community, we should be taking a more positive stance in regard to bi/multilingual learners' placement, especially when contemplating the ramifications of a special education assignment. Child Trends notes that although "the achievement gap between ELL and non-ELL students . . . has been essentially unchanged from 2000 to 2013 . . . , the achievement of former ELL students shows greater progress." What we have neglected to see is that all the affordances of bilingualism "go unrealized when schools and other social institutions lack the understanding required to respond to the particular needs of dual language learners" (Murphey, 2014).

Superintendents' change of mindset from having special education as a de facto placement for multilingual learners when necessary to incentivizing all teachers to become certified language specialists through coursework and professional learning can make a tremendous positive difference for multilingual learners and their families. Coupling this districtwide initiative with incentives for dual language or bilingual certification can fortify and firmly establish an educational program that will yield benefits to multilingual learners for years to come.

FIRST IMPRESSIONS

- In what ways does this scenario resonate with you?

- How are large-scale standardized achievement data interpreted for multilingual learners (in relation to other student groups) in your setting?

- Why is collaboration and mutual understanding between school leadership and teachers especially important in the data interpretation phase of assessment?

- How do you differentiate interpretation among classroom-, school-, district-, and state-level data?

With movement by scholars and practitioners alike toward greater acceptance of multilingualism and its teaching in schools, the need for linguistically and culturally valid assessment of multilingual practices is more important than ever (Basterra, Trumbull, & Solano-Flores, 2011; Leung & Valdés, 2019; López, Turkan, & Guzman-Orth, 2017). However, equity in assessment is not confined to the measures themselves; it also extends to the interpretation of the data generated from assessment. That's the focus of this chapter—phase 3 of the assessment cycle—how educators determine the meaning of the information from assessment in multiple languages and communicate it through feedback. Figure 5.1 highlights this phase of the assessment cycle.

In this chapter, we examine data that are generated from an array of sources for different purposes across the school year. Beginning with annual testing for school and district accountability, we carefully peel away the layers within the educational system to examine interim testing and common assessment that occur

FIGURE 5.1 The Third Phase of the Assessment Cycle: Interpreting Information and Providing Feedback in Multiple Languages

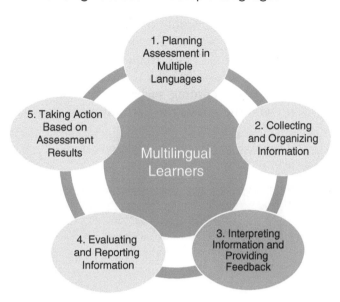

across schools or grades, as well as daily assessment in each and every classroom. In doing so, we maintain an assets-based lens for students through linguistically and culturally responsive methodologies so that interpreting data in multiple languages is always appropriate, fair, and equitable for multilingual learners.

EXAMINING DATA IN MULTIPLE LANGUAGES

Interpreting data for multilingual learners, especially those derived from large-scale measures, is tricky as often it is difficult to detect built-in bias. School administrators have to be sensitive, cautious, and strategic on how data on multilingual learners, whether in one or more languages, are presented, analyzed, and interpreted to inform decision making. Reiterating three points mentioned previously, interpreting data and providing feedback to stakeholders, including teachers, family members, and students, must directly relate to the:

1. Purpose of the assessment and decisions to be made

2. Standards/goals addressed in the assessment

3. Language(s) of the assessment (and its match with instruction)

Another point important during this phase of the assessment cycle is that test data should never be interpreted in isolation. Shohamy (2001) states that high-stakes "tests cannot be viewed as isolated and neutral events, but rather [are always] embedded in educational, social, political, and economic contexts. Therefore, tests need to be interpreted and understood within this complex context" (p. xvi). If the purpose for assessment is to demonstrate content learning, then we need to allow multilingual learners the space to show their knowledge by taking into account their languages, cultures, identities, and experiences, all of which affect learning and how we measure it. In essence, what we assess and the context in which we approach assessment should align with who our students are so ultimately students become empowered in their journey known as school (Montenegro & Jankowski, 2017).

Interpreting Different Types of Data Involving Multilingual Learners

Data are everywhere! How might school leaders think about interpreting the constant flow of data from classrooms, schools, and districts? One way to describe assessment is according to its frequency of occurrence. Using that organizing scheme in Figure 5.2, we can say that assessment falls into four general time-sensitive categories according to level of implementation, from the state to the classroom, with the results used according to its purpose.

FIGURE 5.2 Types of Assessment by Level of Implementation According to Frequency

LEVEL OF IMPLEMENTATION	TYPE OF ASSESSMENT	FREQUENCY OF ASSESSMENT	USE OF ASSESSMENT RESULTS MATCHED TO PURPOSE
State	High-stakes tests	Annually	Meet accountability requirements; apply reclassification criteria; determine growth from year to year
District	Standardized commercial tests	Interim (3–4 times per year)	Predict results on high-stakes annual tests
School	Common prompts, performance tasks, or projects	Monthly/ quarterly	Contribute to local accountability; gain a pulse on student growth over a school year
Classroom	Instructionally embedded and student-centered	Daily	Inform teaching and learning

 Stop-Think-Act-React

Relax and Reflect: How should school and district leaders go about interpreting data from multilingual learners?

Beware. When analyzing and interpreting data that impact multilingual learners, it is important for decision makers (i.e., educators) to realize that what multilingual learners know in English might be masked by extraneous, dense, or complex language that interferes with their understanding of tests in English (Abedi, 2002; Fairbairn & Jones-Vo, 2016). In other words, interpreting assessment results in English for multilingual learners should be done with caution.

Student responses might be confounded by language background variables, or, in technical terms, there might be construct-irrelevant variance in the tests. In addition, multilingual learners' inaccessibility to full comprehension of test items might be attributed to cultural nuances that advantage one student group over another. As you read this chapter, think of this cautionary note as a filter when interpreting standardized achievement testing data in English for multilingual learners.

Looking at the timing of assessment graphically, Figure 5.3 provides an overview of the compendium of assessment information available to school and district leaders over a school year. The side-by-side boxes indicate the availability of English and other languages for annual, interim, common, and daily assessment. The state-level data generated just once a year are broadest in coverage, reflecting grade-level curriculum, followed by districtwide interim testing that occurs about three times per year. Common assessment at a school level generally corresponds to the culmination of a unit of learning, on a monthly to quarterly basis, while classroom data represent everyday lessons.

If we revisit the data available to stakeholders, it is interesting to see the inverse relationship between the frequency of assessment and the type of data that are generated. That is, a state, the largest educational entity, is responsible for conducting assessment on a yearly basis, while if you peek into any classroom at any time, assessment is usually under way. Figure 5.4 illustrates this relationship as inverted triangles, understanding that when interpreting data from multiple sources, leadership must take into account the impact or weighting of data on decision making based on frequency, understanding the inherent underlying hierarchy of the system.

State annual and district interim data, in large part, are equated with large-scale standardized testing with prescribed windows and procedures for administration. The data from these tests are generally quantitative in nature, yielding

FIGURE 5.3 Occurrence of Assessment in Multiple Languages Across a School Year

State-Level Data

Annual Achievement and Language Testing in English and Additional Languages
Annual English Language Proficiency Assessment

District-Level Data in Multiple Languages

| Interim Testing | Interim Testing | Interim Testing |

School-Level Data in Multiple Languages

| Monthly/ Quarterly Common Assessment | Monthly/ Quarterly Common Assessment | Monthly/ Quarterly Common Assessment | Monthly/ Quarterly Common Assessment |

Classroom Data in Multiple Languages . . . Every Day!

FIGURE 5.4 The Inverse Relationship Between the Size of an Educational Entity and the Frequency of Available Assessment Data for Interpretation

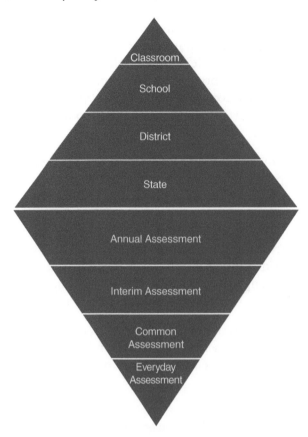

 Stop-Think-Act-React

Relax and Reflect: How might distributive leadership lend itself to the interpretation of assessment data of multilingual learners?

Interpreting data is definitely not a one-person job. There are a variety of configurations of district and school staff who can help in examining assessment results within the context of characteristics, including the languages, of their multilingual learners. Looking at assessment data through an assets-based lens, you might answer questions such as these:

- What can multilingual learners do (with language) in each content area?

- Has there been change in student performance over time? To what might you attribute the change?

- How can we build on multilingual learners' strengths?

- How does information in one language help complement or reinforce that in another language?

- What suggestions do we have to improve teaching and learning of multilingual learners and other minoritized students?

numbers such as scale scores, percentages, quartiles, and confidence bands and, for language proficiency testing, composite scores yielding language proficiency levels. As we'll show in Chapter 6, in some cases these data are contextualized with graphs and descriptors as part of score reports to be shared with families.

Common assessment data share space with interim data as both are summative in nature and often are generated at certain points in the school year. Developed locally by leadership teams, there is a range of common assessment, from responding to a writing prompt for a grade band, to taking an online test, to designing long-term classroom projects. Unlike annual and interim testing, common assessment is more closely associated with school or district curriculum.

Everyday classroom data are embedded in instructional activities and tasks that have been crafted by teachers, with input from multilingual learners. These data can be quantitative, as in numerical; numerical with accompanying descriptors, such as rubrics; or qualitative, as in specific oral or written feedback based on the day's objectives. Figure 5.5 is a series of assessment features anchored by a set of continua associated with annual, interim, common, and classroom data.

Qualitative data analyzed in conjunction with quantitative data yield more comprehensive results than those from just one data source. Qualitative data provide a fuller descriptive picture of the learner, especially if the student's own words contribute to that portrait. Figure 5.6 identifies examples of mixed data sources in one or more languages from everyday classroom, common, interim, and annual assessment in multiple languages that are named in Figures 5.4 and 5.5.

You might be wondering how to organize so much data before launching into interpretation. Figure 5.7 considers the presence of assessment *as*, *for*, and *of* learning according to the type and frequency of data collection (daily, monthly/ quarterly, on an interim basis, or annually). As noted in the figure, assessment *as* learning is largely confined to everyday classroom data and grade-level projects while assessment *for* learning can occur across all levels. Assessment *of* learning, represented by common classroom or interim data, is part of local accountability while assessment *of* learning, represented by annual standardized data, is generally a response to state/federal (i.e., Title I) mandates.

FIGURE 5.5 Continua of Assessment Characteristics Associated With Classroom, Common, Interim, and Annual Data

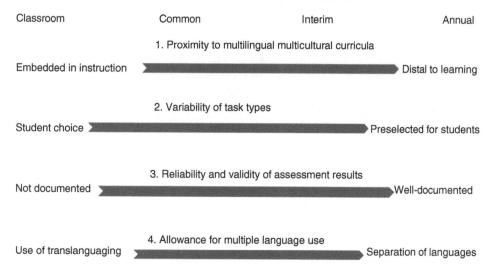

Relax and Reflect: How would you describe data for multilingual learners?

Given the continua in Figure 5.5, where would you place classroom, common, interim, and annual data in your school or district? Decide where you are and where you would like to be along each continuum; then set a goal based on your context for interpreting data.

FIGURE 5.6 Examples of Different Types of Assessment Data Available for Interpretation

EVERYDAY CLASSROOM DATA IN MULTIPLE LANGUAGES	COMMON DATA IN ONE OR MORE LANGUAGES (MONTHLY/ QUARTERLY)	INTERIM DATA IN ONE OR MORE LANGUAGES (2–3 TIMES PER YEAR)	ANNUAL DATA IN ONE OR MORE LANGUAGES
• Observation of student–student interaction • Student self-reflection • Student learning logs in one or more content areas • Oral and written sentence starters across content areas	• Uniform prompts across grade levels or a school • Grade-level products, projects, or performances along with standards-referenced criteria	• Language proficiency testing • Achievement testing—generally in mathematics and reading/language arts • District/school writing prompts or activities	• Language proficiency testing in English • Language proficiency testing in Spanish • Achievement testing—in mathematics, reading/language arts, and science

FIGURE 5.7 Interaction Between Types of Data and Assessment *as, for,* and *of* Learning

	EVERYDAY CLASSROOM DATA	COMMON DATA FROM MONTHLY PROMPTS OR PROJECTS	INTERIM STANDARDIZED TEST DATA	ANNUAL STANDAR-DIZED TEST DATA
Assessment *as* learning	X	X		
Assessment *for* learning	X	X		
Assessment *of* learning		X	X	X

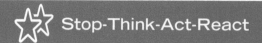
Relax and Reflect: Are you drowning in data?

Spend some time examining the figures in this chapter to help you sort through all the data with which you are bombarded throughout the school year. In your leadership team, use Resource 5.1 to assign different data sources, measures, and languages that you use in assessment *as, for,* and *of* learning on an everyday, monthly/quarterly, interim, and annual basis. Consider producing a summary document to use as guidance for planning, interpreting, and organizing data throughout the school year.

COMMON ASSESSMENT IN MULTIPLE LANGUAGES

As multilingual learners are given increasing freedom to express themselves in multiple languages, there is a growing amount of data to interpret. Observation provides a direct way for school leaders, coaches, and classroom teachers to assess multilingual learners. In bilingual and dual language classrooms that have relatively strict language policies or rely on specific models for language allocation (e.g., 90/10, 50/50, alternate days), teachers have opportunities to gauge student learning in each language, but rarely have the option of determining students' full linguistic and conceptual understandings as the two languages of instruction are not programmed to come in contact. In contrast, in classrooms where translanguaging is an accepted practice and languages are not isolated, multilingual learners' linguistic repertoires are on display all day long. Thus, teachers can more accurately assess students' full range of language use (M. T. Sánchez, García, & Solorza, 2017).

Common assessment can, but does not always, have the identical project, prompt, or test across classrooms. It does, however, have to be based on the identical standards and have a uniform tool or protocol for data interpretation. Figure 5.8, with a blank as Resource 5.2, offers ideas for collecting and interpreting information across classrooms at strategic times (e.g., within an agreed-upon week) in one or more languages. It is suggested that instructional leaders design a set of guidelines to collect, record, and interpret common assessment data in uniform ways.

Interpreting Student Work With Uniform Criteria for Success

"Assessment, if not done with equity in mind, privileges and validates certain types of learning and evidence of learning over others" (Montenegro & Jankowski, 2017, p. 5). These watchwords apply to districts and schools that choose to counteract some of the ill effects of standardized tests with local common assessment. Common assessment can readily afford multilingual learners opportunities to demonstrate their expertise in multiple languages.

Performance descriptors and rubrics are tools for interpreting locally designed common assessment. We recommend establishing and following certain

FIGURE 5.8 Collecting and Interpreting Data on Common Assessment Within and Across the Content Areas

COLLECTING DATA ON ORAL LANGUAGE USE	INTERPRETING ORAL LANGUAGE DATA	COLLECTING DATA ON TRANSLANGUAGING PRACTICES DURING CONTENT LEARNING	COLLECTING DATA ON (MULTI) LITERACIES	INTERPRETING DATA ON (MULTI) LITERACIES
Observing student interaction with each other or technology: • Engaging in academic conversations and discussions • Participating in debates or Socratic seminars • Relating experiences, events, readings, or stories • Asking and answering questions • Conferencing with teachers	Interpreting student interaction with: • Checklists • Rubrics • Criteria for success • Descriptors of expectations • Student self- and peer assessment • Videotaping • Audiotaping	Documenting student interaction in multiple languages: • Comparing linguistic similarities and differences (metalinguistic awareness) • Emphasizing cross-cultural awareness • Sharing multilingual practices • Using learning strategies • Demonstrating conceptual understanding	Documenting student products, such as: • Learning logs • Multimedia projects • Essays • Research reports • Editorials or critiques • Responses to open-ended questions/prompts • Tables, charts, and graphs • Illustrations or diagrams • Content-based writing • Videos	Interpreting student products with: • Project descriptors • Analytic rubrics • Holistic rubrics • Genre-specific rubrics (e.g., argument) • Success criteria • Narratives

SOURCE: Adapted from Gottlieb (2021).

schoolwide or district policy to ensure the maintenance of linguistic and cultural responsiveness when interpreting common assessment. Consider the following suggestions in crafting an interpretative tool, such as a rubric:

• Rely on qualitative descriptions rather than numerical information (e.g., *use colorful, vivid details* vs. *use 2 details*)

• Weigh the descriptors equally unless there is a rationale for not doing so

• Keep the same distance between intervals (e.g., the difference between level 2 and level 3 is the same as between level 3 and level 4)

• Use little to no evaluative language (e.g., *more* or *less*)

- Use positive, assets-based language throughout

- Allow for or include multimodalities for students

- Be inclusive of multiple perspectives

- Focus on examining language, content, or both in context

- Use student samples in multiple languages as anchors or models

Schools may already have specific rubrics in place for different purposes and grade levels. Prior to engaging in interpreting common assessment prompts or projects, leadership teams need to evaluate the rubrics or performance descriptors that are currently in place to ensure that they can be used with confidence to interpret the performance of all students, including multilingual learners in multiple languages. Inspired by Care, Kim, and Sahin (2020), the following list describes the attributes of student-centered rubrics that have been augmented for multiple languages. Resource 5.3 converts it into a checklist for schools.

1. Performance descriptors are simply and clearly stated for all students.

2. The descriptors are in the language(s) the students best understand.

3. Students can paraphrase and give examples of the descriptors in one or more languages.

4. Students can apply the descriptors to self- and peer assessment.

5. The descriptors match the language(s) of assessment.

6. The descriptors give students enough information to move their learning forward.

7. The descriptors allow for students to respond using multiple modes of communication.

8. The descriptors are sufficiently defined to ensure that interpretation is accurate and consistent.

9. The rubric reflects the range of levels at which students can perform the tasks.

10. The rubric is sensitive to multiple linguistic and cultural perspectives.

In Chapter 4, we introduced ideas for different types of multilingual long-term projects for individual grade levels or departments to be aligned with multidisciplinary academic content standards. In Figure 5.9, we offer some examples of multilingual projects that can be adopted or adapted across grades depending on the selection of relevant standards and criteria for success. In Chapter 6, we dive deeper into designing student-centered rubrics for evaluating student work.

FIGURE 5.9 Ideas for Multilingual Projects for Common Assessment and Criteria for Success

EXAMPLE MULTILINGUAL PROJECTS	CORRESPONDING ACADEMIC CONTENT/ LANGUAGE DEVELOPMENT STANDARDS	CRITERIA FOR SUCCESS IN ONE OR MORE LANGUAGES
Student-produced videos, such as reporting on or reenacting events	Multidisciplinary	
Student original performances, such as raps, poetry, music, or screen making	Language arts, humanities, and the arts	
Student-led fairs or exhibitions, such as robotic demonstrations	STEM (science, technology, engineering, and mathematics)	
Student-built theme-based gallery displays around the school; multicultural murals open to the community	Social studies, humanities, and the arts	
Classroom-created websites or contributions to school/ community newsletters	Language arts and technology	

With common assessment in mind, using Resource 5.3 as a guide and Resource 5.4 as a template, we encourage leadership or teacher teams to:

- Select applicable language development and academic content standards in English and Spanish (or other languages, as applicable)

- Flesh out the details and timelines for projects and common descriptors for grade levels or departments

- Apply criteria for success to determine the extent to which students have met their learning goals for their projects

Interpreting Translanguaging in Common Assessment

Interpreting multilingual learners' oral or written language that contains translanguaging is rather tricky when it comes to assigning a score on common assessment. If a school has a language policy that embraces translanguaging, then it should also be an accepted assessment practice. If translanguaging highlights a multilingual learner's metalinguistic curricular insight, it should surely be interpreted in that context. In dual language settings, the common prompt or measure should always be interpreted by a bilingual educator who is knowledgeable about the content and understands the intertwining of content and language. In other words, the interpretation of translanguaging in common assessment is a local decision.

Translanguaging is a more thorny issue on standardized interim or annual tests when often there has been no forethought for multiple language use. If content is being measured, and multilingual learners are able to convey that content in one or more languages, then some provision should be made to acknowledge that understanding. The following offers some considerations for use of translanguaging in large-scale assessment:

- Interpret data through the lens of multilingualism and multilingual learners

- Base interpretation of information on the extent that the overall meaning is conveyed, not the use of one language in relation to another

- Do not insist on translanguaging in assessment if it is not an acceptable classroom or school practice or if it has not been a focus for instruction

- Use data with translanguaging to underscore assets-based decisions for multilingual learners

Interpreting Common Assessment in Multiple Languages With Qualitative Rubrics

Standardized test data provide a quantitative data source; however, to obtain a complete picture, there also must be qualitative data to complement and describe what multilingual learners can do. Qualitative data can document students' academic language use in authentic situations, which is recognized as a hallmark of school success (Gottlieb & Ernst-Slavit, 2014; Ohara, Pritchard, Pitta, & Newton, 2017). Performance-based common assessment provides opportunities for schools to collect and interpret information in multiple languages.

 Stop-Think-Act-React

Relax and Reflect: What is academic language, and should it be present in rubrics?

Academic language is generally equated with the language of school (Gottlieb & Ernst-Slavit, 2014). Recently, however, some scholars have contested the term and its utility in the schooling of multilingual learners that is perplexing to educators on the ground. Is academic language a construct that fosters equity of opportunity for learning among minoritized or marginalized students, or does it perpetuate inequity across racial and ethnic lines? Gibbons (2015), for example, equates academic language with critical thinking and problem solving while Flores (2020b) sees academic language as a raciolinguistic ideology that frames **racialized** students (among them, multilingual learners) as linguistically deficient.

What is your definition of academic language? Should academic language influence rubrics for interpreting common assessment for multilingual learners?

FIGURE 5.10   Using the Dimensions of Language to Annotate Multiple Language Use

DIMENSION OF LANGUAGE WITH EXAMPLE DESCRIPTORS OR CRITERIA	EVIDENCE OF INFLUENCE OF ANOTHER LANGUAGE ON ENGLISH	EVIDENCE OF TRANSLANGUAGING	EVIDENCE OF INFLUENCE OF ENGLISH ON ANOTHER LANGUAGE
Discourse • Representation of ideas • Coherence of ideas • Cohesion of text • Organization	*Ideas presented in a circular fashion rather than directly*		
Sentence • Syntactic order • Prepositional phrases • Complexity		*Interjection of a sentence in students' other language for emphasis*	
Phrase/Word • Cognates • Multiple meanings • Collocations • Idiomatic expressions		*Use of terms of endearment (e.g., mi hijito)*	*Use of words with multiple meanings related to technology (e.g., mouse)*

Figure 5.10, duplicated in Resource 5.5, shows three dimensions of (academic) language—discourse, sentence, and phrase/word—along with some example descriptors that form the backbone of a qualitative rubric designed to capture evidence in multiple languages. Coaches and teachers can independently annotate evidence of a student's language use that has been influenced by another language as well as instances of translanguaging. Then teacher teams can convert the annotations, such as those suggested in the cells, into evidence charts. The intent of this qualitative rubric is to represent portraits of multilingual learners' full linguistic repertoires in school.

Qualitative rubrics provide rich descriptive information that cannot be revealed through numbers, levels, or scores. An important ingredient of interpreting student work with qualitative rubrics is agreement among educators as to what the data mean. This reliability or consistency among educators in interpreting data is maximized when there are built-in opportunities for collaboration.

COLLABORATION IN PROVIDING CONSISTENT FEEDBACK

Collaboration affords the building of consensus from disparate points of view or perspectives and contributes to a sense of ownership in the assessment process. It is a necessary partnership to ensure that assessment practices are congruent within a grade, aligned across grades, or even aligned across schools among:

- Administrators (school and district leadership)

- Teachers and administrators

- Coaches

- Teachers

- Teachers and students

- Students

Although collaboration is essential throughout the assessment cycle, it is especially pertinent in interpreting data, when information from assessment must be thoroughly digested and agreed upon. A critical step in strengthening assessment of multilingual learners is to create ongoing professional learning opportunities to analyze student work. Evidence-based conversations between educators about what students are producing can directly lead to ideas for effective student feedback and instruction (Ottow, 2016).

 Stop-Think-Act-React

Relax and Reflect: How might you improve collaboration around data in your setting?

What can you do if your school's culture is one of silos where language and content teachers have precious little time to collaborate, if at all? What procedure can be put in place when it comes time to interpret common assessment information in multiple languages? Think about how technology, where teachers share documents, can facilitate the process if teachers cannot physically meet.

With teacher guidance, multilingual learners can interact with each other to check for understanding and analyze and interpret their work; if they have a shared language, they have the bonus of being able to communicate in one or both languages. Talking among students is productive! Through thoughtful and collaborative conversations, students can become adept at examining their own and each other's work. Co-teaching and co-assessing give multilingual learners space to grow and learn. Together the students can:

- Apply criteria for success to work samples and defend their interpretation

- Self- and peer assess drafts, such as writing pieces, oral language samples, or visual displays, applying a uniform set of descriptors

- Revise drafts based on self-, peer, and teacher feedback (Gottlieb & Honigsfeld, 2020)

Providing Feedback During Times of Stress and Duress

The crises of 2020 forever changed school as we knew it, bringing equity and social justice to the forefront. School and district leadership, teachers, families, and students alike have had to endure a tremendous amount of uneasiness and anxiety. How can we responsibly add the pressure of assessment as another stressor?

It is more important than ever to view assessment as a process, not an event or a product. The overall intent of this process is to enhance and empower all who are engaged. The first step is for stakeholders to collaborate in formulating and agreeing on a clearly articulated district- or school-level language and assessment policy for multilingual learners. Second is to have teacher leadership teams, along with multilingual learners, craft learning targets in one or more languages that reflect that policy.

After collecting information during instruction, the next step in the process is to provide concrete feedback that helps students move toward meeting the selected target. Whether in a live classroom or a virtual environment, care must be taken to contextualize the information from assessment. That is, when interpreting the data, consideration of multilingual learners' social-emotional state must be taken into account alongside their progress in meeting language and content expectations. Students should always be invited to be part of the process, minimally given time to reflect on their learning and respond to feedback.

Creating a Schoolwide Culture of Critique: Language for Feedback

Designing and enacting a system for providing feedback on learning adds intentionality and commitment to a schoolwide vision of excellence (Wiliam & Leahy, 2015). When all students, teachers, and school leaders have a shared language around interpreting student work, there is a universal understanding of expectations and increased reliability in conveying feedback that, in turn, leads to improved products. Features of effective feedback for multilingual learners and their teachers that might fold into a schoolwide checklist include:

- Descriptive targeted information, preferably in the language best understood by students

- Mutually agreed-upon criteria or clear learning goals

- Ties to instruction

- Modeling of language, content, or behavior in context

- Being:

  - Focused on building student and/or teacher self-efficacy

  - Aimed at creating a community of trust

  - Objective rather than evaluative in nature

  - Attainable and actionable, with specific next steps

- Practical, realistic, and attainable

- Personalized

In the words of Dylan Wiliam (2011), "feedback should cause thinking" (p. 127). For multilingual learners, feedback has the benefit of supporting not only their metacognition, or how they are thinking, but also their metalinguistic awareness, or how they are using language strategically. An example of effective feedback is watching assessment *as* and *for* learning at the Dayton Regional STEM School. Across this middle and high school, everyone uses a color-coded thinking hats protocol, where each hat represents one facet of constructive feedback, such as "green-hat thinking" to make a suggestion or "yellow-hat thinking" to describe what's working.

What is unique about this project-based learning school is that both faculty and students rely on identical protocols for analyzing and interpreting each other's work. For example, in a faculty meeting co-teachers propose a new project to their colleagues that is strengthened through the feedback using the six-color-coded hats protocol. Likewise, in classrooms you see student pairs offer "yellow- and green-hat" feedback on sticky notes. Using this project protocol is a whole-school commitment that, in essence, is a set of common assessment criteria used during critique sessions as part of project development.

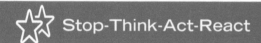
Stop-Think-Act-React

Relax and Reflect: Why is feedback so important?

Black and Wiliam's (1998) groundbreaking research finding is that targeted ongoing feedback makes a positive difference in student achievement. In his series of meta-analyses, Hattie (2012) found that feedback has an effect size of 0.7 (beyond the average effect size of 0.4), meaning that indeed it significantly impacts student learning. Simply stated, teachers are able to "see learning through the eyes of their students to help students become their own teachers" (Hattie, 2012, p. 6). How is feedback systematically incorporated into teaching and learning in your school?

Communicating results from assessment must be understandable to the user who needs to respond and take action, and there has to be sufficient detail to the feedback to guide the learner's actions (Stiggins, 2006). The use of effective feedback—that is, a teacher's or student's timely, direct, and descriptive response to student work or performance with the aim of stimulating learning—has proven to support achievement (Black & William, 1998; Heritage, 2010; C. M. Moss & Brookhart, 2009).

There are generally two sources of feedback—teachers and students—with a unified goal: to spark new learning within a culture of trust. Timely and **descriptive feedback** from teachers serves as instructional scaffolding, offering linguistic or conceptual support for multilingual learners in the form of examples, samples, models, elaborations, or explanations to help move student learning forward. Student-directed feedback either is personal or comes from classmates. After much modeling and practice, asking students to analyze their own work or to give, receive, and thoughtfully use feedback deepens their engagement in learning. For students to provide effective actionable feedback to each other, it must be clear, center on the specific aspect of the work that is being assessed, and have **success criteria** coupled with time to deliver it (Berger, Rugen, & Woodfin, 2014).

☆ Stop-Think-Act-React

Relax and Reflect: How might coaches and teachers give feedback in interpreting data from multilingual learners?

As a principal, how might you interpret the meaning of test scores of multilingual learners in reference to the norming population? What are the implications of the results for teaching and learning for your school? What kind of feedback would you offer teachers?	As a data or instructional coach, how might you apply multilingual learners' learning in multiple languages to contextualize test results to other educators? What kind of feedback would help teachers better understand learning in multiple languages?

INTERIM/ANNUAL ASSESSMENT IN MULTIPLE LANGUAGES

Educators must join forces with developers of interim and annual tests to ensure linguistically and culturally valid measures (Basterra et al., 2011) and push K–12 accountability to embrace acceptance of students' multilingual reality. Some criticism has been pointed at the language testing community for not embracing multilingualism as a testing construct (García & Wei, 2018; Shohamy, 2011). This reticence has impeded the pursuit of large-scale efforts to simultaneously test in multiple languages and to acknowledge the use of translanguaging as a bona fide measure of language proficiency (Chalhoub-Deville, 2019). Most recently, however, this alternate paradigm has been gaining momentum as educators realize that only through the design, development, and use of multilingual large-scale measures will the construct gain legitimacy. According to Chalhoub-Deville (2019), language testers "need to be guided by new thinking and innovations to continue to advance to the changing linguistic landscape of the world" (p. 476).

Considering that translanguaging has only been addressed in the literature and discussed in educational circles in the United States since García's 2009 groundbreaking article, it has had an amazing rapid rise of acknowledgement and use across the educational spectrum. Translanguaging has been the subject of scholarly discussions and publications and has been accompanied by a more visible role in the schooling of multilingual learners. As a precursor to the acceptance of translanguaging, however, educators have had to accept the reality that bi/multilingualism is a global norm and a goal of dual language education programs. This increased focus on the interactive use of two languages by multilingual learners has to be extended to assessment, especially in the interpretation of students' work where two languages contribute to communicating learning.

Relax and Reflect: Are there interim and annual data in multiple languages?

Identify interim and annual student data in your school(s) and district. Where do the data fall on the continuum that follows? Are the measures only in English, in separate languages (i.e., translations or transadaptations of measures administered separately), or in two languages (such as side-by-side assessment)? Do the data match your district's or school's language programs and assessment policy? If not, how might you combine these data with those from local common assessment to create a fuller complement of available data in multiple languages?

The Languages of Large-Scale (Interim and Annual) Assessment Data

One Language—Two Separate Languages—Two Languages, Including Translanguaging

⟶

Throughout this chapter, we have seen how information in one or more languages can be interpreted according to the type of assessment, starting with everyday classroom contexts and moving on to common, interim, and annual assessment. Now we turn to examining how school leaders might interpret interim data from standardized tests in English, occasionally with translated or transadapted versions in other languages. These tests, generally selected at a district level, offer insight into multilingual learners' language proficiency or achievement at strategic points during the year.

Interpreting Language Proficiency Data Through a "Can Do" Lens

As mentioned previously, multilingual learners who are English learners, by definition, have not reached a threshold of English language proficiency; unfortunately, interpreting data often reverts to looking at the negative side of a scale. However, results do not have to reflect a deficit perspective. Since its inception in 2003, WIDA, a consortium of 40 states, territories, and entities as well as approximately 500 international schools, has adopted a "can do" philosophy as one of its values that permeates all products and services.

WIDA MODEL (Measure of Developing English Language) is an English language proficiency assessment for Grades K–12. In the United States, it serves as an interim assessment, providing data to inform instructional planning and, additionally, to predict multilingual learners' performance on its annual English language proficiency test, ACCESS. MODEL's interpretive speaking and writing rubrics (see Figure 5.11) and training materials are illustrative of a strengths-based perspective. For example, in lieu of scoring the oral components of the assessment according to the number or severity of errors, it uses positive attributes to describe what multilingual learners can do (Chapman, Kim, Wei, & Bitterman, 2018).

FIGURE 5.11 The Writing and Speaking Rubrics From WIDA MODEL, an Interim English Language Proficiency Test

	WRITING RUBRIC OF THE WIDA™ CONSORTIUM GRADES 1-12		
LEVEL	**LINGUISTIC COMPLEXITY**	**VOCABULARY USAGE**	**LANGUAGE CONTROL**
6 Reaching	A variety of sentence lengths of varying linguistic complexity in a single tightly organized paragraph or in well-organized extended text; tight cohesion and organization.	Consistent use of just the right word in just the right place; precise Vocabulary usage in general, specific or technical language.	Has reached comparability to that of English proficient peers functioning at the "proficient" level in state-wide assessments.
5 Bridging	A variety of sentence lengths of varying linguistic complexity in a single organized paragraph or in extended text; cohesion and organization.	Usage of technical language related to the content area; evident facility with needed vocabulary.	Approaching comparability to that of English proficient peers; errors don't impede comprehensibility.
4 Expanding	A variety of sentence lengths of varying linguistic complexity; emerging cohesion used to provide detail and clarity.	Usage of specific and some technical language related to the content area; lack of needed vocabulary may be occasionally evident.	Generally comprehensible at all times, errors don't impede the overall meaning; such errors may reflect first language interference.
3 Developing	Simple and expanded sentences that show emerging complexity used to provide detail.	Usage of general and some specific language related to the content area; lack of needed vocabulary may be evident.	Generally comprehensible when writing in sentences; comprehensibility may from time to time be impeded by errors when attempting to produce more complex text.
2 Emerging	Phrases and short sentences; varying amount of text may be copied or adapted; some attempt at organization may be evidenced.	Usage of general language related to the content area; lack of vocabulary may be evident.	Generally comprehensible when text is adapted from model or source text, or when original text is limited to simple text; comprehensibility may be often impeded by errors.
1 Entering	Single words, set phrases or chunks of simple language; varying amounts of text may be copied or adapted; adapted text contains original language.	Usage of highest frequency vocabulary from school setting and content areas.	Generally comprehensible when text is copied or adapted from model or source text; comprehensibility may be significantly impeded in original text.

ASSESSMENT IN MULTIPLE LANGUAGES

	SPEAKING RUBRIC OF THE WIDA™ CONSORTIUM*		
TASK LEVEL	**LINGUISTIC COMPLEXITY**	**VOCABULARY USAGE**	**LANGUAGE CONTROL**
1 Entering	Single words, set phrases or chunks of memorized oral language	Highest frequency vocabulary from school setting and content areas	When using memorized language, is generally comprehensible; communication may be significantly impeded when going beyond the highly familiar
2 Beginning	Phrases, short oral sentences	General language related to the content area; groping for vocabulary when going beyond the highly familiar is evident	When using simple discourse, is generally comprehensible and fluent; communication may be impeded by groping for language structures or by phonological, syntactic or semantic errors when going beyond phrases and short, simple sentences
3 Developing	Simple and expanded oral sentences; responses show emerging complexity used to add detail	General and some specific language related to the content area; may grope for needed vocabulary at times	When communicating in sentences, is generally comprehensible and fluent; communication may from time to time be impeded by groping for language structures or by phonological, syntactic, or semantic errors, especially when attempting more complex oral discourse
4 Expanding	A variety of oral sentence lengths of varying linguistic complexity; responses show emerging cohesion used to provide detail and clarity	Specific and some technical language related to the content area; groping for needed vocabulary may be occasionally evident	At all times generally comprehensible and fluent, though phonological, syntactic, or semantic errors that don't impede the overall meaning of the communication may appear at times; such errors may reflect first language interference
5 Bridging	A variety of sentence lengths of varying linguistic complexity in extended oral discourse; responses show cohesion and organization used to support main ideas	Technical language related to the content area; facility with needed vocabulary is evident	Approaching comparability to that of English proficient peers in terms of comprehensibility and fluency; errors don't impede communication and may be typical of those an English proficient peer might make

SOURCE: WIDA MODEL. (2020).

Relax and Reflect: How would you describe the language used in rubrics for interim measures?

Take a look at the kind of language used in your school's or district's language proficiency or content-based rubrics for interim testing or for other forms of common assessment. Pay close attention to the descriptors at the lower end of the performance scale. Would you say that the rubric is descriptive of an assets or a deficit mindset? What specific evidence do you have? If need be, how might you convert the rubric to one that has a more positive or strengths-based orientation?

STANDARDIZED TESTING: REASSESSING VALIDITY CLAIMS

Standardized testing has been a stronghold of federal accountability and the forbearer of K–12 educational policy for over two decades. As mentioned in Chapter 1, ever since the 1994 reauthorization of the Elementary and Secondary Education Act (ESEA), the Improving America's Schools Act (IASA), there has been statewide required standardized achievement testing aligned with content standards in designated grades. Since 2003 and No Child Left Behind (NCLB), multilingual learners (labeled 'limited English proficient' students back then) have been part of the equation, requiring both English language proficiency standards and an aligned assessment. However, multilingual learners were technically absent from overall accountability until the Every Student Succeeds Act (ESSA) in 2015 when their accountability moved over to Title I from Title III.

Where does validity fit into standardized testing? The classic definition of validity is "the degree to which evidence and theory support the interpretations of test scores entailed by proposed uses of tests" (American Educational Research Association, American Psychological Association, & National Council on Measurement in Education, 2014, p. 9). That is, a test is not valid in itself; rather, it is the interpretations of the test scores that are valid for specific uses. The higher the stakes of a test, the more impactful the consequences, and thus, the levels of evidence must be more convincing. Educational decisions should be predicated on data that are relevant, fair, meaningful, and useful; in other words, when it comes to standardized tests, we need to be able to make valid inferences for multilingual learners and other minoritized students.

Based on the premise that traditional off-the-shelf standardized tests of achievement are becoming increasingly unsatisfactory for guiding learning and evaluating student progress, Mislevy, Almond, and Lukas (2003) have proposed an expanded view of validity to include a principled framework of evidence-centered design to support a wider range of educational assessments. Evidence-centered design is a framework for the development of assessments that considers the collection of validity evidence from the onset of the test design process, thus ensuring a stronger connection with learning.

Given this situation, school and district leaders have to ask the question, "What is the value of making validity claims for high-stakes achievement testing if multilingual learners have not been part of the development process?" Although interpretation of test data and comparison among student groups are inevitable, it should be supplemented by other data sources with proven reliability (and, to the extent feasible, validity) to strengthen the case for the value of standardized achievement measures, especially when in multiple languages.

INTERPRETING DATA IN MULTIPLE LANGUAGES FOR LOCAL ACCOUNTABILITY

Standardized testing results indeed contribute to accountability; however, they are not necessarily an accurate barometer of district- and school-based efforts to showcase teaching and learning for multilingual learners and other minoritized students. School and district leadership should meet with teachers to generate ideas for evidence for local accountability that takes student strengths into account. Capstone or passion projects are often focused on a single learning goal for students, generally at the close of middle or high school, whereas assessment portfolios represent more of a sampling of student growth and can be useful across the K–12 spectrum, especially for showing growth in multiple languages.

Capstone Projects

Capstone projects are an expression of assessment *as*, *for*, and *of* learning all rolled into one. Generally centered on a research question, these projects have specific descriptions and specifications of activities along with a timetable to mark each milestone. For multilingual learners, capstone projects should lend themselves for conducting research in one or more languages, even if the final presentation is only in English.

Feedback from teachers and peers based on a series of rubrics helps move student learning toward the final product. Ultimately, students are encouraged to make a live report on their findings and a personal impact statement to a panel of teachers, school leaders, and community members. The panel often uses an **analytic rubric** of criteria associated with the project's major components, such as the one in Figure 5.12, to interpret each student's presentation.

Culminating projects, often a graduation requirement for high schools, entail learning in action where students engage in service learning, volunteer in the community, or conduct field work to deepen their personal and school experiences. Capstone projects also afford multilingual learners opportunities to reveal their inner feelings about being bilingual/multicultural as they express themselves in multiple languages. Through these projects, multilingual learners can delve into how multiple languages and cultures have helped shape their identities, define their goals, and influence their future.

Student Assessment Portfolios in Multiple Languages

For multilingual learners, student assessment portfolios are anchored in a composite of state academic content and language development standards. Entries can be organized by quarters, semesters, or an entire year to represent a compilation of evidence of learning. These portfolios should highlight multilingual learners' strengths in languages, literacies, content, and character.

FIGURE 5.12 Criteria and Descriptors for a High School Capstone Project and Report

COMPONENT OF PROJECTS AND REPORTS	POSSIBLE CRITERIA FOR MEETING EXPECTATIONS
Literature Review	• Rationale or purpose for the project/personal statement in one or more languages • Introduction of the topic and related literature • Supporting evidence for learning goals found in the literature
Methods/Process/Strategies for Planning and Implementing the Project	• Description of the methods or process aligned to learning goals • Process for development and implementation • Inclusion of a feedback loop by peers or experts
Results/Products/Outcomes	• Match between results/products and learning goals • Match between results/products and methods or development process • Practical/personal application of findings
Discussion/Conclusion and Reflection	• Summary of findings in relation to learning goals • Reference of results/findings to the literature • Discussion of project impact in one or more languages
Significance	• Synthesis of learning, showing novel insights • Statement and application of significance • Personal significance in one or more languages

SOURCE: Adapted from http://www.kumc.edu/Documents/mph/CapstoneReportRubric.pdf

One way of interpreting information from assessment portfolios of multilingual learners is to view it as a student's autobiography of lived experiences, languages, and cultures that celebrates the student's journey of academic, language, and personal (or social-emotional) development. Potential components/entries of student assessment portfolios include:

1. Introductory autobiographical video

2. Learning goals and accomplishments

3. Multimodal entries (e.g., oral, written, graphic, visual, computer-mediated), including self- or peer assessment

4. Entries of different genres (e.g., blogs, learning logs, narratives, arguments), including self- or peer assessment

5. Entries from each or one specific content area or multidisciplinary ones, including self- or peer assessment

6. Evidence and summary of community outreach/field work/interaction with family members

7. Personal reflection on learning in one or more languages

There are several ways for teacher teams or co-teachers to interpret the information from portfolios. Consider:

- Assigning a weight to each component (e.g., entries 1–7) so that students know up front where to center their attention and the total point count magically adds up to 100

- Providing students detailed feedback on the portfolio as a whole

- Giving students opportunities to revise individual entries based on initial teacher (and peer) feedback

- Having students engage in self- and peer assessment on the portfolio as a whole and give an oral or written commentary as to the portfolio's strengths and areas of improvement

The Manhattan International High School, part of the New York Performance Standards Consortium, is a long-standing exemplary program that embraces newcomers from around the world. Like most typical high schools, Grade 12 focuses on requisite coursework for graduation and postsecondary preparedness. Multiple sources of evidence signal these multilingual learners' readiness to graduate: (1) passing the English Language Arts Regents exam (a state requirement), (2) engaging in teacher-developed performance tasks, and (3) presenting a graduation portfolio. When it comes time to interpret student portfolios, members of the coordinating council, the main governing body of the high school that includes the principal, cluster leaders, a guidance counselor, and a teacher union representative along with select parents, coordinate and serve on student presentation panels (MAEC, 2020).

 Stop-Think-Act-React

Relax and Reflect: What is the contribution of student assessment portfolios to local accountability?

Given assessment approaches (as, for, and of learning) and the types of measures (classroom, common, interim, and annual) associated with each, how might leadership and instructional teams work together to devise a student assessment portfolio that is balanced and representative of multilingual learners and their multiple languages and cultures? How can students' strong evidence of learning (in multiple languages) counteract some of the ill effects of standardized testing? How can rubrics be crafted to interpret student assessment portfolios in multiple languages? How can this information contribute to local accountability?

FACING THE ISSUE: NEVER CONSIDER SPECIAL EDUCATION AS AN OPTION FOR MULTILINGUAL LEARNERS (UNLESS DULY WARRANTED)

The pandemic and the subsequent "COVID slide" are one more attempt on the part of educators to measure students' loss of achievement rather than viewing the difference in multilingual learners as loss of opportunity to learn in school. As a result, it is "troublesome for English-language learners, many of whom could [be] fall[ing] farther behind because of a confluence of factors including limited access to the internet and the language support services they often receive in school" (Mitchell, 2020). However, instead of thinking about special education placement for multilingual learners, how about investigating how the students' time at home, and their learning in multiple languages, has benefited their development?

Rather than relying on just one test to make high-stakes educational decisions, we should take the advice from researchers and educators alike who suggest the use of multiple measures that include information gathered from family and student surveys, observational protocols, and tools that meet psychometric requirements (Chester, 2005; Espinosa & García, 2012). Additionally, if interpretation only depends on data from a single achievement test and that test privileges English and proficient English speakers, then schools and districts have lost out on having comparable data in other languages of instruction. Here are some questions for school and district leaders to ponder.

For School Leaders

➤ How might you be proactive, insisting that multilingual learners be observed and assessed in multiple languages (as required) with interpretation by a multilingual team who knows the students if they are being referred to special education services?

➤ How might leadership teams build in time for grade-level sessions for data interpretation to ensure inter-rater reliability (consistency between teachers) in scoring performance assessment?

➤ How can school leaders highlight and display data from multilingual learners in multiple languages for all teachers to interpret?

For District Leaders

➤ To what extent are leadership and teacher teams involved in the interpretation of data in multiple languages at either a school or district level?

➤ How might you advocate for and help design a strengths-driven agenda for interpreting data in multiple languages?

➤ How might leadership teams ensure a realistic weighting of classroom, common, interim, and annual assessment data for school-based decision making for all students, including evidence in multiple languages?

RESOLVING THE DILEMMA: USE MULTIPLE DATA APPROACHES, SOURCES, AND LANGUAGES WHEN ASSESSING MULTILINGUAL LEARNERS!

To diminish the extent of disproportionality of multilingual learners who are potentially dually identified, school and district leaders must be able to distinguish between goals and criteria associated with a multitier system of supports with those services specific for multilingual learners. In addition, having teacher teams interpret data in multiple languages from multiple data sources through a strengths-based lens is a surefire strategy to highlight student evidence of learning. Having a language policy that strategically invites multilingual learners to express themselves in their preferred language is another small step on the road to systemic change.

With increasing numbers of multilingual learners in our schools, all educators should become well versed on the positive impact of using multiple data sources, ideally in multiple languages, and their contribution to decision making. Interpreting data in multiple languages should involve collaboration among teacher teams of classroom, special education, and language teachers who work together in identifying areas for improving teaching and learning across a school. Systemically interpreting classroom, common, interim, and annual data, especially if arranged in an assessment portfolio in multiple languages, provides a true picture of multilingual learners.

National data inevitably filter through states, districts, and schools. Let's assume a "can do" spirit and look at the glass as half-full. For example, when interpreting NAEP data, what is rarely broadcast is achievement data for "former English learners," those multilingual learners who no longer participate but have received language services within the past two to four years. The most recent national data show fourth graders who are former English learners achieved at a level comparable to non–English learners in reading (Murphey, 2014). Just imagine if NAEP data could be available in multiple languages to reflect the current reality in schools that are devoted to students' biliteracy development . . . and how those results would shed a most positive light on multilingual learners and their achievement.

Resources for School and District Leaders

RESOURCE 5.1
Interpreting Classroom, Interim/Common, and Annual Data by Assessment Approach

Map out all the sources of data on your multilingual learners that are accessible to you. You may wish to sort the data by approach (assessment *as*, *for*, or *of* learning), by frequency (everyday, interim/common, or annual), and/or by language. With a leadership or teacher team, you are welcome to slice the data whichever way will yield the most useful results for you to take action.

	EVERYDAY CLASSROOM DATA	INTERIM AND/OR COMMON DATA	ANNUAL DATA
Assessment *as* learning	In multiple languages	In English	In English
		In another language	In another language
Assessment *for* learning	In multiple languages	In English	In English
		In another language	In another language
Assessment *of* learning	In multiple languages	In English	In English
		In another language	In another language

 Available for download at **resources.corwin.com/assessingMLLs-LeadersEdition**

RESOURCE 5.2

Collecting, Recording, and Interpreting Information on Multilingual Learners' Languages and Literacies in Content-Based Assessment

You may wish to dive deeper into classroom assessment and parse out multilingual learners' oral language and literacy development by the instructional activity along with the ways for recording or interpreting data. As always, think about how the context for language use impacts your interpretation.

COLLECTING INFORMATION ON ORAL LANGUAGE USE ACROSS CONTENT AREAS	WAYS OF RECORDING AND INTERPRETING ORAL LANGUAGE	COLLECTING INFORMATION ON TRANS-LANGUAGING PRACTICES	COLLECTING INFORMATION ON (MULTI) LITERACIES ACROSS CONTENT AREAS	WAYS OF RECORDING/ INTERPRETING (MULTI) LITERACIES
Observation of student interaction:	Documentation:	Observation of student interaction:	Student products:	Documentation:

 Available for download at **resources.corwin.com/ assessingMLLs-LeadersEdition**

RESOURCE 5.3
A Checklist of Descriptors for Common Assessment

Apply the following checklist to performance descriptors or rubrics for common assessment to ascertain the extent to which there is sufficient consideration for multilingual learners in multiple languages and ensure confidence in the interpretation of data.

YES/NO	FEATURES OF DESCRIPTORS OR RUBRICS
	1. Are the performance descriptors simply and clearly stated for all students?
	2. Are the descriptors in the language(s) the students best understand?
	3. Can the students paraphrase and give examples of the descriptors in one or more languages?
	4. Can the students apply the descriptors to self- and peer assessment?
	5. Do the descriptors match the language(s) of assessment?
	6. Do the descriptors give students enough information to know their next steps in learning?
	7. Do the descriptors allow for students to respond with multiple modes of communication?
	8. Are the descriptors sufficiently defined to ensure that interpretation is accurate and consistent?
	9. Does the rubric reflect the full range of levels at which students can perform the tasks?
	10. Is the rubric sensitive to and inclusive of multiple language and cultural perspectives?

 Available for download at **resources.corwin.com/assessingMLLs-LeadersEdition**

ASSESSMENT IN MULTIPLE LANGUAGES

RESOURCE 5.4
Ideas for Multilingual Projects for Common Assessment, Standards, and Criteria for Success

Principals, coordinators, or directors may wish to share ideas for multilingual projects with grade-level teacher teams and, as a faculty, select one or two school-wide projects per year based on a curricular focus or a current initiative for common assessment. Based on the selection of projects and using Resource 5.3 as a guide, each grade-level team can then select applicable standards in English and Spanish (as applicable) and craft criteria of success or adapt an existing rubric.

POTENTIAL MULTILINGUAL PROJECTS	STANDARDS ADDRESSED (IN ENGLISH AND SPANISH)	CRITERIA FOR SUCCESS
Student-produced videos, such as reporting on or reenacting events		
Student original performances, such as rapping, reciting poetry, or screen making		
Student-led fairs or exhibitions, such as robotic demonstrations		
Student-built theme-based gallery displays around the school; multicultural murals open to the community		
Classroom-created websites or contributions to school/community newsletters		

online resources — Available for download at **resources.corwin.com/assessingMLLs-LeadersEdition**

RESOURCE 5.5

Annotating Multilingual Learners' Use of Multiple Languages Across Three Dimensions

Over the course of a quarter or a semester, co-teachers may collaborate to offer evidence of student growth in multiple languages. As a grade-level, department, or schoolwide activity, these data can offer insight into multilingual learners' patterns of multiple language use across the discourse, sentence, and word/phrase dimensions.

DIMENSION OF LANGUAGE	EVIDENCE OF INFLUENCE OF ANOTHER LANGUAGE ON ENGLISH	EVIDENCE OF TRANSLANGUAGING	EVIDENCE OF INFLUENCE OF ENGLISH ON ANOTHER LANGUAGE
Discourse • Representation of ideas • Coherence of ideas • Cohesion of text • Organization			
Sentence • Syntactic order • Prepositional phrases • Complexity			
Phrase/Word • Cognates • Multiple meanings • Collocations • Idiomatic expressions			

 Available for download at **resources.corwin.com/assessingMLLs-LeadersEdition**

CHAPTER 6

Evaluating and Reporting Assessment Information

▶ A sign in Seoul, South Korea

Yo no soy mexicano. Yo no soy gringo. Yo no soy chicano. No soy gringo en USA y mexicano en Mexico. Soy chicano en todas partes. No tengo que asimilarme a nada. Tengo mi propia historia.

I am not Mexican. I am not a gringo. I am not Chicano. I am not a gringo in the United States and a Mexican in Mexico. I am Chicano everywhere. I don't have to assimilate to anything. I have my own story.

—Carlos Fuentes

The Dilemma

But how can we evaluate the effectiveness of instruction or programs for multilingual learners in multiple languages if we only depend on results from assessment in one language?

On one level, an evaluation is considered a value statement; what needs to be kept in mind, however, is that every value statement has cultural implications. Take, for example, the "Female Parking First" sign. What are the potential values that underlie it? Does it privilege females, or does it denigrate the entire gender? How is it to be interpreted in light of South Korean culture? It is difficult to make a judgment in regard to the value of this sign if we do not know its purpose, the circumstances that prompted it, or the context for its use.

Now let's make an initial impression or evaluation of our perception of a person rather than an inanimate object, in this case, the sign. If you have never watched the riveting TED Talk "The Danger of a Single Story" by Chimamanda Ngozi Adichie (2009), or have not done so in years, treat yourself and view it again. Then think about the incredible tale of Chimamanda growing up in Nigeria. In essence, what the TED Talk highlights is some of Chimamanda's and others' linguistic and cultural misconceptions based on viewing the world from a singular perspective or a single story.

Finally, let's think about Lisa, a fourth grader, and her dual language classmates. Their teacher, Sra. Sánchez, has just received the "disappointing" results from their state achievement tests in reading and mathematics from her principal, Mr. McMasters. Most of the class is inching toward "proficient" in reading in English according to the measure, the only piece of data that "counts" for accountability purposes. The school's dual language program is evaluated on this one set of scores, and the principal is saying that by fourth grade there should be more "positive" results. Based on this annual achievement test, which students first encountered last spring, Mr. McMasters is threatening to dismantle the entire dual language program, regardless of the research or classroom evidence. This principal is unequivocal in asserting that for him, the school is failing in the eyes of the district, and he cannot accept that reality (the "Danger of a Single Story" syndrome).

Now, let's direct our attention to the educational dilemma of this chapter: the inappropriateness of a principal or any other instructional leader evaluating and reporting assessment results from a single data set or sole perspective. In particular, we have seen time and time again the admonishment of educators based on evaluation of multilingual learners or their programs based on data from a sole language, English. We ask, how might educators be proactive in reporting assessment results that reveal multilingual learners' entire linguistic repertoires to gain a more accurate depiction of bilingual or dual language programs and their goals?

It's true that schools and districts are under increasing pressure to prove themselves academically, especially in difficult times, and many are looking to demonstrate student growth in innovative ways. Mr. McMasters's district has been exploring the use of new technologies and multiple modalities as additional means of learning and assessment, but the pandemic and its aftermath have placed additional stressors on everyone. What can we do to ensure protection of our multilingual learners under the law and their equitable treatment so they can thrive in every environment where learning occurs? How can we secure data from multiple languages in the evaluation of programs serving multilingual learners?

FIRST IMPRESSIONS

- In what ways does this scenario resonate with you?

- How might your school or district design, adopt, or adapt an assessment equity framework for multilingual learners to apply to program evaluation?

- How do dual language perspectives or histories help provide a more comprehensive view of program effectiveness?

- What are some sources for evaluating and reporting assessment data in multiple languages?

Bilingual/multilingual learners are not to be perceived as, nor do they represent, two or more monolingual learners in one (Grosjean, 1989). Only through the combined impact of all their languages on learning will we be able to ascertain their true accomplishments. In cases where language education has biliteracy as a programmatic goal, it is irresponsible and reprehensible not to have large-scale assessment in two languages (if at all possible). The same principle extends to the evaluation of assessment data. Evaluation, as assessment, should always consider students' opportunities to learn in multiple languages coupled with their experiences, bilingualism, biliteracy, and their ways of languaging.

In this chapter, we explore the evaluation and reporting of assessment information within dual language contexts. In revisiting goals for learning, we evaluate the extent to which assessment results are equitable. In addition, we tackle how to establish grading policies for multilingual learners in multiple languages. Lastly, we delve into evaluating data through the eyes of multilingual learners and think about the evolving role of student self- and peer assessment in growing assessment-capable learners. As seen in our assessment cycle in Figure 6.1, we have reached phase 4, *evaluating and reporting assessment information in multiple languages.*

High-stakes tests have come under fire and to some extent rightfully so, especially for minoritized students—even more so during stressful times, as in a pandemic, civil unrest, or a natural disaster. However, when we evaluate assessment data or specific programmatic data, we still can do so with a positive outlook. The large-scale testing data, for example, are useful contributors to federal accountability requirements and serve as baseline data for determining student growth over time. In the name of equity, annual achievement testing attempts to ensure quality education for all students by requiring disaggregation

FIGURE 1 The Fourth Phase of the Assessment Cycle: Evaluating and Reporting Assessment Information

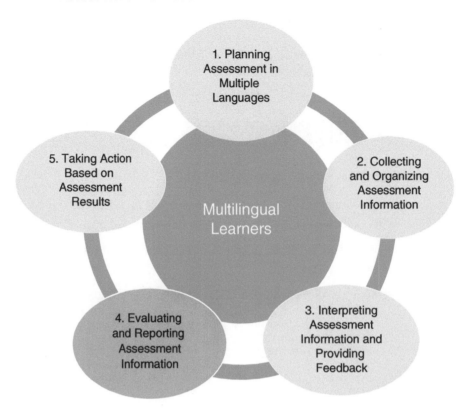

of data by student groups (e.g., English learners, English learners with disabilities, long-term English learners by race and socioeconomic status).

Administrators must be able to see mandated testing as an opportunity to provide accessible and actionable information that can support further learning (Calkins et al., 2018). What is most important, though, is that these summative data cannot stand alone, as high-stakes decisions should never overrely on normative data. This information must be combined with other data sources to form a comprehensive portrait of students, and for multilingual learners, these data must represent the languages of instruction and programmatic goals. Otherwise, when evaluating this information in isolation, such single-source measures can have an insidious effect on students who may already be "behind" (Huff, 2020).

AN EQUITY FRAMEWORK FOR ASSESSING MULTILINGUAL LEARNERS

Given this reality, we might ask to what extent is assessment equitable for multilingual learners who are participating in dual language or bilingual education programs? If equity addresses fairness, access, and opportunity, and it demands that we hold the same high expectations along with quality instruction for all students, it just doesn't seem to work for minoritized students. Here we see the unfolding of a different formula; that is, unequal opportunity coupled with unequal access yields unequal outcomes. This educational disparity in student groups has also been pronounced in assessment, especially when comparing results from standardized achievement testing in English.

Let's admit it: Historically, making meaningful inferences from assessment results for multilingual learners, in essence affirming the validity of testing, has been problematic. In fact, the nature of assessment equity for this group of students has been questioned for years. Rightfully so, as there has been a failure to address many issues that revolve around assessment equity for multilingual learners, including:

1. Expanding the coverage/integration of grade-level content and language standards

2. Minimizing built-in cultural biases/assumptions

3. Responding to issues of language complexity (e.g., density of language, multiple meanings)

4. Tapping students' experiences and interests

5. Increasing accessibility to content (e.g., through scaffolds) and use of multiple languages

6. Acknowledging the interaction between languages

There is a ray of hope, however. LaCelle-Peterson and Rivera (1994) have envisioned a framework for equitable assessment policies for multilingual learners that is inclusive of multiple languages. In it, they specify educational goals, operationalized in distinct program models, that are driven by high academic content standards and corresponding language development standards. These standards, in turn, lead to and define criteria for equity issues that are associated with performance assessment and standardized tests. Figure 6.2 shows an updated framework for assessment equity.

Our job as educators and advocates for multilingual learners is to create and operationalize an equity assessment framework that encompasses multiple languages and fairly represents assessment practices. If an assessment framework is not in place in your school or district, start with evaluating the results of standardized annual or interim tests to determine the extent you trust the data in relation to teachers' judgment of multilingual learners' performance. Then review the issues related to equity, keeping in mind your theory of action, such as the one presented in Chapter 4: *"Linguistically and culturally sustainable schools and classrooms offer students choice and voice that draw from their identities and relationships, fostering collaboration among stakeholders and advocacy for multilingualism and assessment in multiple languages."* The beginning steps to formulating an equity framework for multilingual learners are outlined in Figure 6.3 and elaborated in Resource 6.1.

FIGURE 6.2 A Framework for Equity in Testing Multilingual Learners

EDUCATIONAL GOALS FOR MULTILINGUAL LEARNERS	APPLICABLE PROGRAM MODELS	EQUITY ISSUES RELATED TO PERFORMANCE ASSESSMENT	EQUITY ISSUES RELATED TO STANDARDIZED TESTS
Biliteracy, bilingualism, conceptual understanding, critical reasoning, and problem solving	One-way and two-way dual language immersion; developmental or late-exit bilingual programs	• Are multimodal (e.g., oral, written, visual, graphic, digital) responses considered; are they built into projects? • Are multilingual learners penalized when one of their languages masks their conceptual understanding in their other language?	➤ Do teachers participate in bias and sensitivity reviews of potential items on tests? ➤ Do accommodations scaffold language to maximize English learners' access to content in achievement tests? ➤ Are multilingual learners given adequate preparation on item types? ➤ Are data meaningful for multilingual learners?
English language proficiency (and conceptual understanding) Language proficiency in home languages other than English (and conceptual understanding)	English language development One-way and two-way dual language immersion	• Are data interpreted in light of student characteristics? • Do data reflect the language of content learning? • Is translanguaging an acceptable testing practice, and if so, do results reflect composite use of languages? • Are data presented through an assets-based lens?	➤ Is there strong inter-rater agreement for students' oral and written language? ➤ Are multimodal stimuli/scaffolds considered in test items? ➤ Is the use of assessment data appropriate for the intended purpose? ➤ Do accommodations, match those in the students' individualized education programs?

SOURCE: Adapted from LaCelle-Peterson & Rivera (1994), pp. 63, 65.

FIGURE 6.3 Designing an Equitable Assessment Framework

ASSESSMENT OF MULTILINGUAL LEARNERS	RESULTS FROM STANDARDIZED ACHIEVEMENT TESTS (DISAGGREGATED BY SUBGROUPS OF STUDENTS)	TEACHER JUDGMENT OF THE SAME STUDENTS BASED ON CLASSROOM EVIDENCE IN ONE OR MORE LANGUAGES	SAMPLE EQUITY-RELATED QUESTIONS THAT EMERGE IN COMPARING THE RESULTS
Achievement (language arts/reading, mathematics, and/or science) data in English			What is the trustworthiness and usefulness of the information from these tests for different subgroups of multilingual learners?

ASSESSMENT IN MULTIPLE LANGUAGES

English language proficiency data			How does English learners' English language proficiency affect their content-area performance?
Achievement data in languages other than English			How does multilingual learners' achievement in multiple languages provide a more comprehensive portrait of their content learning?
Language proficiency data in languages other than English			How does multilingual learners' language proficiency in multiple languages provide a more comprehensive portrait of their linguistic repertoires?

Stop-Think-Act-React

Relax and Reflect: How can multilingual learners contribute to designing an equitable assessment framework?

Revisiting your theory of action, determine the extent that student voice counts in developing an equitable assessment framework. Here are some questions that a committee or task force of school leaders might ask students in designing an assessment framework.

1. Do your end-of-unit tests or projects match your expectations?

2. Do your tests or projects make sense to you?

3. Do you think that your tests or projects are fair? Why or why not?

4. Do you feel prepared for taking tests or doing projects?

5. Do you find that knowing two languages is helpful in taking tests? If so, how does it help?

ANOTHER SINGLE STORY, A DIFFERENT SCENARIO: STATE RECLASSIFICATION CRITERIA

Let's turn to another topic that is also tied to the evaluation of assessment data and state assessment policy. Wherever there are multilingual learners who are deemed English learners (ELs), by law there must be language proficiency standards with a strong correspondence to the state's academic content standards and instructional programs that support the integration of students' language and conceptual development. Individual states have the responsibility of determining students' initial EL status and when ELs no longer require English language support. One of the measures that triggers reclassification of ELs' status must be the state's English language proficiency test.

Although the recommendation has always been the use of multiple exit criteria, in a survey of state reclassification criteria Linquanti, Cook, Bailey, and MacDonald (2016) found that 29 states and the District of Columbia use a single criterion—the state's English language proficiency test—for determining which EL students are reclassified. The remaining 21 states have between two and four reclassification criteria, including academic content test achievement (17 states), teacher input or evaluation (15 states), and some form of parental notification or consultation (6 states). There is no mention of proficiency in languages other than English or the **Seal of Biliteracy** (a certificate given to students who achieve a specified literacy level in two languages) as an acceptable reclassification criterion.

Although states must have a uniform set of classification criteria, classroom teachers know the students best. When it comes to reclassification of ELs, a single score generated at one point in time should never be the sole determiner for that critical decision (analogous to the dilemma in the opening vignette). An evaluation process should be put in motion so that multiple stakeholders have a say in making that high-stakes decision. One consideration that does not seem to enter the equation is the voice of our students and their parents/guardians. There is no reason why our students should not have input in this decision as it has direct impact on their learning (and the label on their identities).

The following is a true story that happened many years ago when I was a second-grade Spanish–English bilingual teacher. Back then, language instruction proceeded sequentially—first in the multilingual learners' home language until students reached a predetermined literacy threshold, then English literacy was introduced. In other words, the goal of the transitional "bilingual education" program was to use the students' home language as a springboard for English language development and, at best, to create a sequential bilingual learner.

One day Araceli came up to me and simply said, "Ya." "Ya," I said back. "¿Qué quiere decir 'ya'?" (*What does "ya" mean?*) The shy little girl responded, almost in a whisper, "Ya se leer en español; estoy lista para aprender a leer en inglés."

 Stop-Think-Act-React

Relax and Reflect: What are the reclassification criteria in your state, and how can multilingual learners and their teachers contribute to that critical decision?

School or district leadership might review the effectiveness of services for multilingual learners—in particular, ELs in relation to state exit criteria. What data are used to make that determination? Are the students themselves part of the equation? Are teachers? As an administrator or school leader, even if students are not currently considered, how might you invite them and their teachers, in some small way, to be part of the decision? For multilingual learners participating in dual language programs, how might languages other than English be "counted" as a criterion?

(*I already know how to read in Spanish; I'm ready to learn to read in English.*) I listened and, trusting the little girl's judgment, transitioned Araceli to my English reading group. Indeed, she was motivated and ready; in little time Araceli was biliterate and proud of it! The moral of this story: Student input should be valued in decision making.

CREATING ASSESSMENT-CAPABLE STUDENTS AND SCHOOLS

Just like Araceli, students can and should have input in determining their educational destinies, especially in high-stakes circumstances. The meta-analytic research that culminated in *Visible Learning* indicates that students who are visible learners can engage in self-monitoring, self-evaluation, self-assessment, and self-teaching (Hattie, 2009). The attributes of assessment-capable learners just described can be appropriated to assessment *as* learning, which changes the narrative from a focus on teaching to one on student learning.

Assessment-capable students are members of assessment-capable schools; these schools deeply understand the role of students in their own learning (Frey, Hattie, & Fisher, 2018). When multilingual learners populate these schools, assessment-capable learning must extend to making multiple languages visible during student self-monitoring, self-evaluation, and self-assessment. Figure 6.4, duplicated in Resource 6.2, outlines characteristics of classrooms, schools, and districts with multilingual learners who are assessment capable.

FIGURE 6.4 Applications of Being Assessment Capable to Classrooms, Schools, and Districts

FEATURES OF BEING ASSESSMENT CAPABLE	APPLICATION TO CLASSROOMS WITH MULTILINGUAL LEARNERS	APPLICATION TO SCHOOLS AND DISTRICTS WITH MULTILINGUAL LEARNERS
1. Ensuring curriculum with embedded assessment is linguistically and culturally responsive	*Multilingual learners' languages, cultures, and experiences are visible.*	*School and district committees infuse linguistic and cultural relevance into extant units of learning.*
2. Setting realistic goals for units of learning in one or more languages	*Students have language choice in defining and meeting their goals.*	*Teacher teams set grade-level unit goals for all students.*
3. Crafting learning targets for a series of lessons in one or more languages	*Teachers and students craft integrated targets for content and language learning.*	*Integrated learning targets combine across lessons to create learning goals.*
4. Understanding learning expectations	*Teachers relate learning goals and targets to students, and together they create "I can" statements.*	*Teachers clarify learning expectations and provide additional scaffolding, as necessary.*

(Continued)

(Continued)

5. Monitoring student progress in one or more languages	*Students act on teacher and peer feedback.*	*Teachers maintain records of student growth.*
6. Describing where students are in relation to the criteria associated with learning targets or goals	*Students offer evidence during conversations with teachers.*	*Student assessment data are evaluated and reported on a quarterly basis using a standards-referenced system.*
7. Reflecting on learning	*Student self-assessment is built into teaching and learning.*	*Teachers have opportunities to self-reflect as do students.*
8. Stating the next learning target or goal based on evidence	*Teachers and students evaluate evidence of learning in one or more languages to determine next steps.*	*Schools or districts evaluate evidence of student learning in relation to standards.*

Stop-Think-Act-React

Relax and Reflect: How might you report the results from evaluating your assessment capability?

Districts and schools that are moving toward assessment *as* learning to create assessment-capable learners might take time to evaluate their progress toward that end. When gearing assessment toward student learning, remember that multilingual learners should have the option of responding in their preferred language. Think about student-level data that can help shape standards-referenced evaluation from various sources of evidence, such as:

- End-of-unit project descriptors (e.g., rubrics or narratives and artifacts)

- Protocols for self-assessment

- Student-devised surveys or interviews

- Common grade-level assessment tasks with multicultural perspectives

- Grade-level, school, or district-developed common measures

In striving toward creating assessment-capable students (referring to Figure 6.4), think about the kinds of evaluation questions you might ask students. How might you analyze the data? How might you report the results?

EVALUATING LINGUISTICALLY AND CULTURALLY RESPONSIVE ASSESSMENT PRACTICES

Assessment-capable multilingual learners should be members of linguistically and culturally sustainable schools. In other words, their schools should reflect multicultural frames of reference and a range of student experiences (Ladson-Billings,

1995). One of the most powerful responses of schools to this claim is to ensure that instruction and assessment are congruent with the cultural values of the surrounding communities (Bazron, Osher, & Fleischman, 2005).

But do current assessment practices in schools actually reflect these important tenets? Figure 6.5, replicated in Resource 6.3 as a needs assessment tool, is a three-point rating scale for administrators and school leaders. Its purpose is to evaluate the extent to which their district, schools, and/or classrooms are enacting linguistically and culturally responsive instruction and assessment, and subsequently reporting data in multiple languages.

FIGURE 6.5 Linguistically and Culturally Responsive Assessment and Reporting of Data in Multiple Languages: A Rating Scale

ASSESSMENT IN MULTIPLE LANGUAGES, AS INSTRUCTION, SHOULD . . .	WHERE ARE YOU?		
	AT AN ADVOCACY LEVEL: ENACTED CONSISTENTLY	AT AN ALERTNESS LEVEL: ENACTED ON A SEMIREGULAR BASIS	AT AN AWARENESS LEVEL: ENACTED SPORADICALLY IF AT ALL
1. Foster multiple perspectives and frames of reference			
2. Leverage students' linguistic and cultural backgrounds			
3. Validate students' lived realities			
4. Minimize bias and stereotyping			
5. Allow for varied (multimodal) expressions of learning			
THEREFORE, REPORTING OF ASSESSMENT DATA IN MULTIPLE LANGUAGES SHOULD . . .			
6. Be within a sociocultural context			
7. Include student input, as in self-reflection			
8. Be in reference to grade-level standards or specified criteria			
9. Be equitable, crafted for individual students			
10. Facilitate teachers', students', and family members' contribution to decision making			

THE ROLE OF RUBRICS IN EVALUATING AND REPORTING ASSESSMENT RESULTS

Rubrics, tools for interpreting and evaluating original student work in relation to a set of criteria or descriptors, serve as a valuable source for reporting performance-based assessment data. While rubrics are useful in relating linguistic and culturally relevant practices, there is always an implicit encoding of a value system (Davis, 2013). These hidden cultural values, which can range from a pedagogical approach to the interpretation of data, should act as a springboard for discussion among educators.

Rubrics do not have to be sophisticated or complicated—what is most important is that the learning intentions or targets are visible and understandable. Actually, as a form of success criteria, rubrics can be embedded in instruction and serve to promote student engagement during assessment *as* and *for* learning. In other words, in one capacity, rubrics can readily apply to assessment designed for formative purposes in one or more languages. Rubrics can also capture social-emotional learning, such as in students' feelings toward or reactions to assessment.

An instance of a universal application of a simple rubric might be a tricolor traffic light. To indicate the extent of understanding or as a form of feedback, this traffic light analogy might be applied as follows: red = stop and think; yellow = proceed carefully; green = full speed ahead. (Younger students might start with Stop and Go.) This feedback strategy with its uniform set of criteria can be adopted by an entire school as it can easily be communicated within and across classrooms.

This strategy also applies to assessment-related contexts, such as when students:

- Give opinions of teacher effectiveness in teaching/testing a concept

- Share their understanding of test data/grading procedures

- Estimate their extent of meeting learning targets

- Evaluate each other's work in relation to standards or "I can" statements

- Engage in self- or peer evaluation

- Express their feelings about assessment in one or more languages

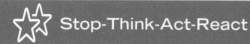

Stop-Think-Act-React

Relax and Reflect: How might you evaluate assessment results based on a traffic light analogy?

Is the traffic light analogy an evaluation strategy that you might consider across classrooms, your school, or even your district? How else might your district or school evaluate assessment results to make them understandable even to the youngest students? How might it bring unity to different stakeholder groups?

Rubrics can actually help to "democratize" the power to evaluate by making explicit criteria visible to students. Additionally, rubrics have the capability of distributing expertise from teachers to students through self- and peer assessment, thus empowering students (Feldman, 2019). When rubrics consist of strengths-based language throughout all levels, they prompt a growth mindset. Research suggests that students actually use rubrics to support their own learning and academic performance (Andrade & Du, 2005).

Designing Student-Centered Rubrics

With such an extensive range of rubrics, which ones provide the most useful information? What are some features that reflect student centeredness, as often students, especially multilingual learners, are not considered? Figure 6.6 points out some characteristics of student-centered rubrics for use with one or more languages. Appearing as Resource 6.4, this tool might be useful for school leadership or teacher groups to determine the extent of student engagement in designing rubrics that account for learning in multiple languages.

Rubrics are most often associated with assessment *of* learning; that is, they are formulated to evaluate student work in relation to a product, performance, or project at the culmination of a unit of learning. Additionally, rubrics are applied to common assessment prompts. The type of rubric and its complexity should reflect the scope of the project and the expected depth

FIGURE 6.6 Designing Student-Centered Rubrics

STUDENT-CENTERED RUBRICS	PRESENT?	WHAT IS THE EVIDENCE?
1. Students have input in creating criteria for success for instruction and assessment in one or more languages.		*Students participate in class discussions.*
2. Students actively engage in instruction and assessment related to the criteria in one or more languages.		*Students interact with each other.*
3. Students' entire linguistic repertoire is captured by the rubric.		*Students perceive that languages are of equal status and worth.*
4. Students are aware of their individual milestones that have been set in one or more languages based on the rubric's criteria.		*Students conference with their teachers.*
5. Students have opportunities to offer focused feedback to each other in the language of their choice.		*Students practice giving positive feedback.*
6. Students pair rubric descriptors with their evidence for learning.		*Student self-assessment is integral to the evaluation process.*
7. Students can restate criteria for success and give an example in the language of their choice.		*Students show understanding of expectations.*
8. Students make judgments about the quality of their work according to the rubric's criteria.		*Students engage in self-assessment.*
9. Students revise their work based on targeted feedback.		*Students submit all drafts along with feedback and the final product.*
10. Students negotiate with teachers to determine the extent to which they have met the rubric's criteria.		*Students have input in the evaluation process.*

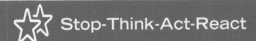

Stop-Think-Act-React

Relax and Reflect: How do rubrics reflect an educational theory or philosophy?

At a staff, grade-level, or department meeting, teachers might analyze some of the rubrics they use to determine the degree of student centeredness. To what extent does your grade-level, department, or school apply student-level data when evaluating a program? How are the multiple languages of multilingual learners considered?

of learning. Creating rubrics is most productive when it is a collaborative process, such as between coaches, grade-level teacher teams, or teachers and students.

There are generally two types of rubrics. Analytic scales have distinct categories or dimensions (such as cohesion of ideas, organization of oral/written text, or precision of language use for expressive language) along with levels of performance. Holistic or overall scales have generalized criteria along with levels of performance. Figure 6.10 is an example of a **holistic rubric** for interpreting and reporting test results.

Characteristics of rubrics that are designed for multilingual learners include:

- Strengths-based language, starting with the earliest levels of performance

- Linguistic and cultural relevant criteria

- Multimodal means of expression

- Integration of content and language

- Recognition of multiple languages and translanguaging

Rubrics are helpful tools for data interpretation and reporting; however, there are additional ways to report assessment results.

REPORTING ASSESSMENT RESULTS

There should always be transparency in reporting assessment results. While multilingual learners are the first and most logical group with whom to share results, other stakeholders should also be involved. Figure 6.7 suggests ways to report assessment results from an array of data sources to different stakeholders.

 Stop-Think-Act-React

Relax and Reflect: How do you report different types of assessment results?

Assessment *of* learning is generally equated with common, interim, and annual assessment. For teachers, assessment *of* learning also extends to classroom-related, long-term projects for units of learning and unit tests. Read the examples of different types of results generated from measures of assessment *of* learning in Figure 6.8. How do the data complement each other to provide a comprehensive portrait of students?

FIGURE 6.7 Reporting Assessment Results to Various Stakeholders

STAKEHOLDER	WAYS TO REPORT ASSESSMENT RESULTS	SUGGESTED DATA SOURCES
Multilingual learners	• During student–teacher remote or face-to-face conferences • As part of goal setting or review of learning goals • During student–family–teacher conferences	• Portfolio entries • Projects, products, or performances with rubrics/criteria for success • Classroom tests • Common and interim tests • Annual tests
Family members	• In score reports with explanations in multiple languages • During meetings at school, in homes, in public places, or remotely in multiple languages	• Portfolios as a whole • Rubrics/criteria for success, such as at the end of units • Common and interim tests • Annual test results in multiple languages
Teachers	• At grade-level or department meetings whether remote or in person • During collaboration time between teachers and co-teacher pairs • During faculty, grade-level, or department meetings • As part of ongoing professional learning	• Portfolio entries • Projects, products, or performances with rubrics/criteria for success • Classroom tests • Common and interim tests • Annual tests
Program directors/coaches	• By grade levels or content areas within and across schools • By English learner subgroups according to federal accountability • By comparing growth of multilingual learners from year to year	• Portfolios • Projects, products, or performances with rubrics/criteria for success • Common assessment • Interim tests • Annual tests
School administrators	• At cabinet meetings for the school district, whether remote or in person • At school faculty meetings • At district principal meetings • At district board meetings	• Portfolios • Common assessment • Capstone projects • Interim tests • Annual tests
The community	• At local meeting points, such as a library, or through technology • Through newsletters, bulletins, and infographics in multiple languages	• Schoolwide portfolios • Capstone projects • Interim tests • Annual tests

SOURCE: Adapted from Gottlieb (2021).

ASSESSMENT IN MULTIPLE LANGUAGES

Common, interim, and annual assessment, all forms of assessment of learning, generate a variety of ways of reporting results. Figure 6.8 outlines these different types of results potentially in multiple languages. Resource 6.5 is a blank form for documenting the reporting of assessment results for your school or setting.

There are a variety of ways to report assessment *of* learning. As you consider the development of your students as expert learners who are becoming agents of their own learning, think about how having fewer targeted and more flexible projects with built-in scaffolding reduces stress and gives more time for reflection, revision, and deeper thinking (Schroeder, 2020). In the next section, we expand on ways to report assessment results for classrooms, schools, and districts.

Classroom Assessment

In today's varied and often changing classroom environments, from in-person to online contexts, teachers may have to consider how to leverage different online platforms that support video or audio to evaluate the evidence and report assessment results. This flexibility allows multilingual learners to have the freedom to

FIGURE 6.8 Reporting Results From Different Measures *of* Assessment of Learning From Classrooms to the State

	CLASSROOM ASSESSMENT (*E.G., END-OF-UNIT PROJECTS OR TESTS*)	COMMON ASSESSMENT	INTERIM SCHOOL OR DISTRICT ASSESSMENT	ANNUAL STATE ASSESSMENT
English	Performance levels based on end-of-unit project descriptors	Analytic or holistic scoring rubric(s) for oral language and/or writing prompts; scores for multiple-choice tests, if applicable	Scale scores/ Lexiles for reading/ language arts; scale scores and language proficiency levels for English language proficiency tests	Scale scores and proficiency levels for reading and mathematics (starting in Grade 3) and science; scale scores and language proficiency levels for English language proficiency tests
Other languages	Performance levels based on end-of-unit project descriptors	Analytic or holistic scoring rubric(s) for oral language and/or writing prompts; scores for multiple-choice tests, if applicable	Scale scores/ proficiency levels for Spanish language arts/ mathematics	Scale scores and proficiency levels for reading and mathematics (in Spanish)

use multimodal representations of their learning in their recordings. Based on these multimodal resources, here are some ways to report classroom-based assessment *of* learning in lieu of grades:

- Standards-referenced reports based on learning goals

- Conversion of criteria of success to scores (such as from 1 to 10)

- Assignment of categorical descriptors (e.g., *emerging, excelling*) from a rubric along with pointed feedback

- Application of school policies, such as Pass or Fail, in specific circumstances

- Summary reports, including scaffolded feedback, based on tasks that culminate in final projects, performances, or products

- Descriptive narratives

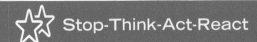

Stop-Think-Act-React

Relax and Reflect: How do you report evaluations of student projects, performances, or products in your classroom?

Given the variety of reports for assessment *of* learning that can be generated by classrooms, which one(s) do you favor? Do you collaborate with other teachers on a project-by-project basis? Do you share different options with your students so that it is a joint decision? How might you adapt what is currently in place for one language to be representative of and equitable for two languages?

Common Assessment Across Classrooms

Rubrics are useful tools for common assessment, both for evaluating and for reporting student achievement on capstone projects that mark the close of elementary, middle, and high school. In addition, when evaluating student assessment portfolios, the leadership team might devise a summary rubric. If common assessment at a school or district level contributes to local accountability, certain steps should be taken to ensure reliability or agreement among reviewers in assigning a score or level and in reporting the results.

Here are some steps for encouraging district and school leadership, teacher–teacher, and teacher–student collaboration in rubric development or redesign for common assessment. Before starting the process, however, school leadership should revisit the purpose for assessment in relation to the project, product, performance, or portfolio to use as evidence for assessment *of* learning.

Suggested Steps in Crafting or Redesigning Rubrics for Common Assessment and Determining Inter-Rater Agreement

1. Review the student-friendly standards (i.e., "I can" statements) derived from academic content and language development standards that were created to generate learning targets.

2. Determine the most appropriate type of rubric (e.g., a holistic or analytic scale) and the languages to apply (e.g., English, English and another language, or only another language) for a project or construct (e.g., oral, written, and/or graphic expression).

3. Decide on the categories (for analytic rubrics) from the selected academic content standards and language development standards.

4. Choose the number of levels of student performance (e.g., developing, extending, reaching, exceeding). Hint: Selecting an even number of levels forces a decision rather than a compromise.

5. Brainstorm descriptors for each category of the rubric with students. Hint: Try to maintain equal intervals of growth between levels.

6. Offer professional learning or joint planning time so that teacher groups or co-teachers can exchange information on their rubrics to form a developmental continuum across grades.

7. Apply a "can do" lens to the descriptors to evaluate the linguistic, cultural, and developmental relevance of the rubric.

8. Pilot the rubric with multilingual learners and other students; include feedback from students to finalize the criteria across performance levels.

9. Collect student samples that represent the midrange of each performance level to serve as anchors.

10. Practice scoring student samples against the rubric descriptors until educators agree on the performance level at least 80% of the time.

As we move to more secure forms of assessment with more rigorous psychometric requirements for scoring and reporting, we realize that results are going to be more distal to what happens in classrooms and schools, yet they tend to count more for accountability purposes. Here is a glimpse into ways for reporting interim and annual assessment.

Interim School or District Assessment

For the most part, the purpose of commercially available interim measures is to predict student performance on the corresponding high-stakes annual test. These online tests, administered two to three times a year, are generally not available in multiple languages; an exception is NWEA's MAP achievement tests in English and Spanish. Domestically, WIDA MODEL, online and in paper forms, serves as an English language proficiency initial screener or interim test that may be given during the school year to provide information for instructional planning and curriculum-related decisions. Internationally, WIDA MODEL is used as a measure for summative purposes. Figure 6.9 is an

FIGURE 6.9 A Sample Individual Student Report for WIDA MODEL Online

English Language Proficiency Test

WIDA MODEL Grades 1–2

Individual Student Report

Report Purpose: This report will provide information about the student's level of English proficiency (ability to listen, speak, read, and write), in both social and academic language. Please refer to the MODEL Interpretive Guide for Score Reports for more detailed information on the scores and score interpretation.

MODEL results by language domain and composite scores:

LANGUAGE DOMAIN	SCALE SCORE (POSSIBLE 100–600)	PROFICIENCY LEVEL (POSSIBLE 1.0–6.0)
Listening		
Speaking		
Writing		
Reading		
Oral Language[A]		
Literacy[B]		
Overall Score[C]		

A. Oral Language = 50% Listening + 50% Speaking; B. Literacy = 50% Writing + 50% Reading; C. Overall Score = 30% Oral Language + 70% Literacy

Overall scores are computed when all four domains have been completed.

DESCRIPTION OF PROFICIENCY LEVELS	
1	**Entering** - Knows and uses minimal social language and minimal academic language with visual and graphic support
2	**Emerging** - Knows and uses some social English and general academic language with visual and graphic support
3	**Developing** - Knows and uses social English and some specific academic language with visual and graphic support
4	**Expanding** - Knows and uses social English and some technical academic language
5	**Bridging** - Knows and uses social English and academic language working with grade-level material
6	**Reaching** - Knows and uses social and academic language at the highest level measured by this test

SOURCE: Adapted from WIDA MODEL. (2020).

example of a partial MODEL student score report. It shows the conversion of scale scores to language proficiency levels for each language domain and composite scores for oral language, literacy, and the overall test along with a proficiency-level descriptor.

☆ Stop-Think-Act-React

Relax and Reflect: What can we learn from action research on school or district large-scale data?

School leadership might collaborate with grade-level cluster or department teams to examine the relationship among assessment *of* learning measures. One group of educators might compare student results between interim and annual tests. Another group might explore the technical manuals of interim and annual tests to investigate the linguistic and cultural relevance of the tests. A third group might compare student evidence from common classroom assessment in relation to that of interim and annual measures. Based on this jigsaw of data, what conclusions might you draw about assessment *of* learning data sources for multilingual learners?

Annual high-stakes assessment is the most familiar form of assessment *of* learning to educators as its consequences are felt from states to classrooms. As mentioned in Chapter 1, it is federal law that calls for annual assessment of achievement (in Grades 3–8 and once in high school) and, for ELs, English language proficiency (in Grades K–12). The ways in which data are reported vary, and there is no reason why reporting needs to be negative in nature.

Annual State Assessment

Chapman, Kim, Wei, and Bitterman (2018) exemplify how assessment for multilingual learners can overcome a deficit mindset by applying WIDA's "can do" philosophy to its high-stakes large-scale writing test as part of ACCESS for ELLs, its annual English language proficiency test. This positive stance permeates the entire test development process, including the writing prompts, rubrics, rater training materials, and the assets-based score report.

The Individual Student Report, such as the partial one in Figure 6.10, details what students can do at their assigned levels of language proficiency. The mockup presented here has been translated into Spanish, one of over 40 languages for family members. In it, there is an icon representing each language domain (listening, speaking, reading, and writing), followed by a language proficiency level (from 1, *Entering*, to 6, *Reaching*) and sample descriptors of what the student can do.

FIGURE 6.10 Individual Student Report for ACCESS, WIDA's Annual English Language Proficiency Test

ACCESS for ELLs 2.0®

Prueba de desempeño lingüístico en inglés (An English language proficiency test)

Informe individual del estudiante (Individual Student Report)

FORMA DE LENGUAJE	EN ESTE NIVEL, LOS ALUMNOS GENERALMENTE PUEDEN HACER LO SIGUIENTE:
Escuchar	Entender el lenguaje oral relacionado con temas frecuentes y específicos en las escuela y participar en discusiones en clase, por ejemplo: • Relacionar ideas habladas con experiencias propias. • Encontrar, seleccionar y organizar información a partir de descripciones orales. • Identificar las causas y los efectos de acontecimientos o situaciones que se discuten de manera oral. • Clasificar las ventajas y las desventajas de temas en discusión.
Hablar	Comunicar ideas e información en inglés de manera oral utilizando un lenguaje que contenga oraciones cortas y palabras y frases cotidianas, por ejemplo: • Compartir sobre qué, cuándo y dónde sucede algo. • Comparar objetos, personas, imágenes y acontecimientos. • Describir los pasos en ciclos o procesos. • Expresar opiniones.
Leer	Entender el lenguaje escrito relacionado con temas familiares y específicos en la escuela y participar en debates en clase, por ejemplo: • Identificar las ideas principales en información escrita. • Identificar los personajes y los acontecimientos principales de historias y textos simples con imágenes o gráficos. • Secuenciar imágenes, acontecimientos o pasos en un proceso. • Distinguir entre una afirmación y una declaración como pruebas.
Escribir	Comunicarse en inglés a través de la escritura utilizando el lenguaje relacionado con temas familiares en la escuela, por ejemplo: • Describir ideas o conceptos utilizando frases u oraciones cortas. • Clasificar ilustraciones describiendo qué, cuándo y dónde sucede algo. • Establecer pasos en procesos o procedimientos. • Expresar opiniones sobre temas o situaciones específicas.

SOURCE: Retrieved from https://wida.wisc.edu/sites/default/files/resource/ACCESS-Sample-Individual-Score-Report-Spanish.pdf

ASSESSMENT IN MULTIPLE LANGUAGES

Relax and Reflect: How can you have confidence in the results from large-scale assessment?

Score reports of state annual tests are generally in the most prevalent languages of family members, which is necessary. However, in large part, these reports represent tests in English, which fail to show a complete linguistic portrait of multilingual learners. When these students are participating in dual language education where instruction is occurring in two languages, it is inequitable to base important decisions on only a single language. Do you agree? How might you (have you) compensate(d) for this inequity?

RECONSIDERING GRADING PRACTICES

The crises that we have faced personally in conjunction with those of our schools, our nation, and the world have given all educators pause for how to evaluate students A standards-based approach to grading that incorporates goal setting and student self-reflection can help advance student learning. However, more humane assessment and grading shouldn't just occur during a pandemic or a time of crisis. After all, a standards-referenced grading system, when coupled with effective instruction, is one of the most equitable ways to report student learning. Whether under unusual circumstances or not, students should demonstrate mastery of various competencies instead of earning points on assignments (Metro, 2020).

The pandemic has spurred most unusual learning conditions that warrant revisiting grading practices, especially for minoritized students who have been most inequitably impacted. According to Feldman (2019), "the ways we grade disproportionately favor students with privilege and harm students with less privilege—students of color, from low-income families, who receive special education services, and English learners" (p. xxii). On one level, however, this tragedy has presented an opportunity to rethink and reset some principles and practices.

Now is the time to take action. The following set of principles for grading multilingual learners in one or more languages might serve as a foundation for redesigning district- or schoolwide policy. Resource 6.6 is set up for leadership teams to evaluate each principle and contemplate its usefulness and applicability to their setting.

Students' attitude, motivation, effort, timeliness, neatness, or attendance may be reported, if warranted, but should not be incorporated into grading. Multilingual learners' social-emotional development, such as their work ethic or persistence on a task, if reported, should be separate from their language and conceptual development. In essence, what is reported should help students focus on what and how they are learning rather than their grades.

Grading Principles for Multilingual Learners

Grading Principle 1: Grades should convey meaning to students and be either **criterion-referenced** or standards-based.

Grading Principle 2: Grades should be a function of programmatic goals (e.g., if a goal of dual language education is biliteracy, grades should be equally weighted for the two languages).

Grading Principle 3: Grades should represent multiple opportunities for students to demonstrate learning based on descriptive, concrete, and actionable feedback.

Grading Principle 4: Grades should show what multilingual learners can do with access to multimodal resources, including multiple languages.

Grading Principle 5: Grades should be an evaluative marker of student growth or performance, not the goal in and of itself.

Grading Principle 6: Grades should reflect multilingual learners' accomplishments based on multiple forms of evidence and should never serve a punitive purpose.

Grading Principle 7: Grades should be negotiated between students and teachers based on their learning goals and evidence for learning in two languages, as applicable.

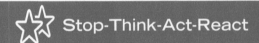 Stop-Think-Act-React

Relax and Reflect: How is grading multilingual learners determined in your setting?

Some educators may feel that the same grading policy should apply to all students. Other educators are of the belief that the grades for multilingual learners, in particular English learners, should take their levels of language proficiency into account. Still others insist on different configurations for assigning grades in multiple languages according to the language allocation of their dual language program. Finally, there are some educators who simply do not believe that grading should occur at all and that evaluation should be in narrative form, especially in primary school. Given these contexts, which of the grading scenarios might you (have you) adopt(ed) for your school, and how might you justify it?

MULTILINGUAL LEARNERS' ROLE IN EVALUATION AND REPORTING

One of the premises of this book is that multilingual learners and their teachers can become empowered through assessment *as*, *for*, and *of* learning. Students, in particular, should be seen and respected as assessment leaders and decision makers, having choices in their language use and in presenting their evidence of learning. In this phase of the assessment cycle, multilingual learners should have opportunities to evaluate and report their evidence based on their learning goals, standards, or criteria for success.

Here is what a district or school might do to initiate the process of being more inclusive of students.

- First, teacher teams select power standards from their state academic content standards, if not previously selected, along with corresponding language development standards.

- Next, schools invite grade-level teams along with students to convert them into "I can" statements.

- Then, strategically throughout the year, students post their standards-related evidence and self-evaluate their work for activities, tasks, and projects (e.g., in their personal portfolios).

- Lastly, teachers or peers affirm or disaffirm each student's evaluation, ideally during teacher–student conferences or conversations.

Figure 6.11 charts this evaluation process and gives some examples.

FIGURE 6.11 An Example of Student Evaluation of Standards-Referenced Evidence in One or More Languages

STATE ACADEMIC CONTENT STANDARD: LANGUAGE ARTS	"I CAN" STATEMENT	EVIDENCE FOR MEETING THE "I CAN" STATEMENT	HOW WELL CAN I DO IT? (CIRCLE ONE)	HOW WELL DOES YOUR TEACHER OR PEER THINK YOU CAN DO IT? (CIRCLE ONE)
Describe *the overall structure* of (multicultural) stories, including describing how *the beginning introduces the story* and *the ending offers closure.*	I can describe each part of stories (from around the world) from beginning to end.	I can write stories in English *y en español.* My stories have beginnings, middles, and ends.	• Amazing • Very well • Well • Pretty well • OK	• Amazing • Very well • Well • Pretty well • OK

FACING THE ISSUE: CONSIDER THE MANY STORIES OF MULTILINGUAL LEARNERS AND THEIR FAMILIES

Evaluating assessment results, from the classroom to the state level, is a sensitive topic as judgment is always part of the equation. In addition, for multilingual learners, issues of linguistic and cultural sensitivity and language proficiency tend to mask equity in evaluation and reporting. Here are some questions to ask school and district leaders in regard to bringing more fairness into this phase of the assessment cycle so that stakeholders are not so quick to make a judgment based on "a single story" or a single language.

For School Leaders

➤ How might you plan for and enact ongoing professional learning for grade-level teams or departments to dive into data from multiple sources and languages to determine the extent to which programmatic goals have been met?

➤ How have recent crises impacted the fidelity of data in multiple languages? For example, what has been the effect of multilingual learners spending more time at home and interacting in languages other than English? How has that been taken into account in evaluating test results in English?

➤ To what extent are you satisfied with your current grading policy? Is it equitable for minoritized students who may lack access to technology or multilingual learners who are learning in two languages? How might you tackle this issue?

For District Leaders

➤ How would you rank the results from the different forms of assessment *of* learning—classroom, common, interim, and annual—in terms of the usefulness of the data that are reported?

➤ How might you revise your districtwide assessment system to be more equitable and inclusive of assessment *as*, *for*, and *of* learning in multiple languages?

➤ How might content teachers collaborate with language teachers to provide the most equitable grades for multilingual learners?

RESOLVING THE DILEMMA: NEVER EVALUATE EVIDENCE OR PROGRAMS FOR MULTILINGUAL LEARNERS BASED ON A SINGLE STORY!

When it comes to evaluating data or programs and reporting results, schools and districts have to avoid the "Danger of a Single Story" syndrome. Lisa, her family, her classmates, and Sra. Sánchez should not be looked down at disparagingly based on assessment results that are solely in English when learning is occurring in two languages. Bilingual or dual language programs should not be penalized for the absence of appropriate assessments and thus the lack of data in multiple languages to prove their effectiveness.

Evaluation data can be very powerful but, as we have seen, also very dangerous. Data that do not match programmatic goals lead to misinterpretation by policy makers. When school and district leaders, such as Mr. McMasters, adopt a monoglossic ideology or one of monolingualism (English), especially when evaluating data from high-stakes assessment, they fail to see the potential of multilingual learners. Just as assessment, evaluation data of multilingual learners and the reporting of results must be balanced and representative of the contexts of languaging and learning.

Resources for School and District Leaders

RESOURCE 6.1
Designing an Equitable Assessment Framework for Multilingual Learners

In seeking to answer policy questions based on evaluation of assessment measures, one of the first steps is to determine the extent to which assessment yields accurate and useful information about multilingual learners. Team leaders for each grade level or department should form a committee or task force to create an assessment framework that is equitable for its multilingual learners and considers their language proficiency and achievement in one or more languages. Here are some steps to follow:

1. Compare the results from a standardized achievement test of the committee's choice with results (evidence) from classroom assessment *of* learning from the same content area.

2. Repeat the activity for assessment *of* learning for tests or measures of language proficiency.

3. Based on the findings, generate questions related to equity across grades, such as those in Figure 6.2.

4. Take a schoolwide poll to collect an array of responses (it could be as easy as creating a rating scale on the usability of the data from each measure).

5. Analyze the responses.

6. Draft an equity assessment framework and present it to the school or district.

7. Evaluate the framework in relation to your theory of action, such as the one proposed in Chapter 4.

ASSESSMENT FOR MULTILINGUAL LEARNERS	RESULTS FROM STANDARDIZED ACHIEVEMENT TESTS (DISAGGREGATED BY GROUPS OF STUDENTS)	TEACHER JUDGMENT OF THE SAME STUDENTS' PERFORMANCE BASED ON CLASSROOM EVIDENCE IN ONE OR MORE LANGUAGES	QUESTIONS OF EQUITY THAT EMERGE IN COMPARING THE RESULTS FROM DIFFERENT DATA SOURCES
Achievement (language arts/reading, mathematics, and/or science) data in English			
English language proficiency data			
Achievement data in languages other than English			
Language proficiency data in languages other than English			

online resources — Available for download at **resources.corwin.com/ assessingMLLs-LeadersEdition**

RESOURCE 6.2

Evaluating Assessment-Capable Classrooms, Schools, and Districts

To what extent do you consider your classroom, school, and/or district to be assessment capable? Use the following checklist or convert it to a rating scale, such as by adding the descriptors (1) *to a great extent*, (2) *to some extent*, and (3) *under consideration*. Based on results of the survey, determine next steps in moving toward becoming more assessment capable.

FEATURES OF BEING ASSESSMENT CAPABLE	FOR CLASSROOMS WITH MULTILINGUAL LEARNERS	FOR SCHOOLS AND DISTRICTS WITH MULTILINGUAL LEARNERS
1. Ensuring curriculum with embedded assessment is linguistically and culturally sustainable		
2. Setting realistic goals for units of learning in one or more languages		
3. Crafting learning targets for a series of lessons in one or more languages		
4. Understanding what is to be learned in one or more languages		
5. Monitoring growth in one or more languages		
6. Describing where students are in relation to the criteria associated with learning targets or goals		
7. Reflecting on teaching and learning		
8. Determining the next learning target or goal based on evidence		

 Available for download at **resources.corwin.com/assessingMLLs-LeadersEdition**

RESOURCE 6.3

Linguistically and Culturally Responsive Assessment and Reporting of Data: A Rating Scale

To what extent are these features for assessment and reporting of data being enacted in classrooms, schools, or districts? For each feature, check a cell indicative of the level of enactment and then discuss responses.

ASSESSMENT IN MULTIPLE LANGUAGES, AS INSTRUCTION, SHOULD . . .	ADVOCACY LEVEL: ENACTED CONSISTENTLY	ALERTNESS LEVEL: ENACTED ON A SEMIREGULAR BASIS	AWARENESS LEVEL: ENACTED SPORADICALLY IF AT ALL
1. Foster multiple perspectives and frames of reference			
2. Leverage students' linguistic and cultural backgrounds			
3. Validate students' lived realities			
4. Minimize bias and stereotyping			
5. Allow for varied (multimodal) expressions of learning			
THEREFORE, REPORTING OF ASSESSMENT DATA IN MULTIPLE LANGUAGES SHOULD . . .			
6. Be within a sociocultural context			
7. Include student self-reflection			
8. Be in reference to grade-level standards or specified criteria			
9. Be equitable, crafted for individual students			
10. Facilitate teachers', students', and family members' contribution to decision making			

online resources ▶ Available for download at **resources.corwin.com/ assessingMLLs-LeadersEdition**

RESOURCE 6.4
Student-Centered Rubrics

Are student-centered rubrics present in your school? For each feature, state whether they are present or not and the evidence you have. Then think about how you might modify existing rubrics to include student voice.

FEATURES OF STUDENT-CENTERED RUBRICS	PRESENT?	WHAT IS THE EVIDENCE?
1. Students have input in criteria for success for instruction and assessment in one or more languages.		
2. Students actively engage in instruction and assessment related to the criteria in one or more languages.		
3. Students' activation of their entire linguistic repertoire is captured by the rubric.		
4. Students are aware of their individual milestones that have been set in one or more languages.		
5. Students have opportunities to offer focused feedback to each other.		
6. Students pair rubric descriptors with their evidence for learning.		
7. Students can restate criteria and give an example in the language of their choice.		
8. Students make judgments about the quality of their work according to the rubric's criteria.		
9. Students revise their work based on targeted feedback.		
10. Students negotiate with teachers to determine the extent to which they have met the rubric's criteria.		

 Available for download at **resources.corwin.com/ assessingMLLs-LeadersEdition**

ASSESSMENT IN MULTIPLE LANGUAGES

RESOURCE 6.5

Reporting Results From Measures of Assessment *of* Learning

Jot down all the measures of assessment *of* learning that apply across classrooms, your school, your district, or your state in English and other languages. Explain why all are necessary and how the results work together to form a comprehensive body of evidence.

	CLASSROOM ASSESSMENT (*E.G., END-OF-UNIT PROJECTS OR TESTS*)	COMMON ASSESSMENT ACROSS CLASSROOMS	INTERIM SCHOOL OR DISTRICT ASSESSMENT	ANNUAL STATE ASSESSMENT
English				
Other languages				

 Available for download at **resources.corwin.com/assessingMLLs-LeadersEdition**

RESOURCE 6.6
Principles for Grading Multilingual Learners

Prioritize the principles of grading practices for your school or district. You are welcome to edit them before reflecting on each principle's potential usefulness and applicability to your setting. Ultimately, you may consider adopting the principles to amend your current grading policy.

Grading Principle 1: Grades should convey meaning to students and be criterion-referenced or standards-based.

Grading Principle 2: Grades should be a function of programmatic goals (e.g., if a goal of dual language education is biliteracy, grades should be equally weighted for the two languages).

Grading Principle 3: Grades should represent multiple opportunities for students to demonstrate learning based on descriptive, concrete, and actionable feedback.

Grading Principle 4: Grades should show what multilingual learners can do with access to multimodal resources.

Grading Principle 5: Grades should be an evaluative marker of student growth or performance, not the goal in and of itself.

Grading Principle 6: Grades should reflect multilingual learners' accomplishments based on multiple forms of evidence and should never serve a punitive purpose.

Grading Principle 7: Grades should be negotiated between students and teachers based on their learning goals and evidence for learning in two languages, as applicable.

GRADING PRINCIPLE	POTENTIAL USEFULNESS (WHY IS IT IMPORTANT?)	APPLICATION TO OUR SETTING (WHAT CAN WE DO?)

 Available for download at **resources.corwin.com/ assessingMLLs-LeadersEdition**

CHAPTER 7

Taking Action Based on Assessment Results

► Con Ganas/We Can is a blog dedicated to amplifying the Latino voice in the education sector (https://www.latinosforeducation.org/blog/)

Inspiration gives no warnings.
La inspiración no da advertencies.

—Gabriel García Marquéz

The Dilemma

The "'COVID slide' may be especially troublesome for English-language learners, the 5 million students still learning English in the nation's K–12 schools" (Mitchell, 2020). How will schools and districts measure multilingual learners' "COVID slide"?

Somehow through all our sadness, exhaustion, worry, and angst over the last year and counting, we have endured and remain resilient in our resolve to be the best educators we can be. Indeed, the COVID-19 pandemic has been devastating for families, students, and educators alike as life suddenly and drastically changed across the globe in the early spring of 2020. Full

(Continued)

(Continued)

recovery still eludes us, and when we finally reach it, we will forever be transformed as people, a nation, and a global community.

It is also true that the challenges that have stemmed from the virus have proven even greater for families of bi/multilingual learners and other minoritized students who have disproportionately felt its effects. Well-known equity gaps due to language, income, race, and immigration status have come into greater focus and are at risk of widening. Exacerbating the problem, the pandemic has triggered new or more serious health and economic insecurities that have compounded disruptions in student learning (Lazarín, 2020). Indeed, it has been the most unusual and perplexing year in recent history.

On the positive side, education has come to embrace the tremendous work of nonprofit community groups, which sprung into action when multilingual families were suddenly faced with multiple crises. Much credit goes to the outreach efforts of local community organizations across the states in helping immigrant families connect with much-needed services and in being critical voices at a time when reports of discrimination have run rampant, especially in Asian communities. In addition, local agencies have made important information available in multiple languages and have served as a voice for public school systems. The realization of the interdependence and interconnection among communities, schools, and classrooms has been a true strength that has grown out of this most horrific time (Zacarian, Calderón, & Gottlieb, 2021).

María Jiménez, the principal of a preK–8 elementary school in the inner city of a major metropolitan area, is very sensitive to the hardship conditions of her families and students. Like all educators, she is facing unprecedented times and unforeseen circumstances. However, rather than looking back, bracing herself for achievement test results that are bound to be regressive, María prefers to be proactive. This principal believes that multilingual practices are a whole-school philosophy and commitment; therefore, the school must act with passion and conviction.

María is fortunate to be taking leadership courses to become a superintendent and has a built-in, albeit remote, cohort to share issues and serve as a think tank. She has been fascinated by the "multilingual turn," a paradigm shift happening in the field of language education that recognizes multilingualism within situated social practice. These new ways of thinking about multilingualism extend to notions of equity, social justice, belonging, and empowerment of learners and teachers where multilingual learners are viewed as multilingual practitioners and language users (Meier, 2016). Specifically, María sets out to explore how to apply this concept to her school and classroom assessment practices.

This forward-thinking educational leader believes that if we accept the premise that multilingualism is intrinsic to multilingual learners and their identities, then as educators it is our responsibility to grow that multilingualism rather than impose monolingual norms and English "nativism" as language goals. Although "formative" assessment tools have been touted as an antidote to learning loss during remote learning (Brookhart, 2020), there is no mention of how assessment in multiple languages can provide more accurate information about multilingual learners. Consequently, if schools only measure English learners' "COVID slide" learning loss in one language (which is a questionable tactic in and of itself) and do not value learning that is occurring at home and in the community in other languages, how do we ever know what our multilingual learners truly can do?

FIRST IMPRESSIONS

- In what ways does this scenario resonate with you?

- How might you take action that can make a difference in the schooling of multilingual learners, given the changes of the past year?

- How might you join forces with other educational leaders and take action at a program, school, or district level?

- How might you, family members, and community organizations take action to improve educational opportunities for multilingual learners?

As witnessed in the vignette, each and every one of us has undergone dramatic change since the international onset of the coronavirus and the turmoil of the crises that ensued. There have been unforeseen challenges, heartaches, increased levels of stress, and utter confusion over what to do. We have seen districts, schools, and classrooms struggle from being in constant flux. Educators have all grappled with the disruption of ever-changing environments, often having to pivot from face-to-face to hybrid to fully remote modes of learning and back again with little notice.

Despite all this upheaval, teachers and other school leaders have become more connected to students and their families. We must remain hopeful so that as we enter a new period beyond crises, we can work together to overcome the inequities that have ravaged our communities, schools, and classrooms (Zacarian et al., 2021). As educators question the traditional role of assessment and the heavy weight of high-stakes testing, we must wonder how we can make a difference by motivating our students to take ownership and action.

Ultimately, it is the actions of educational stakeholders that will enhance opportunities and access for multilingual learners and other minoritized students to learn and lead in improving educational systems. This chapter recaps how assessment in multiple languages helps carry out that mission as it urges stakeholders to take on that challenge. It is the strength of assessment data coupled with the convictions and passions of multilingual learners, their families, and educators that will ultimately reshape our educational landscape. And so, as shown in Figure 7.1, we enter the last phase of the assessment cycle, *taking action based on assessment results.*

We have come full circle in the assessment cycle as we see the extent to which our initial planning efforts have become reality. Armed with goals for learning in multiple languages, we have collected and organized assessment data, applied criteria for success, offered feedback to improve teaching and learning, judged our efforts, and reported the results. We have carefully focused on assessment in multiple languages to gain the full benefits of our multilingual learners' conceptual, linguistic, cultural, and social-emotional development.

FIGURE 7.1 Completing the Assessment Cycle: Using Assessment Results to Take Action

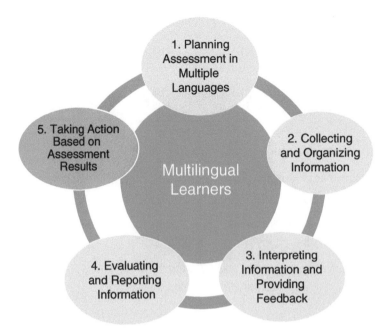

Now is the time to take action in assessing multilingual learners by overlaying multiple languages and cultures onto current educational policies and practices. In portraying the whole child through an assets-based lens, we can assume a positive outlook and more favorable outcomes. This chapter centers on six actions for educational leadership that summarize how assessment in multiple languages can be transformative for multilingual learners and their families, schools, and communities. These actions, also presented in Resource 7.1, are for leadership teams to contemplate in embarking upon changing the current monoglossic assessment paradigm to one that embraces multilingualism.

Taking Action Based on Assessment Results in Multiple Languages

Action 1: Engage in Reflective Practice and Inquiry

Action 2: Determine Priorities in Assessing in Multiple Languages

Action 3: Challenge the Status Quo in Assessment

Action 4: Assess Multilingual Learners From a Strengths-Based Lens

Action 5: Enact Effective Assessment Practices in Multiple Languages

Action 6: Use Assessment Data in Multiple Languages to Leverage Systemic Change

---

ACTION 1: ENGAGE IN REFLECTIVE PRACTICE AND INQUIRY

The lasting effects of the coronavirus on our nation's educators, especially school leaders, is palpable. Stress, anxiety, angst, and uncertainty are commonplace; motivation, engagement, and personal health have often been compromised. The work–life balance of educators remains delicate. Says one leader, "From my kitchen table, I'm running a school with 1,700 students, some of whom we're having trouble finding. I'm also attempting to stay connected to 150 faculty and staff, some of whom have gotten sick and others who are not adjusting well to remote learning. At the same time, I'm attempting to communicate with thousands of frustrated family members who speak dozens of different languages" (Brackett, Cannizzaro, & Levy, 2020). The toll of this decade has been heavy on all of us.

Ever since Dewey's (1933) vision of reflection as movement of a learner from one experience to the next, reflective practice has been part of our educational tradition. Even in today's unusual conditions for teaching and learning, reflective practice continues to be important in fostering and developing principal and teacher leadership as a major ingredient of school improvement (Day & Harris, 2002). When assessment is involved, school leaders need to take the time to be reflective before taking action as there is a tremendous amount of data that impact students and teachers.

The scope of reflective practice broadens when educational inquiry is added and embedded in professional learning. One way to pursue this inquiry is through action research. **Action research** is a reflective process that revolves around inquiry of a self-identified question or a group's pressing issue. The question should be of immediate concern to teaching and assessment, and its resolution serves as a means for instilling change and improvement in everyday policies or practices (Gottlieb, 2021).

For example, a case study on multilingual learners reveals that teachers involved in ongoing inquiry through professional learning shifted their attitudes, perspectives, and beliefs about language in education. In particular, teachers deepened their understanding of learning in multiple languages and increased their openness toward the value of home languages and translanguaging for content learning (Stille, Bethke, Bradley-Brown, Giberson, & Hall, 2016).

In our new reality, educational leaders need to create and extend community, maintain stability, and project resiliency. This is the time to have a sense of a shared mission that unifies and solidifies our commitment to educational equity for all students. Since the onset of the pandemic, different kinds of assessment data have surfaced outside of testing. There has been a refocusing on assessment results that are more learning-centered and educational decisions that have been made based on social-emotional learning rather than test scores. Descriptive data are critical as part of the sociocultural context for understanding the whole student. During unsettling times, schools and districts have been laser focused on these different kinds of data, including the:

- Number of healthy students and faculty vs. those infected with/affected by COVID-19

- Number of teachers and support staff available for instructing others

- Number of families in distress vs. families receiving needed services

- Number of students who have not returned to "school" or who have erratic attendance patterns vs. those with consistent attendance

- Number of students with vs. without access to technology and reliable broadband

- Number and types of community services available to students and families

- Number and types of resources reaching multilingual families in multiple languages

These data are of vital concern to the well-being of our students, families, and educational systems. Time and time again, we have read and heard how personal and school health, safety, and security are of utmost importance. Let's take a moment to center our attention on students' social-emotional well-being as a stepping-stone to full recovery of our schools and how reflective practice can help stakeholders accomplish it.

Reflect on and Inquire About Students' Social-Emotional Learning

During crises and times of despair, care and safety of all students, teachers, and school personnel take priority over assessment, period. The four-point plan set out in the social-emotional learning roadmap speaks to the role of data in supporting the healing process for districts and schools. It entails:

1. Taking time to cultivate and deepen relationships, building partnerships, and planning for social and emotional learning

2. Designing opportunities where educators can connect with and assist students (and their families)

3. Creating empathetic and equitable learning environments that promote all students' social and emotional development

4. Using data to share power, deepen relationships, and continuously support students, families, and staff (see Collaborative for Academic, Social, and Emotional Learning, 2021)

We urge educators of minoritized and multilingual communities to make a special effort to set aside grades and test scores as the only measures of success. Instead, we encourage all stakeholders—students, families, and educators—to be self-reflective and introspective. In particular, we invite multilingual learners to self-assess their social-emotional learning and take action by:

- Helping to set and pursuing learning goals in one or more multiple languages

- Identifying, understanding, and managing their emotions

- Strategizing on how to cope with disappointment and setbacks

- Asking about others and showing empathy

- Establishing and maintaining positive social relationships

- Figuring out how and when to compromise

- Becoming agents of their own learning

- Making responsible choices and decisions

ACTION 2: DETERMINE PRIORITIES IN ASSESSING IN MULTIPLE LANGUAGES

To take action, educational leadership has to have a firm sense of the scope of assessment, especially when more than one language is involved. Even though assessment for state accountability purposes may be on hold due to upheaval to the educational system, assessment is still central to school life. In fact, assessment may be of greater importance at district or school levels so that educators can gain a better sense of how to improve educational opportunities for students and families.

Local priorities most likely have shifted in the last several years, especially for assessment. In many districts and schools, the depth and breadth of the assessment process have expanded to accommodate growing numbers of multilingual learners and other minoritized students. Here are sets of assessment-related variables and related options as a precursor for taking action. Resource 7.2 converts the list to a multiple-choice survey for school or district use.

1. Languages of instruction and assessment (English, students' other languages/dialects, students' other languages and English) with consideration for adjusting time allocation for each language, if applicable

2. Types of assessment (everyday classroom, common, interim, annual)

3. Formats for assessment (online/digital, paper and pencil, multimodal)

4. Conditions for assessment (remote, in person, hybrid)

5. Levels of enacting assessment (classroom, grade-level/department, school, program, district, state)

6. Purposes for assessment (screening, determining growth of language proficiency or content-area achievement, accountability)

7. Assessment approaches and stakeholders—*as* (students), *for* (students and teachers), *of* (teachers and administrators, with input from students) learning

8. Timeline for assessment (weekly, monthly, quarterly, by semester)

9. Recording or storage of assessment results (grade books, e-portfolios, school/district portals)

Before taking next steps, you may wish to discuss these assessment-related variables and their impact on multilingual learners in your setting, their potential influence, and what actions you might take as a leadership team. This discussion also needs to address the changing context of school that has been brought on, in large part, by crises, including:

- Changes to conditions of schooling or learning environments (from face-to-face to hybrid to remote and back again)

- Changes to schedules (due to changes in conditions)

- Changes in faculty and their positions

- Changes in administration or leadership

- Changes in policies

- Changes in student demographics

A Rubik's cube, shown in Figure 7.2, serves as a metaphor for envisioning and mapping the interaction (literally or figuratively) of categories of assessment-related variables for multilingual learners. You might wish to consider which categories (the sides) and variables (the squares of the Rubik) to use in organizing assessment results. Then you might think about designing or revising a policy or an action plan based on your choices or configurations.

Engage in District- and Schoolwide Professional Learning on Assessment Literacy

Assessment in multiple languages is a complex undertaking, and educators must feel confident in undergoing the process. Professional learning is an entrée for unlocking the potential of equity-minded assessment (Montenegro & Jankowski, 2020). Through sustained school-/districtwide professional learning, educators come to recognize the enormous power and influence of language and culture in assessing multilingual learners. Assessment literacy involving multiple languages encompasses understanding the purposes, principles, practices, and procedures involved in the assessment process and how they apply to improving student learning and program effectiveness. We recommend that all stakeholders, including family members, become assessment literate to minimally comprehend the basics of data in one or more languages.

FIGURE 7.2 Using a Rubik's Cube to Envision Assessment for Multilingual Learners

ASSESSMENT IN MULTIPLE LANGUAGES

FIGURE 7.3 A Continuum of Opportunities for Educators to Become Assessment Literate

Occasional meeting with colleagues to discuss data and quickly take immediate next steps	Joint planning time for educators (and coaches) to analyze and interpret data and make short-term plans	Ongoing professional learning communities or networks to analyze data and take action based on evidence	School- or districtwide commitment to courses/long-term professional learning with coaching that leads to lasting change

Professional learning on assessment literacy for teachers and other school leaders can take on many forms; in general, it can be presented along a continuum, such as the one shown in Figure 7.3. At the far right-hand end of the continuum is a carefully planned and sustained series of workshops coupled with coaching (Honigsfeld & Dove, 2015; Zacarian et al., 2021). In the middle range are cooperating teachers who have dedicated time to co-plan, co-assess, and exchange information with their students; participate in ongoing professional learning communities with colleagues; and/or network with administrators on a regular basis. At the beginning of the continuum are teachers with shared students who grab a couple of minutes whenever they have a chance, such as at lunch or before school, to exchange assessment-related information.

For schools and districts, a combination of planning, coaching, and engaging in professional learning could prove effective for all educators. Here are some suggestions for educators to become more knowledgeable about assessment data that revolve around multilingual learners:

- Plan and present a series of workshops or a course on assessment literacy using real data in one or more languages

- Have teachers share strategies for assessment *as*, *for*, and *of* learning at faculty meetings

- Participate in brainstorming projects for units of learning, including common assessment *of* learning options, at grade-level or departmental meetings

- Organize "lunch and learn" sessions to discuss data from various sources

- Observe or mentor individual teachers about using data for decision making

- Graph and manipulate data from annual or interim score reports or from common assessment

- Invite grade-level or content teachers to shadow multilingual learners (Soto, 2012)

- Encourage coaches to demonstrate assessment strategies for multilingual learners in one or more languages followed by a debrief

Relax and Reflect: How might you be proactive regarding professional learning opportunities on assessment literacy that lead to taking action based on data?

The turmoil of recent crises has interrupted professional learning in schools and districts. Teachers and other school leaders have had little to no time to indulge in reflective practice. Use the suggestions listed earlier to begin centering professional learning on assessment literacy, especially for multilingual learners. What might you do to begin renewing professional learning opportunities around the assessment cycle and evaluating local assessment data in one or more languages?

ACTION 3: CHALLENGE THE STATUS QUO IN ASSESSMENT: TAKE THE MULTILINGUAL TURN

Another area ripe for change in assessment is abandoning the idea that monolingual constructs can apply to multilingual contexts and embracing the notion that assessment in multiple languages provides minimally two sources of data and two perspectives. In fact, there have been calls for language testing and assessment to accept multilingual approaches to (1) better reflect the linguistic repertoires of multilingual students and (2) contest the ongoing marginalization, discrimination, and racism that multilingual learners confront. These expanding orientations in content and language assessment by test developers and scholars have stimulated the multilingual turn and illuminated its visibility (Chalhoub-Deville, 2019; Schissel, Leung, & Chalhoub-Deville, 2019; Seed, 2020). As part of phase 5 of the assessment cycle in multiple languages, we urge educational leaders to take action by applying assessment results to the (re)formulation of multilingual assessment policy.

Large-scale assessment at a school, district, or state level, as in classroom assessment, should center on multilingual learners' use of language to make meaning and communicate that meaning to others. In other words, languaging should be viewed as a strength, and the test development process should be inclusive of what multilinguals can do with that asset. Adopting a multilingual perspective allows for taking a fuller account of local language practices and multilingual ways of being (Schissel et al., 2019).

Transform Assessment Practices

A prerequisite for transforming assessment practices across a district or school is reenvisioning educational leadership as change agents. These trailblazers must take on the responsibility for shifting language education ideologies, policies, and practices from a monolingual (or monoglossic) to a multilingual (or heteroglossic) orientation. In essence, educational leaders need to take a "multilingual turn" based on the understanding of language as a multilingual situated social practice (May, 2014; Meier, 2016). Research shows that effective school leaders of multilingual learners who are committed to this ideology:

- Seek ideological changes in adopting favorable multilingual approaches

- Cultivate and sustain a schoolwide ecology of multilingualism

- View bilingualism as a resource in curriculum, instruction, and assessment

- Prompt structural changes in programming and pedagogy

- Alter school leadership structures from hierarchical to collaborative

- Encourage translanguaging strategies that engage the entire linguistic repertoire of multilingual learners in flexible ways (Ascenzi-Moreno, Hesson, & Menken, 2016)

The Translanguaging Classroom (García, Johnson, & Seltzer, 2017) exemplifies transformative practices in bilingual classrooms that can be extended to schools and districts. It introduces three concepts—Stance, Design, and Shift—that are essential for framing translanguaging pedagogy, yet aptly apply to all multilingual educational settings. *Stance* refers to a commitment to bi/multilingual learners' linguistic and cultural identities as a human right and resource. *Design* encompasses establishing and sustaining links across home, school, and community. Finally, *Shift* entails the pivoting of positions that arise from (classroom) interactions. When thinking about assessment in multiple languages in the classroom and beyond, the paradigm shift that this book suggests exemplifies the multilingual turn.

ACTION 4: ASSESS MULTILINGUAL LEARNERS FROM A STRENGTHS-BASED LENS

As part of transforming assessment practices, we have discussed the ways to offset deficit labels that can negatively portray minoritized students (see Chapter 2). We have emphasized the importance of instilling and maintaining an assets-based mindset to the assessment process for all students throughout all phases of the cycle. We have yet to mention, however, how this "can do" spirit of instruction and assessment also affects multilingual learners with suspected disabilities or gifted and talented multilingual learners; we touch upon these important stakeholders here.

Apply an Assets-Based Philosophy to All Multilingual Learners

Under the Every Student Succeeds Act (ESSA) of 2015, qualification of English learners for special education services requires schools to make every effort to assess this population in English *and* their home language(s). While this is a requirement for ELs suspected of having a disability, there is not one for those multilingual learners deemed to be gifted and talented. Therefore, it would be a sound school- or districtwide policy and practice to periodically (as in common assessment) tap all multilingual learners' oral and written language in conjunction with their content-area achievement in multiple languages.

The same detrimental labels for minoritized students tend to be exacerbated for multilingual learners with potential disabilities, where quite often speaking an additional language is considered a barrier or interference. While assessment in multiple languages may be a common practice in schools or districts with formal bilingual programming, Hamayan, Marler, Sánchez-López, and Damico (2013) recommend that all multilingual learners with potential disabilities be minimally assessed in more than one language on an annual basis. Having information on multilingual learners' patterns of language use facilitates school connections with families in their home language(s) and strengthens their partnerships.

Inequity in assessment extends to multilingual learners and other minoritized students who might otherwise qualify for gifted and talented services. These students' inaccessibility to deserved educational opportunities can be attributed, in part, to standardized interim measures and psychological measures that fail to account for linguistic and cultural variation (Basterra, Trumbull, & Solano-Flores, 2011). Considerations for "identifying" gifted and talented multilingual learners should be inclusive of multiple data sources from various stakeholders including evidence of:

- Being inventive with translanguaging

- Demonstrating creativity in one or more languages

- Having strong critical thinking in one or more languages

- Expressing complex ideas through visual arts

- Tackling challenges with enthusiasm

- Making deep connections between the known and unknown

- Possessing leadership qualities

- Engaging in self-initiated learning

- Representing ideas and concepts in multimodal ways

- Showing metalinguistic and metacultural insight

 Stop-Think-Act-React

Relax and Reflect: How might your school or district take action on behalf of multilingual learners who are potentially gifted and talented or have disabilities?

We have already cautioned against attaching labels to different subgroups of multilingual learners; this caveat extends to those who potentially qualify for gifted and talented services or students with intense needs. Although some parameters have been set by federal legislation for students with special needs, there is usually district flexibility in regard to identifying gifted and talented students. Do you think that the identification procedures are equitable in your district? What action might you take based on additional, more linguistically and culturally appropriate, evidence? How might you include use of multiple languages as part of the identification criteria?

ACTION 5: ENACT EFFECTIVE ASSESSMENT PRACTICES IN MULTIPLE LANGUAGES

The National Academies of Sciences, Engineering, and Medicine (2017) advocates for assessment in multiple languages. Specifically, NASEM asserts that accurate assessment of multilingual learners entails obtaining information on the students' language development and instructional demands in multiple languages. Further, this independent, evidence-based scientific body emphasizes the need to measure multilingual learners' academic literacy in the language(s) of school. While NASEM covers minimal requirements of federal and state assessment responsibilities under ESSA, we feel that it does not go far enough in terms of requiring multilingual assessment as part of the schooling of multilingual learners.

One of the lessons learned from the global pandemic is that educators must emphasize student-driven assessment as students are the center of our universe and the hope of our future. We must understand their inner thoughts and emotions along with their skills and competencies. With the continuous growth of the multilingual student population, we must consider the unique characteristics of these students as we (re)configure assessment, but more importantly, we must accept these students as assessment leaders in their own right (Berger, Rugen, & Woodfin, 2014). When we invite students to express themselves, we often can peek into their social-emotional development. As seen in this young child's self-portrait, COVID-19 has truly affected her identity as shown in her image and her view of the world.

▶ The self-portrait of a multilingual toddler during the pandemic of 2020

Exert Locus of Control Through Assessment *as,* *for,* and *of* Learning

Locus of control is a psychological concept that refers to how strongly people believe they can influence the situations and experiences that affect their lives. In education, locus of control typically refers to how students perceive their personal impact on their academic success or failure in school. As shown in Figure 7.4, we see locus of control as analogous to and an expression of assessment *as,* *for,* and *of* learning. Let's review. In assessment *as* learning, students gradually accrue decision-making power and take on actions that are within their control; in assessment *for* learning, students join with teachers to extend their circle of control, and in assessment *of* learning, there is generally an external locus of control outside that of students and teachers.

Students who have an internal locus of control tend to be motivated to learn and attribute their success to their own efforts and abilities. In fact, student engagement is deemed a critical driver for cultivating equitable school climates (Communities in Schools, 2020). Within the context of assessment in multiple languages, multilingual learners who possess an internal locus of control possess greater flexibility in language use, including confidence in their strategic use of translanguaging. Recent empirical research based on meta-analysis of 33 studies highlights the positive impact of student-initiated assessment or assessment *as* learning, where students exert an internal locus of control. Findings indicate that when students are active in their own learning and self-assess, they outperform those students who are subject to general formative strategies (Lee, Chung, Zhang, Abedi, & Warschauer, 2020).

We are familiar with the positive effects of assessment *for* learning, where teachers provide concrete actionable feedback to students, as there is a solid body of research on formative assessment, starting with the groundbreaking study by Black and Wiliam (1998). When an external locus of control is exerted, students believe that they do not have the power to govern their own actions. For example, annual standards-referenced tests (assessment *of* learning) are often anxiety producing as they are outside the control of students.

Let Multilingual Learners Take the Lead

An effective strategy that invites students to showcase their multilingualism is through student-led conferences. This collaboration, facilitated by teachers but

FIGURE 7.4 Locus of Control Applied to Assessment *as,* *for,* and *of* Learning

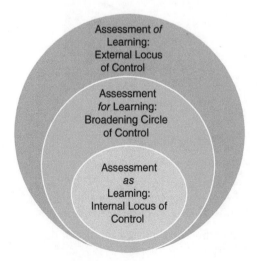

led by students, entails student reflection on their educational accomplishments in relation to their goals, assessment of their growth, and, based on feedback, the setting of new goals. Figure 7.5, replicated in Resource 7.3, is a planning sheet for a student-led conference that includes a family member and a teacher. Depending on the circumstances, the multilingual learner might take on the additional role of translator during the discussion.

FIGURE 7.5 A Planning Sheet for Student-Led Conferences

STUDENT-LED CONFERENCES WITH INPUT FROM A TEACHER AND A FAMILY MEMBER	
Student	*A Teacher and a Family Member*
My Learning Goals: (Introduces "I Can" statements or student-friendly standards)	*Teacher:* (Reviews learning expectations) *Family Member:* (Understands student expectations)
Evidence for Meeting My Goals: (Shows multimodal examples of work or a student portfolio along with criteria for success)	*Teacher:* (Discusses the match between expectations and evidence) *Family Member:* (Offers insight into what the student can do)
Next Steps I Plan to Take: (Indicates how learning goals have been met to help make new goals)	*Teacher:* (Guides presentation of further evidence) *Family Member:* (Describes linguistic and cultural student assets)
What I Want to Learn More About: (Reformulates learning goals)	*Teacher:* (Co-creates new or revises learning goals) *Family Member:* (Helps craft student goals from home or community resources)

 Stop-Think-Act-React

Relax and Reflect: How might the leadership in your setting take action on behalf of multilingual learners and their families?

How can school leaders support student-led conferences for bi/multilingual learners and their family members? How can teachers bolster multilingual learners' confidence in using multiple languages to show evidence of learning? How can teachers encourage family members to provide feedback using one or more languages to reinforce student learning?

Give Teachers Autonomy in Communities of Practice

Communities of practice enable teachers to gain a sense of belonging and camaraderie by connecting with colleagues to share information and knowledge (Wenger, 1998). Today, virtual communities of practice serve as meeting places for educators who wish to explore and expand their expertise around a shared interest or passion (Rock, 2020). Communities of practice can stimulate effective assessment practices.

Let's look at a community of practice around a school reform effort that focuses on the Collaborative Assessment Conference (Seidel, 1996), a teacher-centered process where educators collaborate in examining performance-based pieces of student work. Applicable to one or multiple languages, this seven-step process encourages teachers to look beyond what's on paper (or the screen) to gain insights into the student. It is outlined in the following (adapted from Blythe, Allen, & Powell, 1999):

1. *Getting started.* A group of educators chooses a facilitator who shares the selected student work without giving any background information. The participants read or observe the work in silence, making notes.

2. *Describing the work.* The facilitator asks, "What do you see?" Participants respond without making judgments about the quality of the work or their personal preferences. If judgments emerge, the facilitator asks participants to describe the evidence on which the judgment is based.

3. *Raising questions.* The facilitator asks, "What questions does this work raise for you?" Group members ask questions about the work, the student, and the circumstances of the work.

4. *Proposing images of the student.* The facilitator asks, "What do you think the student is thinking, feeling, or doing while engaged in learning?" Participants offer ideas.

5. *Hearing from the presenting teacher.* The presenting teacher provides one perspective, responds to the questions raised, and adds any other relevant information or insights.

6. *Discussing implications for teaching and learning.* The group discusses thoughts about their own teaching, the student's learning, and ways to support this student.

7. *Reflecting on the conference.* The group reflects on the assessment conference experience.

Determine Program Effectiveness Based on Assessment in Multiple Languages

We have suggested how schools and districts might develop assessment-capable multilingual learners within linguistically and culturally sustainable systems. Now we turn our attention to district and school leaders who are ultimately answerable and accountable for the success of language education programs. As we center our attention on assessment in multiple languages, we address data that are generated from dual language programs. At the same time, we recognize there are other viable means of educating and assessing multilingual learners in multiple languages.

Today the number of dual language education programs, where instruction occurs in two languages, continues to grow exponentially. The latest data from the 2016–2017 school year indicate that dual language education is alive and well in 35 states with a reported 2,000 programs (Mitchell, 2020). There is tremendous variability among programs, the qualification of teachers, the amount of language allocation, and student demographics; however, effective dual language programs all tend to be unified in their mission, vision, standards, and assessment measures (Lindholm-Leary, 2012).

Consider Principles for Assessment in Dual Language Contexts

Two decades ago, Cloud, Genesee, and Hamayan (2001) proposed four qualities of effective assessment in dual language and developmental bilingual education that, to this day, remain pertinent. Although these assessment principles are linked to classrooms, they readily extend to schools and districts. In essence, effective assessment for dual language and developmental bilingual education is:

- Directly linked to improving teaching and learning instructional activities through learning targets (or, for schools and districts, assessment is tied to curriculum and program goals)

- Considerate of multilingual learners' experiences that are based on their assets and interests

- Comprehensive, where instruction allows multilingual learners to provide evidence of learning in multiple languages

- Developmentally, linguistically, and culturally appropriate where multilingual learners see themselves in what they do and relate to what is asked of them

Intended for district leadership, *The Guiding Principles for Dual Language Education* (Howard et al., 2018) is a handbook that examines the effectiveness in enacting major programmatic components in two languages. The program evaluation strand addresses assessment principles for dual language education programs that include:

1. Creating and maintaining an infrastructure that supports an assessment and accountability process

2. Aligning student assessment with program goals and state content and language standards with results used to inform instruction

3. Using multiple measures in both languages of instruction

4. Systematically measuring and reporting student progress toward program goals

5. Communicating program outcomes with appropriate stakeholders

These principles work in conjunction with programmatic norms described as Key Points, namely:

Key Point A: The program systematically collects and analyzes data to determine whether academic, linguistic, and sociocultural goals have been met.

Key Point B: The program engages in ongoing evaluation.

Key Point C: Assessment data are integrated into planning related to ongoing program improvement.

Key Point D: The program systematically collects demographic data from program participants that allow for disaggregated data analysis in order to effectively monitor and serve different student subgroups.

Key Point E: Assessment is consistently conducted in the two languages of the program. (Howard et al., 2016, pp. 78–88)

Outlined in a set of rating scales, these principles and norms help schools and districts evaluate the impact of dual language program components on multilingual learners' growth and achievement. The data from the evaluation offer useful feedback to school leaders for local accountability and ongoing program improvement.

 Stop-Think-Act-React

Relax and Reflect: How might school or district leadership take action based on evaluation of assessment data in dual language programs?

How do the assessment principles outlined earlier apply to your language education program? How might your school or district respond to them? If you were to assign a rating to each Key Point, from 1 (*not at all*) to 4 (*fully*), how would your dual language program fare? What favorable actions might you take to improve assessment in multiple languages?

ACTION 6: USE ASSESSMENT DATA IN MULTIPLE LANGUAGES TO LEVERAGE SYSTEMIC CHANGE

Assessment that drives systemic change at the school, district, or state level must have proven reliability and validity. Yet measures for accountability purposes, namely standardized achievement tests, have questionable psychometric properties for English learners (NASEM, 2017, among many others). The reason for this incongruence is that large-scale assessment has historically been built from a monoglossic or monolingual perspective whose goal has been student performance in English. These forms of assessment simply do not align with, nor do they represent, the linguistic and cultural identities of multilingual learners or the instructional grounding of dual language education.

Evoke Systemic Change Through Assessment

If we are to instill change, specifically if we are to embrace multiple languages as part of an assessment paradigm, the policies, practices, and information generated at the classroom level must contribute to that of the school as a whole.

ASSESSMENT IN MULTIPLE LANGUAGES

The school, in turn, must share assessment data with the district, and ultimately, the district must share such data with the state. When data from one level readily dovetail with data from the next one, whether from the top down or the bottom up, we can say that there is an aligned assessment system. In Figure 7.6, we present a series of nested circles that show how assessment data can infiltrate across an accountability system.

FIGURE 7.6 Viewing Educational Systems From Classrooms to State Education Agencies or From the Inverse

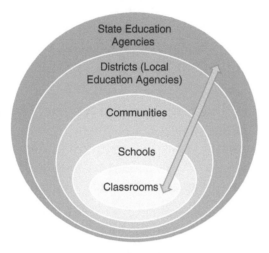

SOURCE: Adopted from Zacarian, Calderón, & Gottlieb (2021).

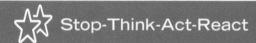

⭐ Stop-Think-Act-React

Relax and Reflect: How aligned is your assessment system?

Think about assessment in multiple languages in your setting, starting at the classroom or school level. How far up the educational ladder is the system aligned? For example, is there acceptance of assessment in multiple languages at the district and state levels? What action might you take to help ensure an aligned assessment system for multilingual learners in multiple languages?

Envision Systemic Change for Multilingual Learners

As opposed to an accountability system, where assessment data often drive educational decisions, let's take some time to think about a learning system with multilingual learners in the center. Cleave (2020), in her research across Australia, the United States, and Canada, uncovers a constellation of themes that underpins current shifts in the education of multilingual learners. Together the five themes, described as follows, constitute a vibrant and equitable learning system. As you read a summary of these critical elements, think about the ways in which you might seamlessly integrate assessment in multiple languages in your setting; use Resource 7.4 to jot down your ideas.

A Learning System Centering on Multilingual Learners

1. **Learner voice:** education systems that engage multilingual learners and their families directly in policy making are more likely to have an equitable approach to language education and diversity, with policies that are conceived, designed and owned by diverse, multilingual communities themselves.

2. **Teacher autonomy:** teacher training programmes that build on teachers' social commitment to making a difference in children's lives, and that encourage autonomy, collaboration, flexibility and innovation when applying language education pedagogies in practice, have created communities of practitioners that value multilingualism in the classroom as a learning resource and as an asset.

3. **Diverse and shared leadership:** leadership strategies that employ principles of shared and distributed leadership, and that actively seek to address institutional racism and structural barriers to broader leadership within the education system, are pro-actively building school leadership teams that are more representative of the diverse, multilingual communities they serve.

4. **Asset-based approaches:** education policies and programmes that actively promote multilingualism as an asset and apply a "can do" philosophy to learner assessment are creating a tangible shift in that way that languages are perceived and valued, moving away from a monolingual, "English only" mindset to a more flexible approach which encourages linguistic diversity in the classroom.

5. **Social justice and equity in education:** education systems that view language education through the lens of social justice, and that promote equitable access to the curriculum in English through clear policies, guidance and assessment practices, demonstrate more comprehensive support and better outcomes for learners.

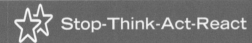 Stop-Think-Act-React

Relax and Reflect: How might you envision systemic change for assessment in multiple languages?

Throughout the book, we have touched on these five research-informed themes that contribute to systemic change for multilingual education: (1) learner voice, (2) teacher autonomy, (3) diverse and shared leadership, (4) assets-based approaches, and (5) social justice and equity in education (Cleave, 2020. p. 10). Which one most resonates with you? Where might you begin changing current assessment practices in multiple languages? How might you create a metaphor for these themes, such as their representation by the Hawaiian plumeria with its five petals emanating from a vivid center, to present to others?

Photo by Lukas Stoermer on Unsplash, https://unsplash.com/photos/2B28K1DksyM

▶ Multilingual learners at the center of a multifaceted learning system

Instill Systemic Equity and Excellence for All Students

Our educational systems have been tremendously disrupted by the coronavirus and racial injustice; in fact, the pandemic has ruthlessly brought systemic inequities more into light. Societal inequities have been exposed, and those impacting marginalized students have been exacerbated. Educational equity remains elusive, as it has been for the last 50 years. "As a country, we must enter a new era. No society can thrive in a technological, knowledge-based economy by starving large segments of its population of learning. Instead, we must provide all of our children with what should be an unquestioned entitlement—a rich and inalienable right to learn" (Darling-Hammond, 2018).

Given the circumstances of today's educational environment, it seems appropriate to shift our attention to assessment inputs—individual learning and development opportunities—rather than rely on standardized outcomes—the results of high-stakes testing—as the basis for systemic equity. Said another way, we should concentrate our assessment efforts on promoting equity, not equality, for all students. Assessment should provide educators insight into who our students are and what they can do rather than serve as a tool for sorting them (Milner, 2018).

Equity-centered assessment entails educators taking the following actions on behalf of their multilingual learners:

1. Identify and be sensitive to personal biases; ask probing reflective questions throughout the assessment process

2. Use multiple sources of evidence that reflect multilingual learners and their languages, cultures, and experiences

3. Include student perspectives and insights from assessment in action planning

4. Make assessment results transparent to stakeholders who are affected and together consider decisions, their consequences, and subsequent policies

5. Ensure that data are meaningful in all circumstances, even their application to subgroups, as part of large-scale testing requirements

6. Make evidence-based changes that address context-specific issues of equity (Montenegro & Jankowski, 2020)

If we are to impart systemic equity throughout the educational arena, it must be grounded in bi/multilingual learners' languages and cultures as a jumpstart for empowering individual students, their families, and teachers. This means that linguistic and cultural sustainability must be the mantra of school systems, because without an ongoing commitment to multilingualism and multiculturalism, assessment in multiple languages will be operating in a vacuum. Simply stated, the words of Blankstein and Newsome (2021) should resonate with every educator—that is, "inequity is not an option."

Apply Assessment *as*, *for*, and *of* Learning in Your Setting

In dismantling inequity and evoking educational change, we invite you to balance assessment approaches—assessment *as*, *for*, and *of* learning—across levels of enactment from the classroom to the boardroom. Infused into every phase of the assessment cycle, as a summary Figure 7.7 offers some tips for embedding these assessment approaches into school- and district-level decision making throughout the assessment cycle.

FIGURE 7.7 Taking Action: Applying Assessment *as*, *for*, and *of* Learning Throughout the Five-Phase Assessment Cycle

PHASE	ASSESSMENT *AS* LEARNING	ASSESSMENT *FOR* LEARNING	ASSESSMENT *OF* LEARNING
1. Planning Assessment	Think about how your multilingual learners might engage in the assessment process using their full linguistic repertoires	Think about how to integrate language and content in common assessment in multiple languages	Think about student use of multiple languages in projects, products, and performances
2. Collecting and Organizing Information	Promote student language choice, voice, and agency	Design a language policy and decide on evidence for learning with students in one or more languages	Pair evidence of learning at the close of a unit with the language(s) of instruction
3. Interpreting Information and Providing Feedback	Create a context for interpretation and feedback by overlaying students' linguistic and cultural perspectives onto data	Match student performance against mutually agreed-upon success criteria in one or more languages	Create a composite of student performance across measures for school or district accountability

4. Evaluating and Reporting Information	Leverage student input in evaluation-related decisions (e.g., grading)	Share assessment information with students (e.g., through conferencing and feedback)	Revisit programmatic goals (e.g., dual language) in light of data with educators and the community
5. Taking action based on assessment results	Use data to illustrate student benefits of multiple language use inside and outside of school	Use data to advocate for assessment in multiple languages and to evoke systemic change	Use data in multiple languages to strengthen the connection among schools, homes, and communities

TAKING ACTION: LESSONS LEARNED FROM CRISES

One of the more positive educational outcomes of the COVID-19 pandemic is that it has blurred boundaries among school, home, and community. The extended period of having students engage in distance or hybrid learning has been an opportune time for educators to try out multilingual ideologies with their multilingual learners and their families. Online schooling has provided a new space for educators to encourage, support, and maintain neglected multilingual practices. It has presented an opportunity for individuals, teachers, and family members to work together in developing positive multilingual dispositions toward learning.

The potential of technology to augment face-to-face interaction in school has post-pandemic staying power. The crises of this decade have hopefully brought about increased access and appreciation for languages and cultures through greater connections, collaboration, communication, and coordination of services. Here are some creative ways to listen to the voices of those historically silenced to ensure equitable assessment for multilingual learners:

- Increase student (and teacher) comfort with online instruction and assessment in one or more languages in synchronous and asynchronous formats

- Use a range of technology as a multimodal resource for students to communicate and provide feedback by fostering and maintaining teacher–student and student–student relationships

- Connect schools and communities by offering a parent university, supporting student e-learning, and extending virtual professional learning to families and service organizations

- Conduct one-on-one video conferences, encourage in-room student collaboration, and spur dialog among students and teachers

- Engage in outside-the-box thinking for assessment *as*, *for*, and *of* learning in multiple languages

- Recruit bilingual staff, including community liaisons, paraprofessionals, coaches, language specialists, and content teachers, and provide online mentoring and support for co-planning, co-instructing, and co-assessing in multiple languages

FACING THE ISSUE: CONSIDER CRISES AS EYE-OPENING OPPORTUNITIES FOR MULTILINGUAL LEARNERS

The path of destruction instigated by the crises of 2020 will be forever etched in our memories as it has lasting and profound effects on every aspect of society, especially for multilingual learners and their families. One positive outcome is that we have witnessed how our students' languages and cultures have proven to be a vehicle of belonging. This book has been devoted to instilling educational change, specifically by examining and advocating for assessing multilingual learners in multiple languages. In some small way, by prompting educators to embrace multilingualism and multiculturalism through assessment, we hope to have expanded multilingual learners' opportunities to build multifaceted identities and more fully engage in learning. Here is a final set of questions to contemplate:

For School Leaders

➢ What actions might you take to continuously improve educational access and opportunity for multilingual learners in your assessment practices?

➢ How does assessment in multiple languages help provide a rationale for accelerated growth for all multilingual learners post-crises?

➢ How might educational stakeholders, from students to teachers, coaches, families, and community members, change the vision of local accountability through assessment *as*, *for*, and *of* learning?

For District Leaders

➢ How might you systemically infuse linguistic and cultural sustainability through comprehensive assessment reform?

➢ How might you convince stakeholders to take the multilingual turn when it comes to assessment of K–12 multilingual learners?

➢ How might you coalesce various stakeholders, including policy makers, educators, and community groups, in formulating a plan for the district or another educational entity based on the six actions suggested in the chapter?

RESOLVING THE DILEMMA: PROVIDE EQUITABLE EDUCATIONAL OPPORTUNITIES TO ALL MINORITIZED STUDENTS, INCLUDING ASSESSMENT IN MULTIPLE LANGUAGES FOR MULTILINGUAL LEARNERS!

Achieving linguistic and cultural equity begins with student access to rigorous and effective instruction, an inherent right of multilingual learners. Having instruction in multiple languages is a precursor to building an equitable assessment framework that is culturally and linguistically sustainable. A retooling of schools' and districts' comprehensive assessment systems begins with assessment

► A poster displayed in Berlin, Germany (2018)

tools that are more aligned with instruction and geared to and representative of the languages and cultures of multilingual learners.

The pandemic has challenged the boundaries between school and home; in a positive way, it has offered educators time and opportunity to shift from monolingual to multilingual ideologies and mindsets. As a result of this shift, online schooling has provided a new space for supporting, maintaining, and developing the often-neglected languages of our multilingual learners at school. In addition, educators and family members have worked together to develop positive cross-linguistic dispositions to enhance and support multilingual learners' languages and cultures.

A multilingual turn in educational policy and practice, as suggested by María Jiménez in the opening vignette, has helped foster the unification of her community, school, and classrooms through language. As we disentangle ourselves from the grips of a global health crisis and racial unrest, let's assume a more positive outlook and opportune time rather than one of loss. As exemplified by María's leadership, let's continue to coalesce our efforts to work together for the good of our students and families.

Throughout this book, we have shown how assessment (especially when multiple languages are involved) is part of an ecosystem of learning (Jones & Saville,

2016). After all, "Assessment is assessment. Any assessment can be used formatively or summatively. In other words, there's nothing magical in the tool itself; it's what you do with it" (Fisher, Frey, & Hattie, 2021, p. 148). We agree that there is a fuzzy distinction between what is called formative assessment and what is called summative assessment (hence assessment *as*, *for*, and *of* learning); more important is that information from assessment must be useful and actionable. Let's remember, for multilingual learners, assessment, as instruction, is much more meaningful when it is in multiple languages as it then becomes a window into their world.

Since its birth, the United States, like many other countries, has been continuously infused with the energy of immigrants and refugees from around the world. Alongside these bi/multilingual newcomers are other multilingual learners who have been born and raised here. As we enter a novel time in our educational history, let's make multilingual learners the centerpiece of comprehensive reform efforts and assessment in multiple languages the means of leveraging their linguistic, cultural, historical, and experiential strengths and resources.

Resources for School and District Leaders

RESOURCE 7.1
Taking Action Based on Assessment Results in Multiple Languages

Reread the section that describes each action. Then jot down some ideas of how your school or district might respond on behalf of its multilingual learners.

ACTION	OUR RESPONSE
1. Engage in Reflective Practice and Inquiry	
2. Determine Priorities in Assessing in Multiple Languages	
3. Challenge the Status Quo in Assessment	
4. Assess Multilingual Learners From a Strengths-Based Lens	
5. Enact Effective Assessment Practices in Multiple Languages	
6. Use Assessment Data in Multiple Languages to Leverage Systemic Change	

online resources 🔖 Available for download at **resources.corwin.com/ assessingMLLs-LeadersEdition**

RESOURCE 7.2
Determining Priorities in Assessing in Multiple Languages

With a leadership team, determine your priorities from the following sets of assessment-related variables and related options. These initial decisions provide the context for taking action.

1. What are the language(s) of instruction?

    - English

    - English and multilingual learners' other languages

    - Languages other than English

2. Which types of assessment prevail in your school/ district?

    - Everyday classroom

    - Common

    - Interim

    - Annual

3. What are the primary formats for assessment?

    - Online

    - Paper and pencil

    - Multimodal

4. What are most prevalent conditions for assessment?

    - Remote

    - In person

    - Hybrid

5. Which levels are emphasized in enacting assessment?

    - Classroom

    - Grade-level/department

    - School

    - Program

    - District

    - State

6. What are the purposes for assessment and how do they match to different measures?

   ○ Screening

   ○ Determine growth in language proficiency and content-area achievement

   ○ Accountability

7. Which approaches are used for assessment?

   ○ Assessment *as* learning (students)

   ○ Assessment *for* learning (students and teachers)

   ○ Assessment *of* learning (teachers and administrators, with input from students)

8. What is the timeline for assessment?

   ○ Weekly

   ○ Monthly

   ○ Quarterly

   ○ By semester

9. Where do teachers record or store assessment results?

   ○ Grade books

   ○ E-portfolios

   ○ School/district portals

 Available for download at **resources.corwin.com/ assessingMLLs-LeadersEdition**

RESOURCE 7.3

Planning a Student-Led Conference Supported by a Teacher and a Family Member

STUDENT	INPUT FROM A TEACHER AND A FAMILY MEMBER
My Learning Goals:	*Teacher:* *Family Member:*
Evidence for Meeting My Goals:	*Teacher:* *Family Member:*
Next Steps I Plan to Take:	*Teacher:* *Family Member:*
What I Want to Learn More About:	*Teacher:* *Family Member:*

RESOURCE 7.4
A Learning System Centering on Multilingual Learners

Reread the components of a learning system that centers on multilingual learners. Then think about an action you might take to optimize the system for your school or district that involves assessment in multiple languages.

CRITICAL ELEMENT OF A LEARNING SYSTEM	APPLICATION TO ASSESSMENT IN MULTIPLE LANGUAGES
1. Learner Voice	
2. Teacher Autonomy	
3. Diverse and Shared Leadership	
4. Asset-Based Approaches	
5. Social Justice and Equity in Education	

Glossary

An Addendum

This glossary is rather unique in that it characterizes the range of terms being used across the fields of education, linguistics, and education rather than the prevalence of a single set of terms that represents one philosophical or theoretical orientation. While the presence of all these terms might create a tension between camps, it is a realistic portrayal of what school and district leaders face. As we undergo a paradigm shift, it would seem remiss not to acknowledge terms that are still in use by these connected communities. Much of the variability of terminology related to multilingual learners and their associated educational programs is found in Chapter 1, although some is sprinkled throughout the book, and a couple of terms are not mentioned at all.

Starting with Chapter 2 and thereafter, we enter the world of bi/multilingualism and multiculturalism. This "multilingual turn" moves away from deficit thinking and labeling to a more assets-based philosophy and stance that are couched in sociocultural theory. This shift toward empowering multilingual learners and their teachers, accentuating students' strengths and giving them agency, and focusing on student-centered assessment practices prevails throughout the remaining pages.

We offer this glossary so that school and district leaders can join forces with other educators in rejecting the negativity that still lingers and taking a more positive stance that promotes multilingualism and advocacy for multilingual learners and their families. As is typical for glossaries, the following words are presented in alphabetical order. Over the course of dissecting the book, however, leadership teams might think about forming some natural categories from the following words and phrases as a means of forming or reinforcing their own educational philosophy, principles, policies, and practices toward assessment in multiple languages.

Academic content standards: the skills and knowledge descriptive of student expectations in school, generally for each grade, such as English language arts, mathematics, and literacy in history/social studies, science, and technical subjects, equated with the generation of state disciplinary standards post 2010

Accountability: a system that holds educational stakeholders responsible for the performance of students, teachers, programs, schools, or districts

Achievement testing: the measurement of subject-area knowledge and skills of students (per ESSA, in language arts/reading, mathematics, and science)

Action research: a reflective process involving inquiry and discussion of pressing issues experienced in classrooms or schools as a means for instilling change and improvement in everyday policies or practices

Additive bilingualism: when multilingual learners' languages continue to develop and are maintained; when there are opportunities for students to grow and use both languages inside and outside of school

Analytic rubric: usually in the form of a matrix, one in which a construct, such as speaking or writing, or a project is defined by multiple dimensions, traits, or criteria and descriptive levels of performance

Anchors: examples of student work that best represent each score point or criterion on a rubric to establish reliability of a task or project

Assessment: the gathering of information from multiple sources over time that, when analyzed, interpreted, and reported, communicates student evidence of learning in relation to standards, targets, or goals

Assessment *as* learning: an approach in which students are agents of their own learning shown through interaction with peers and self-reflection of personal goals in relation to specified criteria for success

Assessment *for* learning: an approach in which teachers along with students plan and use evidence that is internal to their classroom to provide descriptive criterion-referenced feedback to inform teaching and learning

Assessment literacy: understanding why and how to assess what students know and can do, interpret the results, and make decisions that enhance student learning or program effectiveness

Assessment *of* learning: (1) an approach in which school leaders and administrators use data external to the classroom, such as from high-stakes tests, to report on students' language growth and achievement and (2) an approach in which teachers, along with students, design end-of-unit products, performances, and projects along with criteria for success

Assets-based orientation: a strengths-based mindset where multilingual learners' languages, cultures, and resources are viewed in a positive light

Balanced bilinguals: persons who have similar levels of proficiencies in two languages for a given context

Bias: in education circles, the manner in which curricula, materials, and assessments are designed, implemented, or interpreted that advantages (or privileges) some students

Bilinguals: persons who generally have interpretative (listening and reading) and productive (speaking and writing) skills in two languages

Bi/multilingual learners: a way to depict bilingualism and multilingualism as a resource in individuals

Common assessment: mutually agreed-upon tasks or projects (ideally by teachers and students) that are embedded in instruction along with uniform procedures for collecting, analyzing, and interpreting information across multiple classrooms; may also refer to identical prompts (and scoring criteria) administered and applied to specific grade levels

Construct irrelevance: factors that influence test scores that are not related to the construct being measured (e.g., the impact of a student's English language proficiency on a content test)

Content and language integrated learning (CLIL): generally referred to as a program for English as an additional language for students outside the United States, a seamless fusion of language and content where educators are aware how both contribute equally to teaching and learning

Criterion-referenced assessment: a type of measure or test that is based on and reported by established criteria, such as standards, rather than ranking the performance of students

Cross-cultural considerations: the application of cultural assumptions from one language and culture to another one by multilingual learners

Cross-linguistic considerations: the application of linguistic features from one language to a related one by multilinguals (e.g., cognates)

Curriculum design: a way of organizing learning experiences (through themes/units) that are relevant, meaningful, and inclusive of students and their resources

Deficit-based orientation: a negative mindset, often referred to as a medical model, where multilingual learners' languages, cultures, and resources are viewed as barriers to their educational success

Descriptive feedback: a formative assessment strategy whereby students gain understanding of their performance and actions to take in relation to learning targets or criteria for success

Digital literacy: making meaning by navigating, collecting, and evaluating information using a range of technologies, including computers, the internet, educational software, and cell phones

Distributed leadership: a practice generated by the interactions of leaders and other educators that is situation specific or that is shared among a team of individuals around a common mission to spark and sustain a schoolwide culture of learning

Dual language education programs: an enrichment or additive educational model in which multilingual learners learn in English and a partner language for minimally half a day generally through the elementary school grades

Dual language learners: multilingual learners who are participating in dual language education programs in Grades K–8 or any and all multilingual learners participating in early-years education during their preK years

Dynamic bilingualism: multiple language interactions and other linguistic interrelationships among multilingual speakers, including the use of translanguaging

Elite bilinguals: language learners participating in immersion or dual language programs usually from upwardly mobile, highly educated, higher-socioeconomic-status families where English is the sole language at home

Emergent (or emerging) bilinguals: language learners who have the potential of becoming knowledgeable in two languages

English as an additional language (EAL) learners: a term that often refers to English learners outside the United States whose English language development is instructionally supported through international EAL programs

English as a second language (ESL) programs: an instructional model whereby English learners' language instruction is supported and differentiated to promote their English language development

English (or language X) dominant: the supposition or generalization that a person has greater knowledge and use of one language over another rather than examining the person's language use as a function of the topic, audience, and context

English language development (ELD) programs: systematic support (at times with use of multiple languages) to maximize English language learning for English learners in school

English Language Development Standards: grade-level cluster expectations that describe what English learners are to do with language as part of multimodal communication

English (language) learners (ELs): the legal term for a heterogeneous group of bi/multilingual learners who are exposed to multiple languages and cultures, have not reached academic parity with their proficient English peers in English, and, through assessment, qualify for language support services

English learners with disabilities: multilingual learners who have been dually identified, qualifying for language support (including in more than one language) and have an individualized education program (IEP)

Every Student Succeeds Act (ESSA): the U.S. Department of Education's 2015 reauthorization of the Elementary and Secondary Education Act that requires states or consortia to have content standards, minimally in reading/language arts, mathematics, and science, with corresponding English language proficiency/development standards that are aligned to annual state testing of language proficiency in Grades K–12 and achievement in Grades 3–8 and once in high school

Expressive (productive) language: a mode of communication associated with language use—namely, speaking, writing, and illustrating

Feedback: timely descriptive, concrete, actionable information about the performance of students or teachers with the goal to inform teaching and learning

"First" language (L1): sometimes referred to as "native language" or mother tongue, often considered the initial language a person acquires or is exposed to from birth; however, the term does not aptly apply to the many youngsters born in the United States who are developing two or more languages and dialects simultaneously

"Foreign" languages: often referred to as "world" languages, typically the study of a language as a subject area in school

Formative assessment practices/purposes (or assessment as and for learning): providing timely, descriptive, and relevant feedback to students related to their progress toward meeting learning targets or objectives; the gathering of information by teachers during instructional activities to inform teaching and learning

Gifted and talented English learners: dually identified multilingual learners whose assessment of their cognitive abilities in combination with achievement testing and other criteria yield exceptional results

Grading: evaluating/rating the work of students, often referenced to standards, criteria for success, or learning goals

Heritage language learners: students who come from home backgrounds with connections to multiple languages and cultures although the students themselves may not be proficient in a language other than English

Heteroglossic language ideology: one that embraces multilingual learners' full linguistic repertoire and welcomes the many contexts of multiple language use

High-stakes testing: measures that have psychometrically sound properties, but often with (negative) consequences for individual test takers, such as grade retention, or repercussions for teachers and schools

Holistic rubrics: single scales where all criteria of a specified level are considered together when interpreting student work and the rater/teacher/student assigns a single score based on an overall judgment

Improving America's Schools Act (IASA): the U.S. Department of Education's 1994 reauthorization of the Elementary and Secondary Education Act whereby states were first required to develop content standards, minimally in reading/language arts and mathematics, aligned with annual achievement testing in Grades 3–8 and once in high school

Individualized education program (IEP): a legal contract between educators and family members that spells out the school's responsibility in ensuring that all students with special needs receive the maximum amount of accessibility and accommodations permitted under federal law

Individuals with Disabilities Education Improvement Act (IDEA): federal legislation that protects and advances the rights of students with intense learning needs, including bi/multilingual learners with those needs

Integrated goals for learning: combining content and language targets to describe multilingual learners' grade-level learning expectations

Interim assessments: large-scale standardized tests, generally mandated by a district, that teachers administer periodically during a school year to determine where students are in their achievement (generally in reading and mathematics) or language development and to project results on their annual assessments

Interpretive (receptive) language: a mode of communication associated with the processing of language—namely, listening, reading, and viewing

Intersectionality: in education of multilingual learners, generally referred to as the crossover among language, culture, race, and economics

"Intervention" programs: instructional programs that generally focus on bolstering subject-area student performance, such as in reading or math; their appropriacy for English language development is questionable

Language development/proficiency standards: language expectations for multilingual learners marked by grade or grade-level cluster proficiency-level descriptors

Language minority students: those who do not belong to a region's or nation's majority racial or ethnic group; also referred to as minoritized students

Language proficiency testing: demonstration of an English learner's competence in processing (through listening and reading) and using (through speaking, representing, and writing) language at a point in time, such as on an annual basis

Languaging: the use of language to mediate cognitively complex acts; "the process of making meaning and shaping knowledge and experience through language" (Swain, 2006)

Large-scale assessment: use of the identical procedures for collecting, analyzing, and reporting results across grade levels, departments, programs, schools, or districts

Learning goals: decisions about student learning, thinking, and engagement, mutually agreed upon by students and teachers, usually for individual units, that provide long-term pathways to academic success

Learning targets: decisions for student learning, thinking, and engagement, crafted by students and teachers for individual lessons, that provide short-term pathways to academic success

Limited English proficient (LEP) students: a pejorative term, referenced in former Elementary and Secondary Education Act legislation, for individuals not born in the United States or whose "native" language is one other than English

Linguicism: discrimination based on language or dialect; linguistic racism

Linguistic and cultural sustainability: the preservation of languages, literacies, and other cultural practices of students and communities in classrooms and schools

Linguistic equity: the respect for, value of, and fairness of treatment of languages, including their varieties and dialects

Linguistically and culturally diverse students: an umbrella term that denotes individuals who come from home environments where there is a presence of languages and cultures other than English

Locus of control: a psychological concept that refers to how strongly people believe they can regulate the situations and experiences that affect their lives

Long-term English learners (LTELs): multilingual learners who are most likely in middle and high schools, having attended school for more than six years without attaining a threshold of academic language proficiency; they generally are transnational students who move back and forth between the United States and their family's country of origin or have received inconsistent schooling in the United States

Maintenance/late exit/developmental bilingual programs: a developmental educational model whereby English learners receive instruction in English and their partner languages for an extended period of time (generally up to six years) with the goals of bilingualism, biliteracy, and achievement in English

Metacognitive awareness: regulating, reflecting, and expressing one's own thoughts

Metacultural awareness: multilingual learners' sensitivity to and knowledge of their own culture(s) and norms in relation to other cultures

Metalinguistic awareness: understanding and expressing the nuances and uses of language, including the process of reflecting on contrasting features and forms of multiple languages

Minoritized students: those who are considered marginalized

Monoglossic language ideology: one that ignores the presence and contexts of multiple language use by multilingual learners and only sees language through a monolingual lens, which is generally English

Multilingual education: a process of comprehensive school reform within a sociocultural context that at its core is a critical pedagogy inclusive of multilingual learners and social justice

Multilingual learners: an assets-based term that describes a wide range of students who are or have been exposed to multiple languages and cultures inside or outside of school including English learners, English learners with disabilities, heritage language learners, students with interrupted formal education, long-term English learners, and students participating in dual language programs learning languages in addition to English

Multiliteracies: a 21st-century approach to making meaning that relies on different forms of text (e.g., digital, visual, oral, written) that offer multimodal ways for learners to make sense of the world and subsequently communicate and connect with each other

Multimodalities: the many ways of communicating, including the resources available to students, such as the use of images, aural, linguistic, spatial, and visual materials, to meaningfully relate to one another and creatively show their learning

"Native" language ("first" language or mother tongue): originally referred to a person's "first" language or language of the country of birth; however, in recent times, it has been contested as many persons develop and use multiple languages simultaneously

Newcomer students: recent arrivals to the United States (generally within the last two to four years) whose conceptual understanding and communicative skills, in large part, are in a language other than English

No Child Left Behind (NCLB) Act: the U.S. Department of Education's 2002 reauthorization of the Elementary and Secondary Education Act whereby states or consortia were to have content standards, minimally in reading/language arts and mathematics, and were first required to develop corresponding English language proficiency standards aligned to annual state testing of language proficiency in Grades K–12 and achievement in Grades 3–8 and once in high school

One-way dual language immersion program: a language education model in which students from predominantly one language group receive instruction in both English and a partner language

Partner language: the shared language (other than English) between bi/multilingual learners

Peer assessment: descriptive feedback on student work based on specified criteria given by classmates

Performance assessment: the planning, collection, and analysis of data from original hands-on activities, such as curriculum-related projects, that are interpreted based on specified criteria

Plurilingual learners: a term generally used outside the United States that refers to persons who communicate in more than one language or who switch between multiple languages depending on the situation

Portfolio assessment: a purposeful representative collection of student work with criteria for selection and evaluation that conveys a story of student growth, achievement, and/or social-emotional development over time

Proficient English speakers: multilingual learners who are former English language learners or students who are fully functional in English

Racialized bilingualism: when minoritized students speak a language other than or in addition to English at home and learn English at school

Rating scales: a type of rubric where traits, language functions, skills, strategies, or behaviors are defined by their frequency of occurrence (how often) or quality (how well)

Reliability: in performance assessment, the consistency of interpretation of student work from rater to rater

Rubrics: criterion-referenced tools that enable teachers and students to interpret or evaluate student work using a uniform set of descriptors

Scaffolding: temporary supports for multilingual learners to maximize their access to grade-level content material as they gain proficiency in a language

Seal of Biliteracy: an award given by a school, district, or state in recognition of multilingual learners who have met the criteria for proficiency in two or more languages

Self-assessment: students' application of performance criteria or descriptors to monitor and interpret their own work as a means of reflecting on their learning in one or more languages

Sheltered English programs: specialized instructional strategies under the umbrella of content-based instruction that teachers use to scaffold language for multilingual learners who are not yet proficient in English

Simultaneous bilinguals: persons who develop two or more languages at the same time

Social-emotional learning (SEL): "a process through which students acquire and apply the knowledge, attitudes, and skills necessary to understand and manage emotions, set and achieve positive goals, feel and show empathy for others, establish and maintain positive relationships and make responsible decisions" (see Rodel Teacher Council, 2018)

Social justice: the belief in equity obtained through economic, political, and social rights coupled with access and opportunity for every person

Sociocracy: a system of school governance that values harmonious and deep solutions of the ideas of all stakeholders

Sociocultural theory: envisioning language as a social activity that is context dependent with consideration of the topic, audience, and situation, where language development is a fluid dynamic process with no one trajectory to language proficiency

Standardized testing: any examination, generally applied to large-scale achievement tests, that is administered and scored in predetermined standard ways

Structural linguistic theory: envisioning language as a set of atomistic parts and language development as a linear trajectory that leads to "native" proficiency

Structured English immersion (SEI) programs: exclusive use of English during instruction of English language development in order to succeed in mainstream education

Student-led conferences: meetings with family members or with teachers led by the student where the classroom teacher is a facilitator and the student discusses their work in relation to established learning goals

Students with interrupted formal education (SIFE): a label that serves as a classification scheme for multilingual learners who have not had consistent schooling (due to mobility, chronic absence, or refugee status)

Submersion ("sink or swim") programs: a deficit educational model whereby English learners are provided the exact same educational services as their proficient English peers with no built-in language support

Subtractive bilingualism: viewing an additional language as an impediment to learning in English, where English often is treated at the expense of or as a replacement for bi/multilingual learners' other language

Success criteria: statements of what students should know, understand, and be able to do at the end of a lesson or a unit of learning that serve as the basis for interpreting student work

Summative assessment practices/purposes (or assessment *of* learning): the "sum" of evidence of learning gathered over time at the classroom level, such as at the culmination of a unit of study, or at a school or district level, such as an interim or annual test that is often used for accountability purposes

Test: a systematic procedure for collecting a sample of student behavior or performance at one point in time

Transadaptation of a test: a test that contains modified items to fit the cultural and linguistic backgrounds of the students

Transitional bilingual education: a subtractive educational model whereby English learners' home language is gradually removed from instruction, generally within three years, with the goals of assimilation and English language development

Translanguaging: dynamic, normative languaging practices of bilinguals; an interchange between multilingual learners who use the resources of two shared languages; in school, the interaction of students or teachers in two or more languages in naturally occurring or specified learning situations

Two-way dual language immersion programs: an enrichment language education model in which multilingual learners who are fluent in the partner language and English-proficient peers are integrated to receive instruction in both English and the partner language, minimally on a 50/50 basis

Understanding by Design (UbD): a three-stage curricular framework and planning process (conceptualized by Wiggins & McTighe, 2005) that involves (1) identifying desired results, (2) determining assessment evidence, and (3) planning learning experiences that are clearly aligned to each other and standards

Universal Design for Learning (UDL): a set of neuroscience principles that includes multiple means of representation to give students multiple entry points to learning, multiple means of expression, and multiple means of engagement

Validity: the extent to which the assessment and data are appropriate for the decisions to be made; the extent to which a test matches its stated purpose and subsequent results from which inferences are made

World languages: languages spoken internationally that are taught as additional or "foreign" languages in U.S. schools

References

Abedi, J. (2002). Standardized achievement tests and English language learners: Psychometric issues. *Educational Assessment*, *8*(3), 231–257.

Abedi, J. (2004). The No Child Left Behind Act and English language learners: Assessment and accountability issues. *Educational Researcher*, *33*(1), 4–14.

Abedi, J. (2011). Assessing English language learners: Critical issues. In M. R. Basterra, E. Trumbull, & G. Solano-Flores (Eds.), *Cultural validity in assessment: Addressing linguistic and cultural diversity* (pp. 49–71). New York: Routledge.

Adichie, C. N. (2009). *The danger of a single story*. TEDGlobal 2009. Retrieved from https://www.ted.com/talks/chimamanda_ngozi_adichie_the_danger_of_a_single_story?language=en

American Educational Research Association, American Psychological Association, & National Council on Measurement in Education. (2014). *Standards for educational and psychological testing: Essential guidance and key developments in a new era of testing* (6th ed.). Washington, DC: Author.

Andrade, H., & Du, Y. (2005). Student perspectives on rubric-referenced assessment. *Practical Assessment, Research & Evaluation*, *10*(3), 1–11.

Anyon, J. (2005). *Radical possibilities: Public policy, urban education, and a new social movement*. New York: Routledge.

Arellano, B., Liu, F., Stoker, G., & Slama, R. (2018). *Initial Spanish proficiency and English language development among Spanish-speaking English learner students in New Mexico* (REL2018-286). Washington, DC: U.S. Department of Education, Institute of Education Sciences, National Center for Education Evaluation and Regional Assistance, Regional Educational Laboratory Southwest. Retrieved from http://ies.ed.gov/ncee.edlabs

Ascenzi-Moreno, L., Hesson, S., & Menken, K. (2016). School leadership along the trajectory from monolingual to multilingual. *Language and Education*, *30*(3), 197–218.

August, D., Goldenberg, C., & Rueda, R. (2010). Restrictive state language policies: Are they scientifically based? In P. Gándara & M. Hopkins (Eds.), *Forbidden language: English learners and restrictive language policies* (pp. 139–158). New York: Teachers College Press.

Bachman, L. F., & Damböck, B. (2017). *Language assessment for classroom teachers*. Oxford, UK: Oxford University Press.

Bailey, A. L., & Kelly, K. R. (2012). Home language survey practices in the initial identification of English learners in the United States. *Educational Policy, 27(5)*, 770–804.

Baldoni, J. (2020, April). Looking for talent to lead a post-crisis world. *SmartBrief*. Retrieved from https://www.smartbrief.com/original/2020/04/looking-talent-lead-post-crisis-world

Basterra, M., Trumbull, E., & Solano-Flores, G. (Eds.). (2011). *Cultural validity in assessment: Addressing linguistic and cultural diversity.* New York: Routledge.

Bazron, B., Osher, D., & Fleischman, S. (2005). Creating culturally responsive schools. *Educational Leadership, 63(1)*, 83–84.

Berger, R., Rugen, L., & Woodfin, L. (2014). *Leaders of their own learning: Transforming schools through student-engaged assessment.* San Francisco, CA: Jossey-Bass.

Berlak, A., & Berlak, H. (1981). *Dilemmas of schooling: Teaching and social change.* London: Methuen.

Bialystok, E. (2011). Reshaping the mind: The benefits of bilingualism. *Canadian Journal of Experimental Psychology/Revue canadienne de psychologie expérimentale, 65(4)*, 229–235.

Bilingual Education Act (BEA) (81 Stat. 816), Title VII of the Elementary and Secondary Education Amendments of 1967 (Pub. L. 90-247, January 2, 1968).

Bisai, S., & Singh, S. (2018). Rethinking assessment: A multilingual perspective. *Language in India, 18(4)*, 308–319.

Black, P., & Wiliam, D. (1998). *Assessment for learning: Beyond the black box.* Cambridge, UK: University of Cambridge.

Blankstein, A. M., & Newsome, M. J. (2021). *Breakthrough leadership: Six principles guiding schools where inequity is not an option.* Thousand Oaks, CA: Corwin.

Blythe, T., Allen, D., & Powell, B. S. (1999). *Looking together at student work.* New York: Teachers College Press.

Boyle, A., August, D., Tabaku, L., Cole, S., & Simpson-Baird, A. (2015). *Dual language education programs: State policies and practices.* Washington, DC: American Institutes for Research.

Brackett, M., Cannizzaro, M., & Levy, S. (2020). The pandemic's toll on school leaders is palpable. Here's what's needed for a successful school year. *EdSurge*. Retrieved from https://www.edsurge.com/news/2020-07-16-the-pandemic-s-toll-on-school-leaders-is-palpable-here-s-what-s-needed-for-a-successful-school-year

Brookhart, S. M. (2020). *Addressing learning loss: Formative assessment tools aid remote learning.* Learning Sciences International. Retrieved from https://www.learningsciences.com/blog/classroom-formative-assessment-tools-address-learning-loss/

Brooks, K., Adams, S., & Morita-Mullaney, T. (2010). Creating inclusive learning communities for ELL students: Transforming school principals' perspectives. *Theory Into Practice, 49*(2), 145–151.

Brooks, M. D. (2020). *Transforming literacy education for long-term English learners: Recognizing brilliance in the undervalued.* New York: Routledge and NCTE.

Bryk, A. (2010). Organizing schools for improvement. *Phi Delta Kappan, 91*(7), 23–30.

Burr, E. (2019). *Guidance manuals for educators of English learners with disabilities: Ideas and lessons from the field* (NCEO Report 410). Minneapolis: University of Minnesota, National Center on Educational Outcomes.

California Department of Education. (2020). *Improving education for multilingual and English learner students: Research to practice.* Sacramento: Author.

Californians Together. (2021). *The accountability system English learners deserve: Framework for an effective and coherent accountability system for ELs.* Long Beach, CA: Author.

Calkins, A., Conley, D., Heritage, M., Merino, N., Pecheone, R., Pittenger, L., Udall, D., & Wells, J. (2018). *Five elements for assessment design and use to support student autonomy.* Lexington, KY: Center for Innovation in Education.

Care, E., Kim, H., & Sahin, A. G. (2020). *Optimizing assessment for all: Developing 21st century skills-embedded curriculum tasks.* Washington, DC: Brookings Institute.

CASEL District Resource Center. (2021). *SEL as a lever for equity.* Collaborative for Academic, Social, and Emotional Learning. Retrieved from https://drc.casel.org/sel-as-a-lever-for-equity/

Cenoz, J., & Gorter, D. (Eds.). (2015). *Multilingual education: Between language learning and translanguaging.* Cambridge, UK: Cambridge University Press.

Center for Education Policy Analysis. (n.d.). *Racial and ethnic achievement gaps.* Stanford University. Retrieved from https://cepa.stanford.edu/educational-opportunity-monitoring-project/achievement-gaps/race/

Center for Public Education. (2016, January). *Educational equity: What does it mean? How do we know when we reach it?* Retrieved from https://www.nsba.org/-/media/nsba/file/cpe-educational-equity-research-brief-january-2016

Chalhoub-Deville, M. B. (2019). Multilingual testing constructs: Theoretical considerations. *Language Assessment Quarterly, 16*(4–5), 472–480.

Chapman, M., Kim, A. A., Wei, J., & Bitterman, T. (2018). Challenging the deficit mindset: The WIDA Can Do philosophy in a second language writing context. In T. Ruecker & D. Crusan (Eds.), *The politics of English second language assessment* (pp. 216–222). New York: Routledge.

Chester, M. D. (2005). Multiple measures and high-stakes decisions: A framework for combining measures. *Educational Measurement Issues and Practice, 22*(2), 32–41.

Cheuk, T. (2016). Discourse practices in the new standards: The role of argumentation in Common-Core era Next Generation Science Standards classrooms for English language learners. *Electronic Journal of Science Education, 20*(3), 92–111. Retrieved from http://ejse.southwestern.edu

Christenson, S. L., Reschly, A. L., & Wylie, C. (Eds.). (2012). *Handbook of research on student engagement.* New York: Springer.

Cleave, E. (2020). *Language, education and social justice: A movement for multilingual classrooms.* Cambridge, UK: Bell Foundation.

Cloud, N., Genesee, F., & Hamayan, E. (2001). *Dual language instruction: A handbook for enriched education.* Boston, MA: Heinle & Heinle.

Cohan, A., Honigsfeld, A., & Dove, M. G. (2020). *Team up, speak up, fire up.* Alexandria, VA: ASCD.

Collaborative for Academic, Social, and Emotional Learning (CASEL). (2021). *SEL roadmap: Actions for a successful second semester.* Retrieved from https://casel.org/reopening-with-sel/

Collier, V. P., & Thomas, W. P. (2017). The power of bilingual schooling: Thirty-two years of large-scale, longitudinal research. *Annual Review of Applied Linguistics, 37*, 203–217.

Communities in Schools. (2020). *A system disrupted: COVID-19's impact on education (in)equity.* Arlington, VA: Author.

Crawford, J. (1987, April 1). Bilingual education traces its U.S. roots to the colonial era. *Education Week.* Retrieved from https://www.edweek.org/ew/articles/1987/04/01/27early.h06.html

Cummins, J. (1979). Cognitive academic language proficiency, linguistic interdependence, the optimum age question, and some other matters. *Working Papers on Bilingualism, 19*, 121–129.

Cummins, J. (1981). *Bilingualism and minority language children.* Toronto, Canada: Ontario Institute for Studies in Education.

Cummins, J. (2017). Teaching for transfer in multilingual school contexts. In O. García, A. M. Y. Lin, & S. May (Eds.), *Bilingual and multilingual education* (3rd ed., pp. 103–115). New York: Springer.

Darling-Hammond, L. (2018). *Kerner at 50: Educational equity still a dream deferred.* Learning Policy Institute. Retrieved from https://tinyurl.com/y5k4l2co

Davis, L. (2013). Building rubrics democratically. In J. D. Brown (Ed.), *New ways of classroom assessment, revised* (pp. 92–94). Alexandria, VA: TESOL International Association.

Davison, C., & Williams, A. (2013). Integrating language and content: Unresolved issues. In B. Mohan, C. Leung, & C. Davison (Eds.), *English as* a second language in the mainstream: Teaching, learning and identity (pp. 51–69). London, UK: Routledge.

Day, C., & Harris, A. (2002). Teacher leadership, reflective practice, and school improvement. In L. Leithwood et al. (Eds.), *Second international handbook of educational leadership and administration, 8,* 957–977. Dordrecht, Netherlands: Springer.

de Jong, E. (2019a, April). *Taking a multilingual stance.* Paper presented at the American Education Research Association meeting, Toronto, Canada.

de Jong, E. (2019b, May). Quality schooling for English language learners: From past experience to principles for the future. Presentation at the Office of English Language Acquisition, *Multiliteracy Symposium: Celebrating the Diverse Linguistic and Cultural Assets of All Our Students.*

de Mejía, A.-M. (2002). *Power, prestige, and bilingualism: International perspectives on elite bilingual education.* Clevedon, UK: Multilingual Matters.

DeMatthews, D., & Izquierdo, E. (2016). School leadership for dual language education: A social justice approach. *The Educational Forum, 80*(3), 278–293.

Dewey, J. (1933). *How we think: A restatement of the relation of reflective thinking to the educative process.* Boston: D.C. Heath & Co.

Duarte, J. (2016). Translanguaging in mainstream education: A sociocultural approach. *International Journal of Bilingual Education and Bilingualism, 22*(2), 150–164.

Dyer, K. (2015, September 17). *Research proof points: Better student engagement improves student learning.* NWEA Education Blog. Retrieved from https://www.nwea.org/blog/2015/research-proof-points-better-student-engagement-improves-student-learning/

Early, L. M. (2012). *Assessment as learning: Using classroom assessment to maximize student learning* (2nd ed.). Thousand Oaks, CA: Corwin.

Early, L. M., Cummins, J., & Willinsky, J. (2002). *From literacy to multiliteracies: Designing learning environments for knowledge generations within the new economy.* Ottawa, ON: Social Sciences and Humanities Research Council of Canada.

Elementary and Secondary Education Act. (1965). H.R. 2362, 89th Cong., 1st sess., Pub. L. 89-10. Reports, bills, debate and act. Washington, DC: U.S. Government Printing Office.

Escamilla, K. (2006). Monolingual assessment and emerging bilinguals: A case study in the US. In O. Garcia, T. Skutnabb-Kangas, & M. Torres-Guzmán (Eds.), *Imagining multilingual schools* (pp. 184–199). Clevedon, UK: Multilingual Matters.

Escamilla, K., Hopewell, S., Butvilofsky, S., Sparrow, W., Soltero-González, L., Ruiz-Figueroa, O., & Escamilla, M. (2014). *Biliteracy from the start: Literacy squared in action.* Philadelphia, PA: Caslon.

Espinosa, L. M., & García, E. (2012, November). *Developmental assessment of young dual language learners with a focus on kindergarten entry assessments: Implications for state policies.* Working paper #1. Center for Early Care and Education Research–Dual Language (CECER-DLL). Chapel Hill: University of North Carolina, Frank Porter Graham Child Development Institute.

Esteban-Guitart, M., & Moll, L. C. (2014). Funds of identity: A new concept based on the Funds of Knowledge approach. *Culture & Psychology, 20*(1), 31–48.

Every Student Succeeds Act. (2015). Pub. L. No. 114-95 §114 Stat. 1177 (2015–2016). Retrieved from https://www.congress.gov/bill/114th-congress/senate-bill/1177

Fairbairn, S., & Jones-Vo, S. (2016). *Engaging English learners through access to standards.* Thousand Oaks, CA: Corwin.

Feldman, J. (2019). *Grading for equity: What it is, why it matters, and how it can transform schools and classrooms.* Thousand Oaks, CA: Corwin.

Fisher, D., Frey, N., & Hattie, J. (2021). *The distance learning playbook grades K–12: Teaching for engagement & impact in any setting.* Thousand Oaks, CA: Corwin.

Flores, N. (2020a). Do Black lives matter in bilingual education? *The Educational Linguist.* Retrieved from https://educationallinguist.wordpress.com/2016/09/11/do-black-lives-matter-in-bilingual-education

Flores, N. (2020b). From academic language to language architecture: Challenging raciolinguistic ideologies in research and practice. *Theory Into Practice, 59,* 22–31.

Flores, N., & Rosa, J. (2015). Undoing appropriateness: Raciolinguistic ideologies and language diversity in education. *Harvard Education Review, 85*(2), 149–171.

Frey, N., Fisher, D., & Smith, D. (2019). *All learning is social and emotional: Helping students develop essential skills for the classroom and beyond.* Alexandria, VA: ASCD.

Frey, N., Hattie, J., & Fisher, D. (2018). *Developing assessment-capable visible learners: Grades K–12.* Thousand Oaks, CA: Corwin.

Gándara, P. (2015, November 4). The implications of deeper learning for adolescent immigrants and English language learners. *Students at the Center.* Retrieved from https://www.jff.org/resources/implications-deeper-learning-adolescent-immigrants-and-english-language-learners

García, O. (2009). Emergent bilinguals and TESOL: What's in a name? *TESOL Quarterly, 43*(2), 322–326.

García, O., Johnson, S. I., & Seltzer, K. (2017). *The translanguaging classroom: Leveraging student bilingualism for learning.* Philadelphia, PA: Caslon.

García, O., Kleifgen, J. A., & Fachi, L. (2008). From English language learners to emergent bilinguals. *Equity Matters: Research Review 1.* New York: Teachers College, Columbia University.

García, O., & Sung, K. K. (2018). Critically assessing the 1968 Bilingual Education Act at 50 years: Taming tongues and Latinx communities. *Bilingual Research Journal, 41*(4), 318–333.

García, O., & Wei, L. (2018). Translanguaging. *The Encyclopedia of Applied Linguistics*. Retrieved from https://onlinelibrary.wiley.com/doi/full/10.1002/9781405198431.wbeal1488

Gibbons, P. (2015). *Scaffolding language, scaffolding learning: Teaching English language learners in the mainstream classroom* (2nd ed.). Portsmouth, NH: Heinemann.

Goldenberg, C., & Coleman, R. (2010). *Promoting academic achievement among English learners: A guide to the research*. Thousand Oaks, CA: Corwin.

Goldschmidt, P., & Hakuta, K. (2017). *Incorporating English learner progress into state accountability systems*. Washington, DC: Council of Chief State School Officers.

González, N., Moll, L. C., & Amanti, C. (Eds.). (2005). *Funds of knowledge: Theorizing practices in households, communities, and classrooms*. Mahwah, NJ: Lawrence Erlbaum.

González, V. (2012). Assessment of bilingual/multilingual pre-K–grade 12 students: A critical discussion of past, present, and future issues. *Theory Into Practice, 51*(4), 290–296.

Gottlieb, M. (1995). Nurturing student learning through portfolios. *TESOL Journal, 5*(1), 12–14.

Gottlieb, M. (2012). *Common language assessment for English learners*. Bloomington, IN: Solution Tree.

Gottlieb, M. (2016). *Assessing English language learners: Bridges to equity connecting academic language proficiency to student achievement* (2nd ed.). Thousand Oaks, CA: Corwin.

Gottlieb, M. (2017). *Assessing multilingual learners: A month-by-month guide*. Alexandria, VA: ASCD.

Gottlieb, M. (2020). Assessment of English learners. In S. Brookhart (Section Ed.), *The Routledge Encyclopedia of Education*.

Gottlieb, M. (2021). *Classroom assessment in multiple languages: A handbook for teachers*. Thousand Oaks, CA: Corwin.

Gottlieb, M., & Ernst-Slavit, G. (2014). *Academic language in diverse classrooms: Definitions and contexts*. Thousand Oaks, CA: Corwin.

Gottlieb, M., & Ernst-Slavit, G. (2019). Promoting educational equity in assessment practices. In L. C. de Oliveira (Ed.), *The Handbook of TESOL in K–12* (pp. 129–148). Hoboken, NJ: Wiley.

Gottlieb, M., & Hilliard, J. (2019). *A presentation at La CLAVE: An integration of language, culture, and the arts*. Oaxaca, Mexico.

Gottlieb, M., & Honigsfeld, A. (2020). From assessment *of* learning to assessment *for* and *as* learning. In M. Calderón, M. Dove, M. Gottlieb, A. Honigsfeld, T. Singer, I. Soto, S. Slakk, D. Stahr Fenner, & D. Zacarian. *Breaking down the wall: Essential shifts for English learners' success* (pp. 135–160). Thousand Oaks, CA: Corwin.

Gottlieb, M., & Katz, A. (2020). Assessment in the classroom. In C. Chappelle (Ed.), *The concise encyclopedia of applied linguistics*. Hoboken, NJ: Wiley.

Gottlieb, M., & Nguyen, D. (2007). *Assessment and accountability in language education programs: A guide for administrators and teachers*. Philadelphia, PA: Caslon.

Grapin, S. (2018). Multimodality in the new content standards era: Implications for English Learners, *TESOL Quarterly, 53*(1), 30–55.

Graves, K. (2008). The language curriculum: A social contextual perspective. *Language Teach, 41*(2), 147–181.

Graves, K. (2016). Language curriculum design: Possibilities and realities. In G. Hall (Ed.), *The Routledge handbook of English language teaching*. Routledge Handbooks Online.

Green, W. (2015). *Depth of engagement*. Retrieved from http://www.depthof engagement.com/2015/04/a-theory-of-action.html

Grosjean, F. (1989). Neurolinguists, beware! The bilingual is not two monolinguals in one person. *Brain and Language, 36*(1), 3–15.

Gubbins, E. J., Siegle, D., Hamilton, R., Peters, P., Carpenter, A. Y., O'Rourke, P., . . . Estepar-García, W. (2018, June). *Exploratory study on the identification of English learners for gifted and talented programs*. Storrs: University of Connecticut, National Center for Research on Gifted Education.

Guzula, X., McKinney, C., & Tyler, R. (2016). Languaging-for-learning: Legitimising translanguaging and enabling multimodal practices in third spaces. *Southern African Linguistics and Applied Language Studies, 34*(3), 1–16.

Hamayan, E. V., Marler, B., Sánchez-López, C., & Damico, J. (2013). *Special education considerations for English language learners: Delivering a continuum of services* (2nd ed.). Philadelphia, PA: Caslon.

Hattie, J. (2009). *Visible learning: A synthesis of over 800 meta-analyses relating to achievement*. New York: Routledge.

Hattie, J. (2012). *Visible learning for teachers: Maximizing impact on learning*. London: Routledge.

Hattie, J., & Temperley, H. (2007). The power of feedback. *Review of Educational Research, 77*, 81–112.

Hawkins, M. R. (2019). Plurilingual learners and schooling: A sociocultural perspective. In *Handbook of TESOL in K–12*. Hoboken, NJ: Wiley.

Heineke, A., Coleman, E., Ferrell, E., & Kersemeier, C. (2012). Opening doors for bilingual students: Recommendations for building linguistically responsive schools. *Improving Schools, 15*(2), 130–147.

Heineke, A., & McTighe, J. (2018). *Using Understanding by Design in the culturally and linguistically diverse classroom.* Alexandria, VA: ASCD.

Hemphill, F. C., Vanneman, A., & Rahman, T. (2011). *Achievement gaps: How Hispanic and White students in public schools perform in mathematics and reading on the National Assessment of Educational Progress.* Washington, DC: National Center for Educational Statistics. Retrieved from https://nces.ed.gov/nationsreportcard/pubs/studies/2011459.asp

Henry, S. F., Mello, D., Avery, M.-P., Parker, C., & Statford, E. (2017). *Home language survey data quality self-assessment* (REL 2017–198). Washington, DC: U.S. Department of Education, Institute of Education Sciences, National Center for Education Evaluation and Regional Assistance, Regional Educational Laboratory Northeast & Islands. Retrieved from http://ies.ed.gov/ncee/edlabs

Heritage, M. (2010). *Formative assessment: Making it happen in the classroom.* Thousand Oaks, CA: Corwin.

Hilliard, J., & Gottlieb, M. (2018). *Multiliteracy curriculum development.* Presentation at La CLAVE de Oaxaca, Oaxaca, Mexico.

Honigsfeld, A., & Dove, M. G. (2015). *Collaboration and co-teaching for English learners: A leader's guide.* Thousand Oaks, CA: Corwin.

Hopewell, S., & Escamilla, K. (2013). Struggling reader or emerging biliterate student? Reevaluating the criteria for labeling emerging bilingual students as low achieving. *Journal of Literacy Research, 1,* 68–89.

Hornberger, N. H. (Ed.). (2003). *Continua of biliteracy: An ecological framework for educational policy, research, and practice in multilingual setting.* Clevedon, UK: Multilingual Matters.

Hornberger, N. H. (2004). The continua of biliteracy and the bilingual educator. *Educational Linguistics in Practice.* Retrieved from http://repository.upenn.edu/gse_pubs/9

Howard, E. R., Lindholm-Leary, K. J., Rogers, D., Olague, N., Medina, J., Kennedy, D., . . . Christian, D. (2018). *Guiding principles for dual language education* (3rd ed.). Washington, DC: Center for Applied Linguistics.

Huff, K. (2020). How "growth" goals actually hold students back. *EdSurge.* Retrieved from https://www.edsurge.com/news/2020-08-30-how-growth-goals-actually-hold-students-back

Hunt, V. (2011). Learning from success stories: Leadership structures that support dual language programs over time in New York City. *International Journal of Bilingual Education and Bilingualism, 14*(2), 187–206.

Improving America's Schools Act of 1994. (1993–1994). Pub. L. No. 103-382. Washington, DC: Congressional Research Service, Library of Congress.

Jones, N., & Saville, N. (2016). Learning-oriented assessments: A systemic approach. *Studies in Language Testing, 45*. Cambridge, UK: UCLES/Cambridge University Press.

Kaul, M. (2019, June). *Keeping students at the center with culturally relevant performance assessments*. Retrieved from https://www.nextgenlearning.org/articles/keeping-students-at-the-center-with-culturally-relevant-performance-assessments

Kelleher, A. (2010). *Who is a heritage language learner?* Washington, DC: Center for Applied Linguistics. Retrieved from http://www.cal.org/heritage/pdfs/briefs/Who-is-a-Heritage-Language-Learner.pdf

Kibler, A. K., & Valdés, G. (2016). Conceptualizing language learners: Socioinstitutional mechanisms and their consequences. *Modern Language Journal, 100*(S1), 96–116.

Kim, A. A., Molle, D., Kemp, J., & Cook, H. G. (2018). Examination of identification and placement decisions made for K–12 English learners. *WCER Working Paper No. 2018-12*. Madison: Wisconsin Center for Education Research.

Kleyn, T., & García, O. (2019). *Translanguaging as an act of transformation: Restructuring teaching and learning for emergent bilingual students*. Retrieved from https://ofeliagarciadotorg.files.wordpress.com/2019/05/kleyngarcia-2019-translanguaging-as-an-act-of-trans.pdf

Kress, G. (2010). *Multimodality: A social semiotic approach to contemporary communication*. New York: Routledge.

LaCelle-Peterson, M. W., & Rivera, C. (1994). Is it real for all kids? A framework for equitable assessment policies for English language learners. *Harvard Educational Review, 64*(1), 55–75.

Ladson-Billings, G. (1995). Toward a theory of culturally relevant pedagogy. *American Educational Research Journal, 32*(3), 465–491.

Lake, R., & Olson, L. (2020). *Learning as we go: Principles for effective assessment during the COVID-19 pandemic*. Seattle, WA: Center on Reinventing Public Education.

Lazarín, M. (2020, June). *COVID-19 spotlights the inequities facing English Learner students, as nonprofit organizations seek to mitigate challenges*. Migration Policy Institute. Retrieved from https://www.migrationpolicy.org/news/covid-19-inequities-english-learner-students

Lea, K., & Dame, B. (2020, May). Using universal design to create better assessments. *Edutopia*. Retrieved from https://www.edutopia.org/article/using-universal-design-create-better-assessments

Lee, H., Chung, H. Q., Zhang, Y., Abedi, J., & Warschauer, M. (2020). The effectiveness and features of formative assessment in US K–12 education: A systematic review. *Applied Measurement in Education, 33*(2), 124–140.

Leung, C., & Valdés, G. (2019). Translanguaging and the transdisciplinary framework for language teaching and learning in a multilingual world. *The Modern Language Journal, 103*(2), 348–370.

Lindholm-Leary, K. (2012). Success and challenges in dual language education. *Theory Into Practice, 51*(4), 256–262.

Linquanti, R., & Bailey, A. L. (2014). *Reprising the home language survey: Summary of a national working session on policies, practices, and tools for identifying potential English learners.* Washington, DC: Council of Chief State School Officers.

Linquanti, R., & Cook, H. G. (2013). *Toward a "common definition of English learner": Guidance for states and state assessment consortia in defining and addressing policy and technical issues and options.* Washington, DC: Council of Chief State School Officers.

Linquanti, R., Cook, H. G., Bailey, A. L., & MacDonald, R. (2016). *Moving toward a more common definition of English Learner: Collected guidance for states and multi-state assessment consortia.* Washington, DC: Council of Chief State School Officers.

López, A. A., Turkan, S., & Guzman-Orth, D. (2017). Assessing multilingual competence. In E. Shohamy, I. Or, & S. May (Eds.), *Language testing and assessment. Encyclopedia of language and education* (3rd ed., pp. 91–102). New York: Springer.

Lynch, B. K. (2001). Rethinking assessment from a critical perspective. *Language Testing, 18*(4), 351–372.

MAEC. (2019). *Creating new futures for newcomers: Lessons from five schools that serve K–12 immigrants, refugees, and asylees.* Bethesda, MD: Author.

Mahboob, A. (2019). Beyond the native speaker in TESOL. *International Journal of Applied Linguistics, 12*(1), 74–109. Retrieved from http://citeseerx.ist.psu.edu/viewdoc/download?doi=10.1.1.510.2158&rep=rep1&type=pdf

Martell, M. (2020). A framework schools can use to make better decisions. *Edutopia.* Retrieved from https://www.edutopia.org/article/framework-schools-can-use-make-better-decisions

Martínez, R. A. (2018). Beyond the English learner label: Recognizing the richness of bi/multilingual students' linguistic repertoires. *The Reading Teacher, 71*(5), 515–522.

May, S. (2014). Disciplinary divides, knowledge construction, and the multilingual turn. In S. May (Ed.), *The multilingual turn: Implications for SLA, TESOL and bilingual education* (pp. 7–31). New York, NY: Routledge.

McTighe, J., & Willis, J. (2019). *Upgrade your teaching: Understanding by Design meets neuroscience.* Alexandria, VA: ASCD.

Meier, G. S. (2016, August 23). The multilingual turn as a critical movement in education: Assumptions, challenges and a need for reflection. *Applied Linguistics Review, 8*(1), 131–161. Retrieved from https://www.degruyter.com/view/journals/alr/8/1/article-p131.xml

Menken, K. (2008). *English learners left behind: Standardized testing as language policy*. Clevedon, UK: Multilingual Matters.

Menken, K. (2013). Restrictive language education policies and emergent bilingual youth: A perfect storm with imperfect outcomes. *Theory Into Practice*, *52*(3), 160–168.

Menken, K. (2014). Principals as linchpins in bilingual education: The need for prepared school leaders. *International Journal of Bilingual Education and Bilingualism*, *18*(6), 1–22.

Menken, K. (2017). *Leadership in dual language bilingual education*. A National Dual Language Forum White Paper. Washington, DC: Center for Applied Linguistics.

Menken, K., & Solorza, C. (2013). Where have all the bilingual programs gone? Why prepared school leaders are essential for bilingual education. *Journal of Multilingual Education Research*, *4*, 9–39.

Metro, R. (2020). Humane assessment shouldn't happen only during a pandemic. *Inside Higher Ed*. Retrieved from https://www.insidehighered.com/views/ 2020/09/09/new-approaches-assessment-can-promote-student-success-times-crisis-well-normalcy? utm_source=BMC+Newsletter&utm_campaign =489ce74095-EMAIL_CAMPAIGN_2020_04_10_04_59_COPY_01&utm_ medium=email&utm_term=0_e57f11e986-489ce74095-121576637&mc_ cid=489ce74095&mc_eid=a2d1967461

Mid-Atlantic Equity Consortium. (2020). *Educational equity*. Retrieved from https://maec.org/our_work/educational-equity/

Milner, H. R. (2018). Confronting inequity/Assessment for equity. *Educational Leadership*, *75*(5), 88–89.

Mislevy, R. J., Almond, R. G., & Lukas, J. F. (2003). *A brief introduction to evidence-centered design*. Retrieved from http://www.education.umd.edu/ EDMS/mislevy/papers/BriefIntroECD.pdf

Mitchell, C. (2020, June 17). How will schools measure English-learners' "COVID-slide" learning loss? *Education Week*. Retrieved from https://blogs .edweek.org/edweek/learning-the-language/2020/06/learning_loss_english_ learners_native_language_assessments.html

Mohan, B. (1986). *Language and content*. Reading, MA: Addison-Wesley.

Montenegro, E., & Jankowski, N. A. (2017). *Equity and assessment: Moving towards culturally responsive assessment*. Urbana-Champaign, IL: National Institute for Learning Outcomes Assessment.

Montenegro, E., & Jankowski, N. A. (2020, January). *A new decade for assessment: Embedding equity into assessment praxis* (Occasional Paper No. 42). Urbana: University of Illinois and Indiana University, National Institute for Learning Outcomes Assessment (NILOA).

Moss, C. M., & Brookhart, S. M. (2009). *Advancing formative assessment in every classroom: A guide for instructional leaders*. Alexandria, VA: ASCD.

Moss, P. (2008). Sociocultural implications for assessment: Classroom assessment. In P. Moss, D. C. Pullin, J. P. Gee, E. H. Haertel, & L. J. Young (Eds.), *Assessment, equity, and opportunity to learn* (pp. 222–258). Cambridge, UK: Cambridge University Press.

Mun, R. U., Dulong Langley, S., Ware, S., Gubbins, E. J., Siegle, D., Callahan, C. M., . . . Hamilton, R. (2016). *Effective practices for identifying and serving English learners in gifted education: A systematic review of the literature.* Storrs, CT: National Center for Research on Gifted Education.

Murphey, D. (2014). *The academic achievement of English language learners: Data for the U.S. and each of the states.* Child Trends. Retrieved from https://www.childtrends.org/wp-content/uploads/2015/07/2014-62Academic AchievementEnglish.pdf

National Academies of Sciences, Engineering, and Medicine. (2017). *Promoting the educational success of children and youth learning English: Promising futures.* Washington, DC: Author.

National Education Association. (2020, June 23). *English language learners: What you need to know.* Retrieved from https://www.nea.org/professional-excellence/student-engagement/tools-tips/english-language-learners-what-you-need-know

New London Group. (1996). A pedagogy of multiliteracies: Designing social futures. *Harvard Educational Review, 66*(1), 60–92.

Newhall, P. W. (2012). Language-based learning disabilities. In P. W. Newhall (Ed.), *Language-based teaching series.* Prides Crossing, MA: Landmark School Outreach Program.

Nieto, S. (2018). *Language, culture, and teaching: Critical perspectives* (3rd ed.). New York: Routledge.

No Child Left Behind Act of 2001. (2002). Pub. L. No. 107-110, § 115, Stat. 1425-2094.

Ohara, S., Pritchard, R., Pitta, D., & Newton, R. N. (2017). Academic language and literacy in every setting: Strengthening the STEM learning ecosystem. In A. Oliveira & M. Weingurgh (Eds.), *Science teacher preparation in content-based second language acquisition* (pp. 199–213). New York: Springer.

Ortega, L. (2014). Ways forward for a bi/multilingual turn in SLA. In S. May (Ed.), *The multilingual turn: Implications for SLA, TESOL and bilingual education* (pp. 32–61). New York: Routledge.

Otheguy, R., García, O., & Reid, W. (2015). Clarifying translanguaging and deconstructing languages: A perspective from linguistics. *Applied Linguistics Review, 6*(3), 8–19.

Ottow, S. (2016). *Supporting English language learners with formative assessments.* Retrieved from https://www.gettingsmart.com/2016/04/supporting -ells-with-formative-assessments/

Palmer, D. K., Cervantes-Soon, C., Dorner, L., & Heiman, D. (2019). Bilingualism, biliteracy, biculturalism . . . and critical consciousness for all: Proposing a fourth fundamental principle for two-way dual language education. *Theory Into Practice, 58*(2), 121–133.

Paradis, J., Genesee, F., & Crago, M. B. (2011). *Communication and language intervention series. Dual language development & disorders: A handbook on bilingualism & second language learning* (2nd ed.). Baltimore, MD: Paul H Brookes.

Paris, D. (2012). Culturally sustaining pedagogy: A needed change in stance, terminology, and practice. *Educational Research, 41*(3), 93–97.

Park, S., Martinez, M., & Chou, F. (2017). *CCSSO English learners with disabilities guide.* Washington, DC: Council of Chief State School Officers.

Pimentel, S. (2018). *English learners and content-rich curricula.* John Hopkins School of Education: Institute for Education Policy.

Posey, A. (2020). *Universal Design for Learning (UDL): A teacher's guide.* Retrieved from https://www.understood.org/en/school-learning/for-educators/universal-design-for-learning/understanding-universal-design-for-learning

Reeves, D. (2004). *Accountability for learning: How teachers and school leaders can take charge.* Alexandria, VA: ASCD.

Relyea, J. E., & Amendum, S. J. (2019, July 16). English reading growth in Spanish-speaking bilingual students: Moderating effect of English proficiency on cross-linguistic influence. *Child Development.* Advance online publication. Retrieved from https://doi.org/10.1111/cdev.13288

Reynolds, D. (2019). *Language policy in globalized contexts.* Carnegie Mellon University Qatar: WISE.

RoadMap. (2018). *Shifting power from the inside out: Lessons on becoming member-led from Mujeres Unidas y Activas.* Retrieved from https://roadmapconsulting.org/resource/the-five-core-practices-of-effective-leadership-for-social-justice/

Robinson, V. (2008). Forging the links between distributed leadership and educational outcomes. *Journal of Educational Administration, 46*(2), 241–256.

Rock, P. (2020, February). Communities of practice: Virtual learning and collaboration opportunities. *Participate Learning.* Retrieved from https://www.participatelearning.com/blog/communities-of-practice/

Rodel Teacher Council. (2018). *Creating a common language for social and emotional learning in Delaware.* Rodel Foundation of Delaware. Retrieved from http://www.rodelfoundationde.org/wp-content/uploads/2018/06/SEL-Brief-2-_-final.pdf

Ruíz, R. (1984). Orientations in language planning. *NABE Journal, 8*(2), 15–34.

Ruíz, R. (1988). Orientations in language planning. In S. McKay & S. C. Wong (Eds.), *Language and diversity: Problem or resource?* (pp. 3–26). Boston: Heinle & Heinle.

Sánchez, M. T., García, O., & Solorza, C. (2017). Reframing language allocation policy in dual language bilingual education. *Bilingual Research Journal, 41*(1), 1–15.

Sánchez, S. V., Rodríguez, B. J., Soto-Huerta, M. E., Villarreal, F. C., Guerra, N. S., & Flores, B. B. (2013). A case for multidimensional bilingual assessment. *Language Assessment Quarterly, 10*(2), 160–177.

Sánchez-López, C., & Young, T. (2018). *Focus on special educational needs.* Oxford, UK: Oxford University Press.

Scanlan, M., & López, F. (2012). ¡Vamos! How school leaders promote equity and excellence for bilingual students. *Educational Administration Quarterly, 48*(4), 583–625.

Schissel, J. L., Leung, C., & Chalhoub-Deville, M. (2019). The construct of multilingualism in language testing. *Language Assessment Quarterly, 16*(2), 1–6.

Schroeder, S. (2020). How to help students focus on what they're learning, not the grade. *Edutopia.*

Seed, G. (2020). What does plurilingualism mean for language assessment? *Cambridge Assessment English Research Notes, 78,* 5–15.

Seidel, S. (1996). *Learning from looking.* Cambridge, MA: Harvard Project Zero.

Seltzer, K. (2019). Reconceptualizing "home" and "school" language: Taking a critical translingual approach in the English classroom. *TESOL Quarterly, 53*(4), 986–1007.

Shepard, L. (2005). *Formative assessment: Caveat emptor.* ETS Invitational Conference. Retrieved from http://www.csai-online.com/sites/default/files/resource/imported/shepard%20formative%20assessment%20caveat%20emptor.pdf

Shohamy, E. (2001). *The power of tests: A critical perspective on the uses of language tests.* London, UK: Longman.

Shohamy, E. (2011). Assessing multilingual competencies: Adopting construct valid assessment policies. *The Modern Language Journal, 95*(3), 418–429.

Sireci, S. G., & Faulkner-Bond, M. (2015). Promoting validity in the assessment of English learners. *Review of Research in Education, 39*(1), 215–252.

Sleeter, C. E., & Carmona, J. F. (2017). *Un-standardizing curriculum: Multicultural teaching in the standards-based classroom* (2nd ed.). New York: Teachers College Press.

Soto, I. (2012). *ELL shadowing as a catalyst for change.* Thousand Oaks, CA: Corwin.

Smith, F., Mihalakis, V., & Slamp, A. (2017). *4 key things to know about distributive leadership.* Retrieved from http://k12education.gatesfoundation.org/blog/4-key-things-know-distributed-leadership/

Snow, M. A., Met, M., & Genesee, F. (1989). A conceptual framework for the integration of language and content in second/ foreign language instruction. *TESOL Quarterly*, 23(2), 201–217.

Solano-Flores, G., & Hakuta, K. (2017). *Assessing students in their home language*. Palo Alto, CA: Stanford University, Understanding Language. Retrieved from https://stanford.app.box.com/s/uvwlgjbmeeuokts6c2 wnibucms4up9c2

Solano-Flores, W. (2011). Assessing the cultural validity of assessment practices: An introduction. In M. R. Basterra, E. Trumbull, & G. Solano-Flores (Eds.), *Cultural validity in assessment: Addressing linguistic and cultural diversity* (pp. 3–21). New York: Routledge.

Souto-Manning, M., Madrigal, R., Malik, K., & Martell, J. (2016). Bridging languages, cultures, and worlds through culturally relevant leadership. In S. Long, M. Souto-Manning, & V. Vasquez (Eds.), *Courageous leadership in early childhood education: Taking a stand for social justice* (pp. 57–68). New York: Teachers College Press.

Spillane, J. (2006). *Distributed leadership*. San Francisco, CA: Jossey-Bass.

Stefanakis, E. H. (2002). *Multiple intelligences and portfolios: A window into the learner's mind*. Portsmouth, NH: Heinemann.

Stiggins, R. (2006, November/December). Assessment for learning: A key to motivation and achievement. *Phi Delta Kappa International*, 2(2), 1–19.

Stiggins, R. (2008). *Assessment manifesto: A call for the development of balanced assessment systems*. Portland, OR: Educational Testing Service.

Stille, S. V. V., Bethke, R., Bradley-Brown, J., Giberson, J., & Hall, G. (2016). Broadening educational practice to include translanguaging: An outcome of educator inquiry into multilingual students' learning needs. *The Canadian Modern Language Review*, 72(4), 480–503.

Sugarman, J., & Villegas, L. (2020, June). *Native language assessments for K–12 English learners: Policy considerations and state practices*. Migration Policy Institute. Retrieved from https://www.migrationpolicy.org/research/ native-language-assessments-english-learners

Suskie, L. (2018). *Assessing student learning: A common sense guide* (3rd ed.). San Francisco, CA: Jossey-Bass.

Swain, M. (2006). Languaging, agency and collaboration in advanced second language learning. In H. Byrnes (Ed.), *Advancing language learning: The contributions of Halliday and Vygotsky* (pp. 95–108). London: Continuum.

Tabaku, L., Carbuccia-Abbott, M., & Saavedra, E. (2018). *State assessments in languages other than English: Preliminary report*. Chicago: Midwest Comprehensive Center.

The Douglas Fir Group. (2016). A transdisciplinary framework for SLA within a multilingual world. *The Modern Language Journal*, 100 (51), 19–47.

The Institute. (2017). *Hiding in plain sight: Leveraging curriculum to improve student learning.* Retrieved from https://edpolicy.education.jhu.edu/hiding-in-plain-sight-leveraging-curriculum-to-improve-student-learning/

Umansky, I., & Dumont, H. (2019). *English learner labeling: How English learner status shapes teacher perceptions of student skills and the moderating influence of bilingual instructional settings* (Ed Working Paper No. 19-94). Providence, RI: Annenberg Institute at Brown University.

UNESCO. (2014). *Multilingual education: Why is it important? How to implement it?* Retrieved from https://unesdoc.unesco.org/ark:/48223/pf0000226554

U.S. Department of Education. (n.d.). *Individuals with Disabilities Education Act.* Retrieved from https://sites.ed.gov/idea/statuteregulations/

U.S. Department of Education. (2016, March 4). *ESEA of 1965 as amended by the ESSA Negotiated Rulemaking Committee issue paper 5a.* Retrieved from https://www2.ed.gov/policy/elsec/leg/essa/session/nrmissuepaper532016.pdf

U.S. Department of Education, Office of English Language Acquisition. (2015). *English learner tool kit.* Retrieved from https://www2.ed.gov/about/offices/list/oela/english-learner-toolkit/index.html

Valdés, G., & Figueroa, R. A. (1994). *Bilingualism and testing: A special case of bias.* New York: Ablex.

Valentino, R. A., & Reardon, S. F. (2015). Effectiveness of four instructional programs designed to serve English learners' variation by ethnicity and initial English proficiency. *Educational Evaluation and Policy Analysis, 37*(4), 612–637.

Villa, R. A., Thousand, J. S., & Nevin, A. I. (2008). *A guide to co-teaching: Practical tips for facilitating student learning* (2nd ed.). Corwin and Council for Exceptional Children.

Walsh, S. (2011). *Exploring classroom discourse: Language in action.* New York: Routledge.

Ward Singer, T., & Staehr Fenner, D. (2020). From watering down to challenging. In M. Calderón, M. Dove, M. Gottlieb, A. Honigsfeld, T. Singer, I. Soto, S. Slakk, D. Stahr Fenner, & D. Zacarian. *Breaking down the wall: Essential shifts for English learners' success* (pp. 47–72). Thousand Oaks, CA: Corwin.

Wenger, E. (1998). *Communities of practice: Learning, meaning, and identity.* Cambridge, UK: Cambridge University Press.

WIDA MODEL. (2020). *Interpretive guide for score reports: Grades K–12.* Retrieved from https://wida.wisc.edu/sites/default/files/resource/MODEL-Interpretive-Guide-Score-Reports.pdf

Wiese, A., & García, E. E. (1998). The Bilingual Education Act: Language minority students and equal education opportunity. *Bilingual Research Journal, 22*(1), 1–18.

Wiggins, G. (2012). Seven keys to effective feedback. *Educational Leadership, 70*(1), 10–16.

Wiggins, G., & McTighe, J. (2005). *Understanding by Design* (2nd ed.). Alexandria, VA: ASCD.

Wiliam, D. (2011). *Embedded formative assessment*. Bloomington, IN: Solution Tree.

Wiliam, D. (2020, December 1). *Using assessment to accelerate student learning post COVID-19*. Webinar sponsored by Learning Sciences International.

Wiliam, D., & Leahy, S. (2015). *Embedding formative assessment: Practical techniques for K–12 classrooms*. West Palm Beach, FL: Learning Sciences International.

Williams, C. P. (2020, May 12). English learners are home with their home language and that's okay. *The Century Foundation*. Retrieved from https://tcf.org/content/commentary/english-learners-home-home-languages-thats-okay/?agreed=1

Wilson, D. M. (2011). Dual language programs on the rise. *Harvard Education Letter*, 27(2). Retrieved from https://www.hepg.org/hel-home/issues/27_2/helarticle/dual-language-programs-on-the-rise#home

Wong, S. (2016). Multilingualism as a tool for closing achievement gaps. *American Councils*. Retrieved from https://www.americancouncils.org/news/language-news/multilingualism-tool-closing-achievement-gaps

Zacarian, D., Calderón, M., & Gottlieb, M. (2021). *Beyond crises: Overcoming linguistic and cultural inequities for communities, schools, and classrooms*. Thousand Oaks, CA: Corwin.

Index

Academic content standards, 6

Academic language, 135–136, 154

Accountability, xxiv, 6–7, 45, 145–147

Achievement gap, 3–4, 123

Achievement testing, 7, 10, 41, 157–158

Action phase, taking. *See* Taking action phase

Action research, 193

Adams, S., 33 (figure)

Additive bilingualism, 14

Aligned assessment system, 36, 36 (figure), 207

Almond, R. G., 144

Analytic rubrics, 145, 169

Anchors, xxvii, 133, 173

Annual assessment, 140–144, 150, 175

Annual standardized tests, 46 (figure)

Assessment, 3

Assessment *as* learning, 43–44, 43 (figure), 56, 62, 109, 163
  assessment cycle and, 210–211 (figure)
  data collection during, 110 (figure)
  data interpretation, 129, 130 (figure)
  locus of control, through, 202, 202 (figure)
  multilingual portfolios across, 80 (figure), 89
  multiliteracies, 104 (figure), 117
  multimodal resources for, 102–103, 104 (figure), 117
  translanguaging, 105–106
  UDL and, 98
  units of learning and, 64

Assessment audit, 51

Assessment-capable classrooms/ schools/districts, 163–164, 184

Assessment-capable students, 163

Assessment data
  collaborative planning and, 60
  levels of, 36, 36 (figure)
  multilingual learners across school year, for, 41 (figure), 53
  multilingual learner subgroups with, 11, 11 (figure), 27
  systemic change and, 206

Assessment *for* learning, 43 (figure), 44–45, 56, 62, 109
  assessment cycle and, 210–211 (figure)
  data collection during, 110 (figure)
  data interpretation, 129, 130 (figure)
  locus of control, through, 202, 202 (figure)
  multilingual portfolios across, 80 (figure), 89
  multiliteracies, 104 (figure), 117
  multimodal resources for, 102–103, 104 (figure), 117
  units of learning and, 64

Assessment in multiple languages
  aligned system, 36
  co-assessment, 108 (figure)
  common, 75–78, 87–88
  curriculum, planning, 57–90
  cycle, 35–37, 37 (figure)
  distributive leadership, through, 60
  effective, 201–206
  families and community in, 50
  federal legislation and, 7–10
  information collection/organization phase, 54–55, 91–121
  information evaluation/reporting phase, 155–188
  information interpretation/feedback phase, 122–154
  instructional models and, 13–15
  language planning, 32–33, 35–36

language policy, 21–22, 32–33, 35–36
linguistically and culturally responsive, 164–165, 185
multilingual resources, 50
planning phase, 57–90
purposes, 37–42
reliability in, 48
taking action phase, 189–219
theoretical orientation, 18–21
theory of action, 92–93, 95–96, 96 (figure), 114–115
tips for, xxviii–xxix, 23–24
transformation of, 198–199
units of learning, for, 63–64, 86
Assessment literacy, 76
professional learning on, 196–197
Assessment *of* learning, 43 (figure), 45–46, 109
assessment cycle and, 210–211 (figure)
basics of, 46–48
classroom-based, 172
common assessment, 45, 72–78
curriculum, in, 62
data collection during, 110 (figure)
data interpretation, 129, 130 (figure)
internal accountability, 45
large-scale, 46 (figure)
locus of control, through, 201–202, 202 (figure)
multilingual portfolios across, 80 (figure), 89
multiliteracies, 104 (figure), 117
multimodal resources for, 102–103, 104 (figure), 117
purposes, 45
reliability, 48
reporting results, 169, 171, 187
rubrics and, 167
stakeholders and, 56
translanguaging in, 106
units of learning and, 64
validity for, 46–48
Assessment policies, 21–23
Assessment portfolio, 78–81, 172
components of, 112, 146–147
considerations, 121
data interpretation, 145–147
organizing and assembling, 111–112
Assets-based orientation, 3

Assets-based philosophy, 199–200, 208
Assets-based terminology, 14
Assistive Technology Act, 65

Bachelard, G., 91
Backward mapping/planning, 61
Bailey, A. L., 162
Balanced bilinguals, 12–13
Baldoni, J., 34
Beginning-of-Year Data, 41 (figure)
Bialystok, E., 18 (figure)
Biases, 14
Bilingual education, 17, 18 (figure), 205
Bilingual Education Act of 1968, 5, 5 (figure)
Bilingualism, 4–5, 17, 105
Bilingual learners, 4, 12
Bilinguals, 3
Biliteracy continua, 105
Bi/multilingual learners, 3, 7
home languages for, 6
Bitterman, T., 175
Black, P., 44, 139, 202
Blankstein, A. M., 113, 210
Bouthot, M., 30
Brainstorming, 25, 104
Breakthrough Leadership (Blankstein and Newsome), 113
Brooks, K., 33 (figure)
Brooks, M. D., 9

"Can do" philosophy, 58, 141–143, 175, 208
Capstone projects, 78, 145, 146 (figure)
Care, E., 133
Carmona, J. F., 61
CASEL. *See* Collaborative for Academic, Social, and Emotional Learning (CASEL)
Cenoz, J., 17
Center for Education Equity, xxvii
Chalhoub-Deville, M. B., 140
Chapman, M., 175
Classroom assessment, 78
data interpretation, 150
reporting results, 171–172
translanguaging in, 64
Cleave, E., 207
CLIL. *See* Content and language integrated learning (CLIL)
Cloud, N., 205

Co-assessment, 108 (figure)
Cohan, A., 49
Coleman, E., 33 (figure)
Coleman, R., 18 (figure)
Collaboration
  data interpretation, in, 137
  feedback, in providing, 136–140
  teamwork and, 49
Collaborative Assessment
    Conference, 203–204
Collaborative for Academic, Social,
    and Emotional Learning
    (CASEL), 23
Collaborative planning, 49, 60
Collection, information. *See* Data
    collection/organization
Collier, V. P., 18 (figure)
Common assessment, 42, 45,
    46 (figure)
  checklist, 88
  collection and organization of,
      107–110
  co-planning, 75–78
  data collection for, 102, 107–110
  features of, 76
  initial data collection, 120
  interim assessment, 42, 78, 97
  multimodal communication
      channels to, 119
  planning, 72–78, 87
  rating scale, 87
  reporting results, 172–173
  using images for data
      collection, 116
Common assessment interpretation,
    131–136, 150
  content areas, within and across,
      132 (figure)
  criteria, 131–134
  multilingual projects,
      134 (figure), 153
  performance descriptors, 131,
      133, 152
  qualitative rubrics, with, 135–136
  rubric, with, 132–133, 135–136, 152
  tools, 131
  translanguaging, 134–135
Communities of practice, 203–204
Construct irrelevance, 47–48
Content and language integrated
    learning (CLIL), 29
Cook, H. G., 162

Co-planning
  common assessment, 75–78
  data collection, 106–107, 118
Counterstructuralist language
    assessment, 19
COVID-19 pandemic, xxii, xxxi, 58,
    177, 189–191, 201, 209, 211
  data collection in (post) pandemic,
      96–98
  educational leader traits in, 34
Crago, M. B., 18 (figure)
Crawford, J., 4
Criterion-referenced assessment, 178
Cross-cultural consideration, 63, 71
Cross-linguistic consideration, 63, 71
Cummins, J., 18, 18 (figure)
Curriculum and assessment
  assessment integration within
      curriculum, 62–63, 84–85
  assessment *of* learning and, 62
  backward planning, 61
  classroom and, 64
  common assessment, 72–78
  curriculum design, 61–66
  distributive leadership, 60
  EL ESPEJO, 69 (figure), 70
  features of, 62–63
  high-quality curricula, 62
  integrated learning
      goals/targets, 70–72
  language and content integration, 62
  linguistic and cultural sustainability
      of, 61–62, 68–72
  multilingual framework, 68–72
  multilingual learners accessibility to,
      65–66
  multiliteracies resources, 66
  multimodal resources, 67
  planning, 57–90
  purposes for assessment, 63–64
  research on, 61–62
  resources for, 66–68
  translanguaging, 67–68
  UbD, 61
  UDL, 65–66
  units of learning, 63–64, 86
Curriculum design, 61–66

Damico, J., 200
Data collection/organization, 91–121
  accessibility in, improving, 98–99
  common assessment, 102, 107–110

co-planning, 106–107, 118
district/school leadership and, 110
leadership role in, 95–96
multiliteracies in, 100–101
multimodalities in, 101–103
(post) pandemic world, in, 96–98
portfolios, 111–113
resources for, 94, 99–106,
    113–114
technology for, 110
theory of action, 92–93, 95–96,
    96 (figure), 114–115
translanguaging in, 94, 103–106
Data evaluation, 155–188
linguistic and cultural sustainability,
    164–165, 185
multilingual learners' role in, 179
rubrics role in, 166–169
state reclassification criteria,
    161–163
traffic light analogy, 166
Data interpretation, 122–154
annual assessment, 140–144, 150
assessment *as/for/of* learning and,
    129, 130 (figure)
assessment characteristic continua
    of, 129, 129 (figure)
assessment occurrence across school
    year, 127, 127 (figure)
assessment portfolios, 145–147
collaboration in, 137
collecting, recording and,
    132 (figure), 151
common assessment, 131–136, 150
data types for, 130 (figure)
distributive leadership and, 128
implementation level and
    assessment, 126–127,
    126 (figure)
interim assessment, 140–144, 150
language proficiency, 141–143
local accountability, for, 145–147
overview, 124–130
standardized testing, 144–145
Deficit-based terminology, 14
DeMatthews, D., 33 (figure)
Descriptive feedback, 139–140
Dewey, J., 193
Digital literacy, 66
Disabilities, English learners
    with, 8–9
Discrimination, xxix–xxx, 92–93, 114

Distributed/distributive leadership,
    33, 44, 60, 208
District language policy, 22
District level assessment,
    38 (figure), 42
Dove, M. G., 49
Dual language, 15
bilingual education, 15
education, 4, 17
educational leaders in,
    33–34 (figure)
effective assessment in, 205–206
learners, 12
Dual language education programs,
    13, 42, 204
translanguaging and, 105
Duarte, J., 23
Dynamic bilingualism, 105

EAL learners. *See* English as an
    additional language (EAL)
    learners
Educational leaders, 11, 32, 193
character traits, 34
collaboration framework, 49
dual language, research on,
    33–34 (figure)
inequality/social injustice,
    counteracting, xxi–xxii
literacy to multiliteracies, 100
multilingual turn, 198–199
qualities, 35
Educational leadership. *See*
    Leadership
Education models, language, 13–16,
    24–25, 29
Effective assessment in multiple
    languages, 201–206
communities of practice, 203–204
dual language, in, 205–206
locus of control, 202
program effectiveness
    determination, 204–205
student-led conferences, 202, 203
    (figure), 218
Effective leadership, 33–34
ELD programs. *See* English language
    development (ELD) programs
Elementary and Secondary Education
    Act (ESEA), 4–7, 144
Elite bilinguals, 13
ELs. *See* English learners (ELs)

Embedded Language Expectations for Systemic Planning, Enacting and Justifying Outcomes (EL ESPEJO), 69 (figure), 70
Emergent (or emerging) bilinguals, 12
End-of-Year Data, 41 (figure)
English as an additional language (EAL) learners, 28
English as a second language (ESL) programs, 13
English (or language X) dominant, 28
English Language Arts, 37, 39 (figure)
English language development (ELD) programs, 13–14
English Language Development Standards, 37, 39 (figure)
English Language Proficiency Screener, 39
English language proficiency test, 142 (figure), 162, 175
English learners (ELs), 5 (figure), 6–7
    definition, 7
    disabilities, with, 8–9
    exited, 12
    former, 12
    gifted and talented, 10
    heritage language learners, 12
    label for, 2–3, 10–13
    LTELs, 9–10
    never, 12–13
    proficient, 12
    recently arrived, 10
    reclassification of, 161–162
    subgroups, 8–10, 8 (figure)
    subgroups with assessment data, 11, 11 (figure)
English, standards in, 37–38, 39 (figure)
Enrollment process, 40
    language sample collection in, 52
    screening process, 38
    surveys for, 38, 52
e-Portfolio, 112
Equitable assessment, 25–26, 158–161, 211
    framework, 158–161, 182–183
Equity, xxi–xxii, xxvii, 208
    systemic, 209–210
Escamilla, K., 18 (figure)
ESEA. See Elementary and Secondary Education Act (ESEA)

ESL programs. See English as a second language (ESL) programs
Evaluation, information. See Data evaluation
Every Student Succeeds Act (ESSA), 5 (figure), 6, 36, 65, 199
    English learners, 5 (figure), 6–10
    state assessment and, 7
Exited English learners, 12
Expressive (productive) language, 101
External locus of control, 202

Federal legislation
    directives/policy, 4–7
    educational accountability, xxiv
    EL definition, 7
    implications for assessment, 7–10
Federal terminology, 4–17, 24–25
Feedback, 35, 44
    collaboration in providing, 136–140
    descriptive, 139–140
    features of effective, 138–139
    importance of, 139
    language for, 138–140
    sources of, 139
    stress and duress, during, 138
    student-directed, 140
    traffic light analogy, 166
Fellini, F., 122
Ferrell, E., 33 (figure)
"First" language (L1), 29
Flores, N., 92, 135
"Foreign" languages, 29
Formative assessment, 43–44, 43 (figure), 214
Formative feedback, 44
Former English learners, 12
Freire, P., 1
Fuentes, C., 155

García, O., 105
Genesee, F., 18 (figure), 62, 205
Gibbons, P., 62, 135
Gifted and talented English learners, 10, 11 (figure)
Goldenberg, C., 18 (figure)
Gorter, D., 17
Grading, 37, 177
    principles, 178, 188
Guiding Principles for Dual Language Education, The (Howard et al.), 205

Hamayan, E. V., 200, 205
Hattie, J., 44, 139
Heineke, A., 33 (figure)
Heritage language learners, 12
Heteroglossic language ideology, 48
High-stakes testing, 10, 38, 157, 209
Holistic rubric, 169
Home Language Survey, 38–39
Home Language Survey Data Quality Self-Assessment, 40
Honigsfeld, A., 49
Hopewell, S., 18 (figure)
Hornberger, N. H., 105
Howard, E. R., 33 (figure)
Hunt, V., 34 (figure)

Improving America's Schools Act (IASA), 5 (figure), 6, 144
Individualized education programs (IEPs), 8–9, 11 (figure)
Individual Student Report, 175, 176 (figure)
Individuals with Disabilities Education Act (IDEA), 65
Individuals with Disabilities Education Improvement Act of 2004, 9
Inequality, xxi–xxiii
    assessment, in, xxix–xxx
Information collection/organization. *See* Data collection/organization
Information evaluation. *See* Data evaluation
Information interpretation. *See* Data interpretation
Instructional models, 13–15, 14 (figure)
Integrated goals for learning, 68, 70–72
Interim assessments, 42, 78, 97, 140–144, 150, 173–175
Interim English language proficiency test, 142–143 (figure)
Interim standardized tests, 46 (figure)
Internal locus of control, 202
Interpretation, information. *See* Data interpretation
Interpretive (receptive) language, 101
Intersectionality, 23–24
Intervention programs, 15
Izquierdo, E., 33 (figure)

Kersemeier, C., 33 (figure)
Kim, A. A., 175
Kim, H., 133

Labels, 2–3, 10–13
LaCelle-Peterson, M. W., 159
Language
    academic, 135–136, 154
    content integration, and, 62
    development/proficiency standards, 37
    dimensions of, 136, 136 (figure), 154
    dual. *See* Dual language
    education models, 13–16, 24–25, 29
    expressive (productive), 101
    feedback, for, 138–140
    "first" language (L1), 29
    "foreign" languages, 29
    heteroglossic language ideology, 48
    interpretive (receptive), 101
    learning, 18–21, 81–82
    minority students, 4
    monoglossic language ideology, 11
    native, 6
    partner, 13
    planning, 32–33, 35–36
    policy, 21–22, 32–33, 35–36
    sample collection, 52
    translanguage. *See* Translanguage/ translanguaging
    world languages, 29
Language proficiency, 35, 38
    data interpretation, 141–143
Language Use Survey, 38–39
Languaging, 19–20, 67, 83, 157, 198
Large-scale assessment, 3, 198, 206
    results, 177
    translanguaging in, 135
Large-scale assessment *of* learning, 46 (figure)
    validity for, 46–48
Leadership, 32–33
    collaboration, 49
    data collection, role in, 95–96
    distributed/distributive, 33, 44, 60, 208
    diverse and shared, 208
    effectiveness in dual language, 33–34 (figure), 48
    planning common assessment, in, 72

principals, 61
theory of action, 95–96, 96 (figure)
Leadership for Educational Equity, xxvii
Learning goals, 61
integrated, 70–72
Learning objectives, 71
Learning system, 208, 219
Learning targets, 62
integrated, 70–72
Limited English proficiency (LEP), 5 (figure), 6, 144
Limited English speaking ability (LESA), 5 (figure)
Linguicism, 92
Linguistically and culturally diverse students, 28
Linguistic and cultural sustainability, 15
curriculum, 61–62, 68–72
data evaluation and reporting, 164–165
schools, 16–17
Linguistic equity, 3
Linquanti, R., 162
Locus of control, 202
Long-term English learners (LTELs), 9–10, 11 (figure)
López, F., 34 (figure)
Lukas, J. F., 144

MacDonald, R., 162
Madrigal, R., 34 (figure)
Maintenance/late exit/developmental bilingual programs, 29
Malik, K., 34 (figure)
Manhattan International High School, 147
Marginalized students, xxi–xxii
Marler, B., 200
Marquéz, G. G., 189
Martell, J., 34 (figure)
Menken, K., 34 (figure)
Met, M., 62
Metacognitive awareness, 43
Metacultural awareness, 43
Metalinguistic awareness, 43
Midyear Data, 41 (figure)
Minoritized students, 2, 113, 157, 199–200
Mislevy, R. J., 144

Mohan, B., 62
Monoglossic language ideology, 11
Morita-Mullaney, T., 33 (figure)
Mujeres Unidas y Activas, 48
Multiculturalism, 3, 17, 21, 25–26, 32, 49, 66, 92–93, 114
Multilingual education, 15, 17, 18 (figure)
Multilingualism, 5, 17, 21, 25–26, 28–29, 32, 49, 92–93, 114
Multilingual learners, 3, 7
assessment as, for and of learning, xxv (figure)
curriculum. See Curriculum and assessment
ELs. See English learners (ELs)
ESEA and terminology for, 4–7
federal terminology, 4–17, 24–25
home languages for, 6
instructional models, 13–15
K-12 school systems, 12–13, 13 (figure)
label for, 10–13
language education models, 13–16, 24–25, 29
learning system, 208, 219
social-emotional learning, and, 23
subgroups, 11–13
teachers of, 29
terminology, 4–17, 24–25, 28
Multilingual learners assessment, 37–42
assessment audit, 51
assets-based philosophy to, 199–200
district level, 42
enrollment process, 38, 40
equity framework for, 158–161, 182–183, 211
initial assessment, 38–42
interim assessments, 42
language sample collection, 52
purposes for, 37, 38 (figure), 64
Rubik's cube and, 196 (figure)
school level, 42
standardized testing, 20, 40–41
standards, 37–38, 39 (figure)
state level, 40–42
Multilingual signs, xxviii
Multilingual theory, 18
Multiliteracies, 66

assessment *as, for* and *of* learning, 104 (figure), 117
curriculum, 66
data collection, 94, 99–101
Multimodalities, 67
assessment *as, for* and *of* learning, 102–103, 104 (figure), 117
common assessment, 119
curriculum, 67
data collection, 94, 101–103

National Academies of Sciences, Engineering, and Medicine, 201
National Education Association, 123
Native language, 6
NCLB. *See* No Child Left Behind Act (NCLB)
Never English learners, 12–13
Newcomer students, 10
Newsome, M. J., 113, 210
New York Performance Standards Consortium, 147
No Child Left Behind Act (NCLB), 5 (figure), 6, 144

One-way dual language immersion program, 13, 15
Online schooling, 211, 213
Opening vignette
data collection/organization, 92–93, 114
data evaluation, 156–157, 180–181
data interpretation, 123–124, 149
English learners label, 2–3, 25–26
inequality and social injustice, xxi–xxiii, xxx–xxxi
monolingual teacher, 30–31, 50
planning assessment, 58–59, 82–83
taking action, 189–191, 212–213
Organization, information. *See* Data collection/organization

Paradis, J., 18 (figure)
Partner language, 13
Peer assessment, 64
Performance assessment, 48, 52
Performance descriptors, 131, 133, 152

Planning phase, 57–90. *See also* Curriculum and assessment
Plurilingual learners, 28
Portfolio assessment, 59, 78–81
assessment *as, for* and *of* learning, across, 80 (figure), 89–90
considerations, 121
data interpretation, 145–147
organizing and assembling, 111–112
Professional learning, 196–197
Proficient English learners, 12
Proficient English speakers, 10
Projects, assessment *of* learning for, 45 (figure)
Prompts, assessment *of* learning for, 45 (figure)

Qualitative rubrics, 135–136

Racial injustice and inequality, xxi–xxii
Racialized bilingualism, 135
Rating scale, 62
assessment integration within curriculum, 84–85
common assessment, 87
linguistically and culturally responsive assessment, 164 (figure)
Reardon, S. F., 18 (figure)
Recently arrived English learners, 10
Reflective practice, 192–195
Reliability, tests, 46, 48
Reporting, assessment data, 157
multilingual learners' role in, 179
rating scale, 165 (figure), 185
Reporting, assessment results, 169–177
annual assessment, 175
classroom assessment, 171–172
common assessment, 172–173
interim assessment, 173–175
rubrics role in, 166–169
stakeholders, to, 170 (figure)
Research
action, 193
assessment *for* learning, 44
assessment policies, 23
bilingualism/multilingualism, 17, 18 (figure)

curriculum, 61–62
educational leaders in dual
    language, 33–34 (figure)
Resources
    curriculum and assessment, 66–68
    data collection, 94, 99–106,
        113–114
    multilingual learners with
        disabilities, 9
Rivera, C., 159
Rubric, 132–133, 172
    analytic, 145, 169
    characteristics of, 169
    checklist of, 152
    data evaluation and reporting, in,
        166–169
    definition, 166
    holistic, 169
    qualitative, 135–136
    redesigning, 173
    student-centered, 133, 167–169, 186
    types of, 169
    writing and speaking,
        142–143 (figure)
Ruíz, R., 32

Sahin, A. G., 133
Sánchez, M. T., 105
Sánchez-López, C., 200
Scaffolding, 47
Scanlan, M., 34 (figure)
School language policy, 21–22
School level assessment, 38 (figure), 42
Seal of Biliteracy, 162
SEI programs. *See* Structured English
    immersion (SEI) programs
SEL. *See* Social-emotional
    learning (SEL)
Self-assessment, 43, 64
Sheltered English programs, 13
Shohamy, E., 23, 125
SIFE. *See* Students with interrupted
    formal education (SIFE)
Simultaneous bilinguals, 12
Sleeter, C. E., 61
Snow, M. A., 62
Social-emotional learning (SEL),
    23, 194–195
Social justice, xxi–xxiii, xxvii, 3,
    17, 208
    systemic change through, 48–49

Sociocracy, 60
Sociocultural theory, 19
Solorza, C., 34 (figure), 105
Souto-Manning, M., 34 (figure)
Spanish Language Arts, 37,
    39 (figure)
Spanish Language Development, 37,
    39 (figure)
Spanish, standards in, 37–38,
    39 (figure)
Special education, 123–124, 148
Spillane, J., 34 (figure)
Standardized testing, 20, 40–41,
    46 (figure), 144–145
Standards in English/Spanish, 37–38,
    39 (figure)
Standards-referenced grading
    system, 177
State level assessment, 38 (figure),
    40–42
State reclassification criteria,
    161–163
Stop-Think-Act-React activity
    aligned assessment system, 207
    assessment-capable learners, 164
    assessment *of* learning data, 175
    assessment portfolio, 113, 147
    collaboration, 137
    common assessment, 76
    construct irrelevance and test
        validity, 47
    curriculum, 63, 65
    data interpretation, 126, 128,
        130–131
    distributive leadership, 128
    district/school leadership data
        collection, 110
    eligibility criteria for multilingual
        learners subgroups, 12
    envision systemic change, 208
    equitable assessment
        framework, 161
    federal definition of EL, 8
    federal legislation, 7
    feedback, 139–140
    grading, 178
    interim/annual assessment
        data, 141
    language education programs, 16
    language planning, 33
    large-scale assessment results, 177

linguistic and cultural sustainability, 16
literacy data, 109
literacy to multiliteracies, 100
multilingual education, 95
multilingual learners assessment, 40
multilingual learners terminology, 14
multimodal resources, 102–103
professional learning on assessment literacy, 196–197
reporting, 169, 172
rubrics, 135, 144, 168
state reclassification criteria, 162
student portfolio, 81
taking action, 200, 203, 206
teacher configurations and co-planning, 107
theoretical orientation for assessment, 21
theory of action, 95
traffic light analogy and data evaluation, 166
translanguaging, 105
Structural linguistics, 19
Structured English immersion (SEI) programs, 13
Student assessment portfolios. *See* Assessment portfolio
Student-centered rubrics, 133, 167–169, 186
Student-directed feedback, 140
Student-led conferences, 111, 202, 203 (figure), 218
Students with interrupted formal education (SIFE), 9, 11 (figure)
Submersion ("sink or swim") programs, 13
Subtractive bilingualism, 14
Success criteria, 131–134, 140, 166
Summative assessment, 43, 43 (figure), 214
Suskie, L., 62
Systemic assessment, xxviii–xxix
Systemic change, xxviii, 48–49, 206–211
Systemic equity, 209–210

Taking action phase, 189–219
assets-based philosophy, 199–200
effective assessment practices, enacting, 201–206

multilingual turn, 198–199
priority determination, 195–197, 216–217
reflective practice and inquiry, 192–195
Teacher autonomy, 203–204, 208
Temperley, H., 44
Terminology
categorization, 28–29
federal, 4–17, 24–25
Tests/testing, 5
achievement, 7, 10, 41, 157–158
annual standardized, 46 (figure)
assessment *of* learning for, 45 (figure)
high-stakes, 10, 38, 157, 209
interim standardized, 46 (figure)
large-scale, 46–48
reliability, 46, 48
standardized, 20, 40–41, 46 (figure), 144–145
validity, 46–48
Theory of action, 92–93, 95–96, 96 (figure), 114–115
Thomas, W. P., 18 (figure)
Title VI of the Civil Rights Act of 1964, 5
Transadaptation, 7
Transitional bilingual programs, 14
Translanguage/translanguaging, 15, 19–20, 43, 64, 67–68, 71, 140, 199
curriculum, 67–68
data collection, 94, 103–106
dual language education programs and, 105
interpretation in common assessment, 134–135
Translanguaging Classroom, The (García, Johnson & Seltzer), 199
Two-way dual language immersion programs, 13, 15

Understanding by Design (UbD), 61
Units of learning, 63–64, 86, 106
Universal Design for Learning (UDL), 65–66, 98–99

Valentino, R. A., 18 (figure)
Validity, tests, 46–48
definition, 46, 144

standardized testing, 144–145
Visible learners, 163
Visible Learning (Hattie), 163

Wei, J., 175
WIDA MODEL, 141–143, 173–175,
   174 (figure)

Wiliam, D., 44, 139, 202
Williams, C. P., 58
Wong, S., 3–4
World languages, 29

A SAGE Publishing Company

Helping educators make the greatest impact

CORWIN HAS ONE MISSION: to enhance education through intentional professional learning.

We build long-term relationships with our authors, educators, clients, and associations who partner with us to develop and continuously improve the best evidence-based practices that establish and support lifelong learning.